SOM journal 10

HATJE CANTZ

Contents

Thomas De Monchaux, Sylvia Lavin, Zoe Ryan, and Brandon Haw outside La Tourette, April 17, 2015

On Ethos

Thomas De Monchaux

Ignorance of the past does not guarantee freedom from its imperfections.

—Reinhold Niebuhr, pastoral journal, 1928

"Okay, okay, okay," observed SOM jury cycle 10 juror Sylvia Lavin, acknowledging but deflecting a flurry of praise around the table for a building's elegant sculptural forms and intricate surface patterns, "but the question is what has it left behind." It was a pivotal moment in the jury's deliberations, not only about that building—the Chhatrapati Shivaji International Airport Terminal 2 in Mumbai, India, which would go on to become one of the jury's selected finalists—but in the more general discourse suggested by all the work under consideration. It was a conversation not only about the resonance between every project on the table, but also—prompted by the roundly-numerical and handily-digital number 10 of the jury cycle—about what a built legacy amounts to. And also, within the specific history of Skidmore, Owings & Merrill as an architecture firm, a conversation about how that built legacy, since 1936 an estimated 10,000 buildings around the world, can be understood not only as a kind of monumental museum—something to forever record the aspirations and tactics of particular times and places, especially of the American mid-twentieth century of the firm at its canonical maximum—but a living archive: a shared intelligence, an ethos, a kind of collective unconscious for the conscious design decisions of today.

The question of what has been left behind, and equally of what is behind the visible and tangible forms and surfaces of the built environment, is the essential query for the critique of architecture, and for the relationship between criticism and practice. SOM's annual internal jury, of which this journal is a record, is a ritual of asking of this question. The phrase, of course, works both ways: what's left behind can mean what's enduring and what remains, but also what has been abandoned or displaced. Lavin was asking not about the artifact of the building itself—left behind, once designed and built, by its architects—but about what might yet be the social, cultural, or economical ripple-effect, upstream and downstream, of the event of its building: the potential infusion of investment or recalibration of opportunity that its construction may have occasioned.

Behind the Beautiful Forevers is the title of Pulitzer-Prize-winning journalist Katherine Boo's account, based on three years of on-site reporting, of the community of Annawadi, an informal settlement—3000 people in about three hundred dwelling-places in about a third of an acre tucked behind a high reinforced concrete wall along an approach road—on marshy land owned by the Airports Authority of India, some of which reverted to the site of the new Terminal 2 itself. It might seem that the story is one of an indigenous local village, its territory displaced by this vast new artifact of contemporaneity and the globalized world. But the real story is more complicated. The settlement of Annawadi had its roots not entirely in time immemorial, but in the dwelling places of migrant workers gathered for the construction of an earlier phase of the airport's development, in 1991. It was something left behind, and as modern as the airport itself. Architecture is the art, among much else, of side effects and unintended consequences; and yet we also look to it to make seemingly permanent and concrete, figuratively and often literally, all that would otherwise be unstable, ephemeral, and elusive. "Beautiful, Forever," were the words that repeated over and over on signage on the wall behind which Annawadi was situated: an advertisement for a particular brand of shiny and durable ceramic tiles.

The airport, along with the willfully iconic downtown skyscraper, is the typology that, from the mid-twentieth century to today, is most enduringly modern. Technologically, it requires and supports perhaps the most perfected large-scale mechanical device of twentieth-century engineering: the post-Boeing-747-scaled commercial jet airliner; socially and experientially, the airport offers an increasingly paradoxical promise. On the one hand, a seamless transition from local to global, ground to air, stasis to motion; and on the other, a relentless sorting and ordering, policing and securing of passengers and cargo, arrivals and departures, migrations and customs, ever-more overlaid with the agencies of the private corporation and the public nation state. In this paradoxical promise, there is in a single typology the axis of hope and fear along which the condition of modernity in design, since it first became recognizable in the years following World War I, can be best described. There is the ecstatic bird's-eye-view release from the tubercular and congested ground abhorred by the likes of Le Corbusier and his generation, undertaken in a tensile and fluid aesthetic inspired by the components of cars and ships and above all planes themselves: "The airplane is the symbol of the new age," Corbusier wrote in his canonical May 1935 essay on the subject, "The Airplane Indicts." He celebrates, with a near-instant nostalgia, his first encounter of the airport typology in 1928: "I arrived one day at the airport of Amsterdam, the meeting-place of several great lines. I was invited into the look-out of the commandant. I saw a station full of traffic. [The planes] come to rest at the entrance to the station. They take up position for departure. A signal, a color here, a flare there, the airplane is off again, they are all off but new ones are landing." And yet, for all the seeming liberties of arrival and departure in perpetual motion, there is that commandant and his look-out: the surveilling and ordering impulse that, over time, also was attached to whatever we mean by modernism in design—especially by those who imagined the possibility of supplanting it with some new sense or sensibility: the mechanizing that surpasses mere efficiency or felicity into something relentless, the systematizing that surpasses the merely technocratic or corporate into a different kind of authority.

These kinds of paradoxes near the heart of the modern in design, are touched on, in different ways, by several of the essayists contributing to this edition of the *SOM Journal*. As many have observed, SOM during its mid-twentieth-century heyday mirrored and modeled the established institutional mode of the private corporations that were, from Lever Brothers onwards, its most significant clients (and who were also, in the form of Time, Inc, its most significant popularizers): an ideal of systemic subjectivity, of orderly creativity, of house voice. In "I Think I Said What They Probably Said: Rhetorical Ethos in the Work and Words of Gordon Bunshaft", writer Oren Abeles addresses ethos as a mode of speech to be found in a canonical 1989 oral history by that design partner who was SOM's most famously anonymous author: "unerringly rational but simultaneously inspired and artistic; he was methodical but messy; confrontational but quiet; dictatorial but collaborative. Some of the ambiguity around Bunshaft is simply the result of his having provided an unusually restricted account of his work, in interviews or writings, speech or text." In "You Young Men Are So Sure": Architectural Ethos at Walter Severinghaus' Chapel House, architectural historian Nicholas Adams examines both hearsay and anecdote to restore our attention to an overlooked but essential work by the Bunshaft contemporary known least for his work as a designer—an act of critical reconstruction and rehabilitation that coincides, ironically, with a substantial present-day renovation of the building in question. Adams cites the paradoxical assertion of adaptive tradition, by theologian Reinhold Niebuhr—whose essay "Tradition and Today's Ethos in the Architectural Forum" of December 1953, suggested that, "Architecture, as every artistic discipline, requires the forming power of a great tradition and sufficient vitality to insure the adaption of that tradition to current interests … i.e. to the temper and functional requirements of a technical age." It was also precisely in that same year that the earliest citation of "mid-century modernism" was self-consciously applied to design; in "When Mid-Century Met Modernism," journalist Karrie Jacobs addresses a paradox of style and substance in which a particular notion of the modern in design—epitomized in the Breueresque stone walls and Miesian flanged columns of Severinghaus' Chapel House—has moved from connoting a futurity that transcends historical contingency itself, to a kind of constant retrospection. To an enduring nostalgia even more acute that Le Corbusier's 1935 recollection of the new airports of a decade earlier: "Even if you detach it from mid-century," writes Jacobs, "the word 'modernism' itself is redolent of the past. In our present moment, 'modern' sounds oddly quaint, the signifier of a future that didn't quite pan out." Jacobs questions, "whether 'mid-century' circa 1953 actually implies the cloudless optimism I associate with it today, or whether the notion of "mid-century" also incorporates the looming threat of the bomb, much as the idea of the Millennium, a half

century later, carried with it a hint of apocalypse."

Unavoidably, that hint of the apocalyptic is a reminder that in 2016, the airport terminal—with its potent global symbolism but its local permeability is also a new default target not of the Cold War strategists of the past, but in the multipolar and asymmetrical conflicts that characterize today's version of the modern world. The first cycle of the *SOM Journal* took place some fifteen years ago in March 2001, around the historical turn of the millennium itself, and the large-scale projects it featured were conceived before the terrorist attacks of September of that year added a new context to any consideration of the monumentally scaled civic typologies, from skyscrapers to airports, in which today's SOM specializes—and that feature equally but differently in that edition of the *Journal*, and in this one. There is, if one seeks it, a poignancy to the questions that edition of the *Journal*'s editor, Wilfried Wang, hoped that that jury's selections would prompt: "How does a building synthesize operational demands with modes of awareness? Where are the realms of freedom for architecture at a time when structure, cladding, and services have all become part of the optimizing package of development? How can long-term projects [establish] valid terms for some time to come?" The decade and a half during which SOM has so far undertaken the annual institutional introspection of its jury has, with the unprecedented speed and scale of global events, illuminated above all the *slowness* of the art of architecture, even relative to what Wang characterized as architecture's own, "fast-changing, ever-evolving discourse." Architecture, more than ever in our fast times—spiky, jittery, digitally-animated, interconnectedly hyper-reactive—always arrives, thanks to the relatively slow pace of its conception and construction, slightly behind the times. It always already embodies the ethos of the recent past. And in that sense, intentionally or not, it serves as a steadying as well as animating presence. It answers the questions we used to ask. It may be that, in our era of accelerating urbanization, this paradoxical quality of forward-looking delay could become an increasingly and consciously intentional driver of design.

For the first time, in this cycle of SOM's annual jury, designers of submitted projects were invited to directly cite which projects from the firm's own history may have most directly informed their work. While the firm's charismatically structurally-expressive skyscrapers of the 1960s and '70s (especially architect Bruce Graham and engineer Fazlur R. Kahn's John Hancock Center tower of 1970 [Chicago], and the not dissimilar ALCOA tower of 1967 [San Francisco]) figured prominently in those citations, along with designer Walter Netsch's boldly tessellated 1962 Air Force Academy Chapel, the most common shared denominator—whether by architects working on airports or other programs—was the 1981 Hajj Terminal at King Abdul Aziz International Airport in Jeddah, Saudi Arabia. That project, primarily attributed to architects and engineer Bunshaft, Gordon Wildermuth, and Fazlur R. Kahn, was a response to a tenfold increase in pilgrimages to Mecca over the previous decade. The terminal, some 3,000,000 square feet of it, organizes typical transit functions like immigration and customs into linear perimeter air-conditioned blocks. But the heart of the complex is a vast internal open-air courtyard, of over a hundred acres, sheltered by some 200 semi-conical tent-like structures, each composed of twenty-one segments of Teflon-coated fiberglass, rising from sixty-six feet above the ground to a steel-ringed oculus at 110 feet, suspended around a central 150-foot-tall tapered steel column, on a 150-foot square grid. This softly monumental indoor-outdoor landscape, with sculptural street furniture and basic infrastructure at ground level, affords a staging area for the cycle of life—assembly and wandering, food preparation and ritual ablution, trade and talk, and rest—with qualities of the public square, World's Fair grounds, souk, caravansaries, and what is effectively a permanently temporary tent city in miniature, an informal settlement established by a globally diverse population of pilgrims, sustaining social, cultural, commercial, and other interactions over the typical peak twenty-four to thirty-six-hour waiting period between arrival by plane and departure for the bus ride—typically to a larger-scaled temporary settlement in the form of a dedicated tent city for global pilgrims, closer to the center of Mecca itself.

There are many reasons why this airport terminal may be a building to look at right now—if we seek an ethos of the transhistorically modern and a living legacy of SOM at its most adept, within what Niebuhr, no stranger to pilgrims and seekers, described in 1953 as, "the forming power of a great tradition [of] sufficient vitality to insure the adaption of that tradition to current interests." The Hajj Terminal's strategy of a deployed and iterated module, its aesthetic of tensile softness and luminously translucent materiality—all this appeals to today's moment of parametrically optimized and versioned form-finding, often extended along cellular or modular arrays that drift from a grid towards more organic-seeming Voronoi and relatedly self-similar formations. Less discursively, the building represents a straightforward vision of operational environmental sustainability that transcends the admirable but pedantically quantified certifications with which we are more familiar: the stack effects and airflow management, the permeability of light and heat through those overhead canopies, which reflect seventy-six percent of solar radiation, are calibrated to sustain a tolerable 80-degree Fahrenheit temperature below, while daytime heat can otherwise reach more than 130 degrees; the seven percent of sunlight transmitted through the fabric keeps visibility and illumination within an optimal range. Culturally and globally speaking, poised somewhere between corporation and kingdom, secular and sacred, the project does inevitably risk the Orientalist encounter of a Western designer and an Eastern client; and yet the tensile canopy landscape, while uncompromisingly modern as a purely functional formal expression of cable profiles and anchors, still evokes without pastiche, for those who may choose to seek it, the vernacular or natural landscapes of Bedouin tents or wind-blown dunes, or other dreams and visions of the desert.

Here and now in 2016, with one's mind on the acute juxtapositions of an informal settlement like Mumbai's Annawadi and its formal airport terminal buildings like Chhatrapati Shivaji's Terminal 2, it is possible to project onto historical images of the Jeddah Hajj Terminal an aspiration for what could happen if these conditions were not walled off from each other, but integrated: for ever more overlap and encounter between the formal and informal, the outdoor and the indoor, the technical and the personal, the high and the low, the top-down and the bottom-up, the possessed and the dispossessed. It's an aspiration somewhat out of the visionary 1960s and '70s proposals of the British collective Archigram, and the Japanese practitioners grouped under the Metabolist sobriquet—for architecture as a kind of canopy of possibility, an infrastructural delivery system that catalyzed dynamically self-organized and improvised settlements and occupations, gatherings and happenings. In *Behind the Beautiful Forevers*, Boo describes awkward moments along the landscape of the airport's property where, "new India and old India collided and made new India late"; one wonders how that notional collision, choreographed by the always already delayed and incidental effects of architecture, could be staged in such a way as to not be the detention or suspension of the future by the past—or of the possible by the actual—but to constitute a complex and emergent and continuous reciprocity.

The airport terminal selected by the first ever SOM jury offers a vision of this kind of encounter, in form and in one critical dimension of its function: the Terminal 3 Building of the Changi International Airport at Singapore, designed in 2000 and 2001 (and opening, with the usual time lapse, in 2007), features a scintillating reinterpretation of the standard Miesian big floating roof: a four-meter-deep deep overhead canopy, a twenty-two-acre pixel- or voxelated-seeming steel-and-glass array of 260 meter long cable-braced steel trusses, dappled with a system of skylights and butterfly-like louver panels, translucent and reflective, above and below the building enclosure; calibrated by software that maps and adapts to the daily daylighting conditions, the continuous opening, closing, and tilting of these mechanical butterflies—like the adjustable aerilon flight control surfaces on the early airplanes beloved of Le Corbusier—ensures a daily eight hours of natural daylighting and optimal indoor visibility, collaborating with the weather outside in a continuous operation of exposing and enclosing, revealing and sheltering. While the architectural conditions below are more conventional, one could imagine such an adaptive and collaborative infrastructure extending cloud-like downward from an overhead plane to an occupy-able volume, and adapting itself responsively and catalytically not only to daylighting, but to all of the building's operations: to circulation and transportation and all the complex behaviors of the natural and artificial world, to the most essential moods and needs and wisdoms of the crowds and pilgrims below. In his essay "On Modern Memory: A Case Study in Brick," in this issue, memoirist Marco Roth recalls Louis Kahn's aspiration for an architecture that operates as, "Ruins in reverse [...] the would-be reversal of ruination with its aesthetic equal." Kahn's putative project may have been only aesthetic: to achieve in scale and Platonic order, and in literal and figurative weight, contemporary work that had the qualities of endurance, permanence, and transcendence that he saw in the classical ruins of the Grand Tour; but the vision of a reverse ruin—of a structure in constant adaptive transformation perpetually between making and unmaking, evokes the potential ethos of such an architecture, fully realized.

As a matter of style, the big roof at Singapore's Terminal 3 is all lightness, seemingly an intricate reinterpretation of late-Miesian glass-and-steel, while the big roof of Mumbai's Terminal 2, fifteen years and ten *Journals* later, is all heaviness, seemingly an intricate reinterpretation of the other modernist idiom of late-Corbusian plastically modeled cast concrete (although, as juror Brandon Haw would point out, given all the structural steel within that actually hollow head house, it's something of an elegant deception); the plasticity of the overhead form means that the roof, in form if not function, can and has been drawn down to ground level, in the form of massive columns that stretch and attenuate that overhead geometry, passing through, in perhaps inadvertent recollection of each Hajj Terminal tent's central oculus around its steel column, openings in the seeming ground plane of the departures concourse to land at the arrivals level below. One only ever fully understands this cross-section when one's visit to the city has come full circle. At Mumbai, as at Singapore, as at any number of modern or modernist buildings of all scales from Breuer's Cape Cod to Neutra's Palm Springs, the last bay of that roof extends out into the open air, beyond the suspended and visually incidental curtain wall in glass—suggesting, in the classically modern way, some implication of a line that, briefly materially held by the building itself, goes on forever.

I remember my last visit to Mumbai, returning to that very terminal, my rattletrap black-and-yellow taxi careening through the hazy and fluorescent dark, through the hot and humid midnight, the driver continuously honking the horn, in the local way, in one near-unbroken note, for the whole ride; the taxi's dashboard a miniature mobile shrine to the relevant gods, plastic gold and fresh-cut flowers all braided together at the feet of an illuminated picture of watchful elephant-headed Ganesh. I remember honking past the teeming city, past the radical juxtapositions of density and intensity, of ephemeral and eternal, of shit and sandalwood, of the seemingly too-late past and the seemingly too-early future—all that this city, to its visitors, presents. Once we were underneath that last open bay of Terminal 2's big roof, that brilliantly uplit canopy, my taxi was momentarily blocked by the taxi in front, which had broken down; manifesting out of the complex chaotic-seeming currents of the crowd, as I worked my way toward the icy air-conditioning on the other side of the wall of glass, I saw a dozen men and women, young and not, barefoot and not, uniformed and not, suddenly and spontaneously emerge and converge and place their hands along the taxi's metal surface—maybe a momentary intersubjective self-transcendence of the kind Niebuhr would have sought and celebrated, maybe just one thing after another—to push the silent car along, to sustain its motion as seamlessly as if its engine had never stopped, to carry it forward and ensure that, in this way at least, it would never be left behind.

Jury Observations

Thomas De Monchaux

The institution of the jury is as central to architecture as it is to law: the disputatious and self-conscious soul of the practice. If you went to architecture school and care to remember it, you may recall the ritual of the jury review with a combination of affection and affliction. Affection, because this central ritual of discourse gathers the acute shoulder-to-shoulder attention of a collective intelligence onto design work that can be a surprisingly lonely endeavor. And sometimes they go easy on you. Affliction, because the jury review can be, and long has been, a gantlet, a kind of institutionalized bullying, a ritual hazing—and although that shameful history, along with much else of the old boys' club, is fading away from our profession, it still lingers enough that the nickname for the primary pin-up space in more than one of America's architecture schools is "the shooting gallery."

But there is another kind of jury review to recall with affection. It's the one when, by tacit consensus, the jurors know that the work is strong enough to be interrogated in a higher gear; to be addressed not as a case study in compliance or competence or even mere excellence, but as a way to look for an ethos: something both defined by, but beyond, the project itself. The kid gloves are off. This kind of conversation is sometimes, at its very best, a cruel-to-be-kind interrogation of whether any given project has met, or could ever meet, the highest of the aspirations that it has acknowledged—and further, of what aspirations are worthy of such endeavor. I believe that the jury conversation for the tenth cycle of the SOM jury and *Journal*—drawn equally from architectural theory, history, journalism, criticism, curatorship, and practice—was a jury of this kind: sharp, idealistic, and searching. We sought projects that not only demonstrated how far something had come, but also how much further it may be possible to go.

Our jury was aware both of the admirably self-reflective fifteen-year legacy of the SOM jury and *Journal*, and of the substantial history and scale of SOM as a global architectural practice—a history and scale that carries with it both glory and duty. There is the reflected glory of what one observer of SOM has described as being, "the kids of rock stars": the lineal descendants of Gordon Bunshaft and his peers, who over a half century from the 1930s to the 1980s—through some overdetermined synthesis of mid-twentieth-century establishment consensus and its opposite, the fluky flowering of passions and obsessions in one-shot touchstone projects (like Walter Netsch's Air Force Academy Chapel or Walter Severinghaus's Chapel house, featured in this issue)—gave modern America its buildings. And there is the duty, given that legacy and the institutional resources for which it was the foundation, to figure out how to carry that forward. As some of the essayists in this issue note, that duty is especially complex when one is looking back to a legacy of the modern in design that is itself, definitively and sometimes enervatingly, forward-looking.

For the most part, our jury was drawn to projects that combined a certain no-nonsense robustness—expressed structural systems, toughness about the service of form to function, ability to operate in unforgiving or unlovely sites or settings—with a visible, or visible-seeming, delicacy around the human scale. The two skyscraper projects that got our attention, the CITIC Financial Center and the Shenzhen Rural Commercial Bank Headquarters, both located in Shenzhen, China, seemed to have something of that quality. Although we noted that a duty to the natural environment was tacitly or explicitly expressed in almost all projects, we were aware that no new-build project, especially at the scale of skyscrapers, is without impact on the complex systems of our global ecology, and we lamented some project presentations' reduction of the language of sustainability to a merely marketable or certifiable metric. We were drawn to projects that mediated between a macro-architectural scale and a micro-urban scale, as with a piece of transportation infrastructure like the Denver Union Station, or the miniature city-in-a-box that is the New School University Center in New York City, a kind of mini-megastructure that accommodates a vertical campus in a dynamic and demanding urban setting. In such projects, the so-called plinths or podiums—with one ever-more-complex cross-section reaching out, ever further below or higher above grade, to the next—becomes more and more critical; the once-iconic freestanding tower, less and less critical. In our new century of climate catastrophe and rapid urbanization, such projects' sense of interdependence and connectedness—visual, structural, operational—will only become more important.

In this critical ecological and economic context, there was a sober, tough-minded, and even austere feeling on our jury that a firm of SOM's capacity needs to think, and work, big—that it must apply itself at scale; that it must not get cute. That it must not pretend to be a different kind of practice from what it is. We singled out (along with a systems project and a research project that both seemed to think big), two big skyscraper developments, a big airport terminal, a big educational complex, a big cultural complex, and a big train station. The clients were banks, universities, development authorities, civic administrations. They cost a lot. They take time. They are not subtle. They are not radical. But they present existing and enduring conditions to which extraordinary subtlety, and even radicality, of architectural observation and intervention must be brought.

In architecture, style can be substance and form can be content. The buildings that drew our interest had both a kind of simplicity and a kind of subtlety. They tended to apply to straightforward and restrained volumes an intricate patterning that was more than skin-deep. We saw prisms and blocks, sometimes gradually deflected (purposefully but not willfully) toward obliques and curves, with finely inscribed and screened and scored and punctured and articulated surfaces. And we saw something formal and functional about those articulations carry from surface to volume, from skin to core. Whether this was the calibrated porosity of the Al Ahmadi Cultural Center in Mahboula, Kuwait; the textured canopy of the Chhatravati Shivaji International Airport Terminal 2 in Mumbai, India, or the linear striations mediating fenestration and function in the New School University Center in New York City, this procedure of patterning is a promising path in SOM's body of work. This tendency of finely woven patterning that inscribes and interrogates a restrained prismatic volume harks back aesthetically to the relationship between surface and volume in the curtain walls of Lever House. But it also points forward toward something more interesting: the deep registration of field conditions, repetitions and variations, calibrations and complications—like currents through a pool of water—whereby a simple building can mediate and animate the complex behaviors of its occupants and sites. It points to an emerging and continuing design ethos for SOM in which seeming decoration is actually a fine-grain and functional registration, against a volume of deliberate simplicity, of complex eventfulness. Call it a deep surface; call it ornamented minimalism; call it what you want. But, just as if you're back in front of that architecture school jury, find out if it's a way forward.

Al Ahmadi Cultural Center: "A rich tradition of modernism"

Al Ahmadi, Kuwait

Box versus blob. That was the shorthand for the competing formalist and stylist architectural discourses of the late 1990s and early 2000s: a shorthand for a tendency toward the putative rigor of seemingly minimalist restraint, and alternately the performative liberty of seemingly expressive, and expensively engineered, formal drama: the box suggests hidden mysteries, the blob forces inside that cannot be contained. At the Al Ahmadi Cultural Center, a self-contained mall-like complex of performance, exhibition, and related spaces, there is a visible conceit of a sealed and inscribed and even forbidding box that has, through moments of plasticity, yielded to environmental and operational influences, as a sail yields in the wind: a roofs cape of curvy scoops reach upward and outward to redirect daylight, hopefully also with some substantially sustainable airflow and climatic effect, while another significant curve yields inward to mark what appears to be a significant pedestrian entrance—although in a seemingly primarily automotive-and-air-conditioned landscape that grade-level entry may be more symbolic. The evocation of calligraphy and latticework in the pale porous skin might also reference, however distantly, the notionally vernacular. Although, as the jury looked closer, we wondered if the local vernacular was really a global modernism, of which this building was—perhaps, to a point, willfully—unaware.

"The entry suggests a slippage," observed juror Zoe Ryan, "that you might slip in off the sidewalk," but whether there may be any such human-scaled sidewalk to slip and slide along, and what type of security rituals contravened that formal rhetoric of sly and subtle entry, was left to the jury's imagination. In a larger sense, we wondered what kind of public realm—what kind of civic idea, if any—was being accommodated in this inward-looking building. "I found this to be interesting, as a typology, as a building," said juror Brandon Haw, "But, having said that, you have to work to discover the public realm, to get inside of it, but maybe that is appropriate given the climate. I think in more a formal analysis, one could talk about better and deeper articulation, it's a little bland, there's a bit of a one line all over it. But I found it an interesting and more complex piece of architecture for its function and appropriate to its location: "Maybe, the public realm is nonexistent in terms of what its context is."

"Well, my comment," noted juror Sylvia Lavin, "given where we are, is that it's hard not to see the massing of La Tourette in there and I thought that the discourse on concrete was a little underdeveloped in that context. This was one of the projects that made me ask about its relationship to other contemporary buildings. I thought this would be one to compare with, say, Reiser Umemoto," a firm whose work shares an interest in the porosity and curvilinear modulation of thick wrapper-like enclosures featured in this project. "It's got a lot of the same discourse, similar context, although all the buildings are very different. The one other thing about it—and I know nothing about the Middle East, though I happen to know something about Kuwait, and the history of modernism in Kuwait, which is very particular—it has a context of lots of significant buildings and commissions. There's, "Jørn Utzon's Kuwait National Assembly building of 1972–82," a composition in a different formal vocabulary, but also of curves pulling at boxes. "There was a major competition for the new city that involved the bulldozing of the old city," continued Lavin, "But it's really where the Smithson Mat Building," the woven-seeming micro-urban permutated figure-ground typology proposed by Alison Smithson in the mid-1970s, "developed in relation to Kuwait." But, Lavin continued, "I just thought it was funny not to see any reference to the strong modern tradition in Kuwait in the presentation of the thinking," behind this building. " "This would be a question I would have for SOM more broadly speaking, which is to say: what has a firm like SOM learned about the importation of modernism into this part of the world, since this is not the first wave, it is at least the second, if not the third? And it would seem to me that there would be lessons learned from that would warrant some discussion here. Maybe that's just a broader comment, not about this project particularly, but not all places in the Middle East happen to have such a rich tradition of modernism already there."

"I would concur with that," I added then, "and it starts an interesting debate about what we were just talking about and what do you do with the modernist context in what's actually not a beautiful, bleak desert. So it starts a conversation." I would add further, now, that the building's plan *partis* is a conventionally high modernist pinwheel-like arrangement of cinemas and halls around a central court, but the whole is wrapped in an articulated and variably porous skin that sometimes thickens and intricately articulates for lighting and circulation effects in a way that records a later generation of practitioners in the modern mode. "It's interesting," concluded Ryan, "like a shopping mall, it's a whole complex within the inside. It's interesting that when you get to cultural projects that the wedded-ness of the landscape is not shown. With tall buildings we are given much more views of how they sit in the landscape, but we have no clue of context here. I am assuming most people are driving to this building and then being inside, but there's no clue about what the building is contributing to that neighborhood, it's very internal. It's not at all about seeing what's going on inside."

CITIC Financial Center: "Something well thought through"

Shenzhen, China

Do what you do. Over the course of its deliberations the jury took an interest less and less in projects and prototypes—generally cultural and single-residential—where SOM seemingly attempted, with variable success, to miniaturize itself to undertake work that generally provides the discursive breakthroughs for hungry small and emerging midsize firms. We took more and more of an interest in the conventional but essential typologies for which SOM, given its history, its resources, and its processing power, should by default excel: we sought skyscrapers and corporate campuses, terminals and stations, conference halls and convention centers. "Something well thought through," in the words of juror Haw about this project, but perhaps equally about the kind of work the group was more generally seeking, "a professional body of work." We looked for skyscraper projects that represented a certain kind of radical competence: structurally straightforward but not timid; as sustainable as any new construction can be; and with the kind of legibility and density that makes buildings of this scale good public citizens—especially in the rapidly growing cities of the Pacific Rim.

At the CITIC Financial Center, a mixed-use commercial and residential dual-towered complex in Shenzhen, China, the jury found a praiseworthy effort at a kind of micro-urbanism, an urban design in miniature that might catalyze a certain level of experiential complexity and spatial diversity in a townscape so far not abundant in those qualities. "I find it interesting," noted Ryan, "that like this one, most of the skyscrapers we're looking at are not singular buildings. Though the familiar signature image is a single building, what we have are intricate complexes with portals, with connections to other buildings, most of which are both servicing and served by them; the complexity of program is," realized in the intricacies of cross-section buried in the podium and subfloors, but is, "elsewhere," from the imagery of the singular icon. The angular landscaping relative to the splayed angles of the tower façade structures, mediated by the somewhat willfully green roofs of the podium-level of the complex, suggests a greater coherence, in a gauzy aerial rendering, than the eventual user may feel. "At least," I added, "they included the bottom—how the building meets the ground and the city—in the rendering." But the structural exoskeleton, recalling robust precedents in SOM's work like the 1970 John Hancock Center tower in Chicago, provides a graphic mediation stretching and reaching between the urban and the human scale.

"I bet they had a whole thing about stretching," said Lavin about the base-to-top attenuated folate pattern of the cross-bracing on the shorter and taller paired towers, "which I thought was an interesting way to relate two buildings that are not related and are not the same size and one is not just being made smaller than the other, but the webbing gets stretched." Noting the more performative and less expressive operations of that perimeter structural frame, Haw concluded, "this really shows a technological shift in the way skyscrapers are being designed today. It has a good analysis, its been drawn out here, with the context and the greenery. It's thoughtful, I think."

Closed Cavity Façade: "Beyond the scale of the monumental"

System developed for multi-site applications, 2012–14

The jury took a pointed interest in any design project conceived and presented as a "building system"—iterated and reproducible, permutated and adaptable, suggesting the kind of house-style mass standardization and in-house kit-of-parts that SOM should be good at and should have at hand. In projects that, as with our interest in complex large-scale typologies like skyscrapers and airports, fulfills what should be a minimum baseline expectation for the bandwidth and processing power of a design firm of SOM's scale and complexity. It's a potential that, we worried, is mostly unfulfilled. Attuned especially to the ethos of the firm's own history, we took an interest especially in a building system that addressed the idea of façade; that reconsidered the glass curtain wall and the metal-and-glass spandrel-and-fenestration systems that, dating back to Lever House of 1950 and the nearby Pepsi-Cola Corporation headquarters of 1960, have been fundamental to the creativity and imagery of SOM—and for which the firm therefore may have an institutional obligation to advance, to question, to reinvent. Although the submission and consideration was narrowly of the façade system and not of the building on which it happened to be deployed, a certain reluctant appreciation for the micro-macro resonances of triangulated and diagonal geometries was unavoidable, especially when viewed, in photography, in a picturesquely low oblique.

"I appreciated the technical idea of having a building system," said Lavin, "I feel like at this point a thing that a firm like SOM can be doing is developing systems that other people could be using. I also thought that a lot of the towers or glazed buildings," in this cycle of submission, "suffered from having an overly exuberant exoskeleton with then a very standardized mullion system behind it, which drives me crazy. And so this seems to me a way to think that through more thoroughly and I appreciated that." "I appreciate that too," I said, and added, "I think it really offers a critique of those other projects in which the exuberant and the standardized are juxtaposed, but in no way reconciled to each other."

Haw both appreciated and cautioned the subtlety of the detailing, and the standard practices of its problem solving at a fine grain and one-to-one scale, issues of reflection, refraction, drainage, weathering, and structure. "It's a response to the standard code," he noted, "so what this one is doing in a very subtle way is still some kind of grid on the side of the building. It's just responding to the need to reduce cooling loads by tilting the glass away from the side, and that does quite a lot. There are lots of ways of doing that with architecture and thermal and this is one response, which is a very simple and elegant response; but it's not entirely original and it's not entirely unique." "For me," Ryan added, this where SOM's experimentation lies, in this kind of systems thinking. The SOM Tools," another cited submission from this cycle, "were some of the most interesting things we've seen, but this work also kind of goes back to their roots in developing these kind of façades."

"But, added Lavin, "it's also kind of like SOM's roots reconsidered: it may just be beyond the traditional architectural scale of the building and it may be better to go back to systems—which I don't think of as particularly or uniquely SOM project—but turning to systems and tools as a way to recognize that the legacy of monumental modernist buildings is maybe giving way to a new way of thinking about structural systems, forms of aggregation, etc. And beyond the scale of the monumental. So the fact that this one represents itself as prototypical, applicable, shareable is something I really appreciate here."

Denver Union Station: "Most stations work exactly the opposite way"

Denver, Colorado, USA

A tensile fabric superstructure gives this critical piece of infrastructure a soft monumentality, with a suggestion of seams stitched and opened to the city, that encourages a feeling of movement, and discourages the casual pomposity to which this kind of project is often otherwise subject—the quaint illuminated signage and historical presence of the existing civic building, to which this intervention rightly reads as a supplement, does the work of landmark: dome or spire or other symbol. The steel-and-fabric mode builds on a sturdy and familiar high-tech style applied to transportation facilities around the world over the last twenty years; here, it speaks to the thread- or ribbon-like trajectories of trains and passengers, and enables a reading of the building not as in independently freestanding monument, but as an in-between intervention, mediating between different speeds, modes, and levels of movement. It is an awkward but essential scale of operation, between big and small. We were struck how the project, like many that we singled out, attempted to operate at a macro-architectural or micro-urban scale, mediating between body and city, human and urban—in this case through the singular gesture of conceiving of the train station platform covering and perimeter as, figuratively, opening blossoms or breathing gills—addressing the traveler's attention to the nearby skyline and distant horizon. But for all the confidence and deference of the grand urban gesture and intermodal weaving, we worried about the needlework and the fine detailing, where something may have begun to fray.

The jury followed those ribbons and threads, loose and otherwise. Lavin: "I liked this—it's the half-eaten sausage. After seeing so many projects claim [SOM's 1982 Hajj Terminal at] Jeddah as their precedents, this one actually seemed to fit." Haw: "At the macro level, the thing that I find disappointing, which happens a lot with these kinds of infrastructure projects, particularly in the USA, there is an undercroft image that really makes it look like a shopping mall, makes it looks like every other station. And I just think that's so depressing. To me that's the Achilles' heel of this project." Ryan: "What I love, though, is you arrive and you can look up and open up and around and get a sense of where you are in the city; an eye on the city." Haw: "Urbanistically, I think it is very successful." Lavin: Most train stations work exactly the opposite way. Where you're enclosed when you get out of the train and then there are openings at the other end. This is different." De Monchaux: "You're right. Someone has obviously thought about the sequence of experience." Ryan: "And the destination doesn't become the train station itself, necessarily: it becomes that view to the city that you are expecting." De Monchaux: "In a way there is a certain humility to the project, that it defers to a little bit anti-monumental. I would love to have seen something showing a little more thinking about the link between old and the new, this little bridging component they have is forlorn; this little thing is the saddest thing in the world." Ryan: "It's quite chunky still, quite robust. It's a skeleton." Haw: "Yes, there was something very inelegant about this element as well. I think the parti at the macro level is very nice, [but] it's letting itself down in the details." Ryan: "It has such a light touch when you look at it up here" from the bird's-eye view there's so much accomplished with so little." De Monchaux: "But the lightness doesn't hold up as you get closer and closer." Haw: "You look at the details and think: they let the big idea down."

Chhatravati Shivaji International Airport Terminal 2: "A big old fashioned SOM project"

Mumbai, India

The jury was charmed, at first glance, by this visually-charismatic project; and by the geometrical and operational resonances at multiple scales; by how surface patterning translated seamlessly into volumetric modeling; and by how, in a very specific mid-twentieth-century-modernist tradition to which SOM is especially heir, the building seemed to solve—yet perhaps also create—all its problems with one big roof. De Monchaux: "I like this one." Lavin: "Me, too." De Monchaux: "And it's like a big old-fashioned SOM project."

But on closer look, we wondered about the building—considered as a design exercise from that old-fashioned modernist form-follows-function point of view—about whether there was a rigorous economy of means within that visual expression. It's a building that strongly evokes the canonical mid-twentieth-century ferroconcrete airport terminals of Eero Saarinen and Minoru Yamasaki and I. M. Pei, with all the rigor of span and moment that they embodied. And yet we worried that all was not as it seemed. Haw: "My feeling was a bit disappointed in as much as it is a sort of wrapper, when I saw the structural diagram," which reveals metal trusses inside all that indeterminate render, "and I felt: okay that's the structure and then they covered it all up. It's all wallpapered." De Monchaux: It's kind of steel frame masquerading as cast-in-place?" Haw: "Yes, it's not really solid; it's a lightweight structure. It's not honest. It's a big massive frame that's been wrapped." De Monchaux: "It's a beautiful lie." Lavin: "How can an airport be honest or dishonest? I totally understand the legacy of what you are talking about, but at this point …"

At this point, the notion of honest and dishonest is one of those familiar moments where the language of architectural aesthetics borrows from, and perhaps even distorts or is distorted by, the language of ethics itself—what is the significance of a dishonest detail? De Monchaux: "how can an airport be honest or why should it be honest?" Another facet of this question has to do with what puzzled the jury about the Al Ahmadi Cultural Center in Kuwait: the question of context: immediate and adjacent urban settings and settlements; historical and cultural context; vernacular and modern; local and global; national and international—confluences at which airports among typologies are acutely—and perhaps uniquely—positioned. Viscerally—rightly or wrongly—one might be given pause by the contrast between the clinically clean and bright and open spaces of international travel and the density and intensity of human occupation in much of the city beyond, and in the informal settlements, what used to be called slums, right next door. But perhaps the question is less whether one is a mask for the other, since both conditions are honest truths. At this literally and figuratively transporting place, maybe we ask a question about the relationship between personal and universal, national and international, and what is left changed and unchanged over time—and what happens when you get down to the ordinary ground, or even below grade, far from the spectacular, but perhaps only visual, shelter of the big roof.

Studying the development plan that was part of this project's submission, Ryan observed in passing, "I was intrigued about whether the national and international terminals could be interchanged? Is everything truly possible under one roof?" Haw took that provocatively operational question in more conceptual terms: "But the international/national terminal debate is an interesting one: how you differentiate national and international, and that may be another question of detailing. This," the monumental departures hall under its debatably sculptural roof, "is the great space, but then when you go to that image," of secondary spaces, lounges, interstitial circulation, and much else, "again it's the same concern. I have the same fear as I did with the station," that the singular big idea of the building's general gesture hasn't been carried through, with the same conviction or distinction, to every detail. And, as Haw observed, it is precisely in the detailing that these sometimes seemingly irreconcilable distinctions can be addressed, even in the sturdy high-modernist practice of seemingly translating old-fashioned references—tiled or inscribed pavilion walls, the geometry of a peacock feather—into new-fashioned morphologies.

"But," concluded Lavin, "that's the problem with all of these big roof buildings: that it is only at the great main level that you get the roof effects and the big idea." And then, she said, "at a certain point you are going to go below grade."

Shenzhen Rural Commercial Bank Headquarters: "Back to basics"

Shenzhen, China

The default historical reference for the legacy projects of SOM are the gracile Park Avenue towers: Lever House and, some ten blocks north and ten years later, the Pepsi-Cola headquarters. Both buildings developed the typology of an attenuated curtain wall, with subtle lines of spandrels and window frames, all around a dense efficient core. But there is another legacy typology from a generation later: the tough, post-Miesian towers of the late 1960s and early 1970s—several of the best in Chicago, like the tall, dark, and handsome mixed-use John Hancock Center tower of 1970, on North Michigan Avenue, which featured a moment-frame façade with dramatic diagonal members intersecting with corner columns at structural floors, and perhaps the very best in San Francisco, the ALCOA Building of 1967, which featured a surface diagonal bracing frame offset outside from a glass curtain wall within. Perhaps these were high-tech buildings *avant le letre*, without a formal polemic, but with a timelessly Modern conception of solving complex performative problems with systems in steel and glass, which animate a cascade of tributary systems: solar shading, circulation, environmental systems, inhabitation.

The dense and vast cities of our century will require, as much or more as the last, skyscrapers. And, maybe, skyscrapers that are simple, that occupy a larger complexity at the scale of the city, and are occupied by a finer complexity at the scale of their human users. It was, in part, with this robust typology of 1967 and 1970 in mind that the jury looked closer at this skyscraper. Here, we theorized, was SOM doing what SOM does, and well: a tough, clear, no-nonsense skyscraper that worked forward and backward from structure above all. In 2016, alas to some, the bracing is a little lacier, the palette a little more pearlescent—all is not a 1970s vision of oxidizing steel and bronze. But that's okay; maybe they're getting back to something. The jury's discussion was as direct as, perhaps, we wished the building itself to be. Haw: "It's a very direct, very simple concept." Lavin: It's most "SOM-ish." Haw: "It's just very pleasant, back to basics. And I quite like it for that simplicity."

SOM Tools: "Design as research"

SOM HPD Methodology + SOM Wind Tunnel 260, 2011–12

Design, at best, is always research. The jury included this project by, as it were, acclaim; without the kind of comprehensive technical interrogation or conceptual discussion that, to be sure, it clearly merits. To discuss the current cutting-edge work of SOM that this research represents is to recover—because of the firm's institutional history and mid-twentieth-century-position at the center of the development of the idea of the modern in architecture—something essential and timeless about the modern project: an interest in technology that transcends a taste for an industrial aesthetic. Not buildings that necessarily resemble machines, but buildings that participate in the mindset of iterative experimentation and empirical observation that gave us, since the era of Isambard Kingdom Brunel and Joseph Paxton, our mechanical world. The ongoing global ecological catastrophe that is one legacy of that world calls for, of course, a deflected but deepened application of the same sensibility. By designers of the built environment, above all. The jury affirmed, with this selection, the obligation of design firms of SOM's scale and resources to be, as it were, a second academy, an institute in practice that is an incubator and engine of possibility.

The University Center at The New School: "Busying around"

New York, New York, USA

A puzzle box. An urban campus building without, in the traditional bucolic sense, a campus. An eye-catcher without a prospect. A lot of fire stairs. A lot to talk about. The jury admired the synthesis of a complex and ambitious program on an uncompromising and in some ways unpromising site, but we recalled educational buildings of the recent past that imaged how the provocations of pedagogy could drive and be driven by transformations in the typology itself.

De Monchaux began, "Living not too far from there, I think that it solves some of the local urban problems convincingly." But, countered Haw, "I think it's unclear. A bit of a mess. Aesthetically I'm not too sure of what I am looking at, it's rather gimmicky, it's not a classic, it's more a fashionable type of project." De Monchaux: "The gimmick is the graphic façade?" Haw: "Yes, it's a bit messy and doesn't have enough gravitas for me. A lot of the insides don't translate out. If we are looking in the context of SOM's work, the resolution of those things should be a lot better."

Lavin: "On the one hand, I thought it was another example of how SOM, at least in this selection of projects, did not seem to be doing as well on smaller-scale projects where a different kind of finesse is needed. On the other hand, I thought this is a building that I would not have thought was done by SOM—and I like it for that reason. And I thought it could be done by a smaller younger firm; now, that could be a kiss of death but it spoke of a weird ambition that was not maybe realized. I do think that there are a lot of school buildings being done now. The part that is very SOM-like is that there is no," evidence in the building's programming of, "innovation in pedagogy; it's really standard." Personally, I think the "subtle innovation would be the expansion and blurring of lines between a kind of expanded circulation space and informal classroom space."

Lavin: "Yes, but if you think of the Morphosis building at Cooper Union [2009's 41 Cooper Square] for example, and we've gone beyond that. And if you even go back twenty years to Venturi at Wu Hall [at Princeton University] that's now its own standard for innovation; or I was thinking of," Diller, Scofidio + Renfro's 2011 Granoff Center for the Creative Arts at Brown University, which, "takes a very bizarre circulation system and uses that to provoke a very interesting set of pedagogical premises. It also made me feel like the SOM-ness of it was betrayed by the way it maximally fulfilled the program requirements of the client and didn't push back or add or resist in any way. So I think of work like that of Lacaton & Vassal, which has had to do with saying you have to have empty space for X or Y, or you do various things to expand its possibilities. So I think [this project] didn't do any of those things, but I thought it might be a project about which one could raise that demand, if that's a useful way to use the jury." De Monchaux: "I see some of that same awkwardness, yet it's a project trying to do something, it's by no means complacent, it doesn't exude the serene self-satisfaction that some other projects do. These deep angles when you are on the sidewalk, they create sight lines as you are adjacent to the building, which is the more typical new york perspective, you are never frontal to a building on an avenue. So these steep angles of the façade really allow this kind of deeply shallow oblique transparency. Which is interesting."

Ryan addressed the urban scale and setting: "I agree with Sylvia," about wondering whether the building could more fully architecturally prompt or enable innovation in pedagogy, about the need for, "dialogue in rethinking these types of projects, in questioning and communicating. And when you come to the images of the interior, it's standard. But as an urban element, mediating between the scales of building, campus, and city, the street level, "seems actually quite lively and it brings something to this very dense streetscape. But the lines here—It looks more exciting from the outside, urbanistically." De Monchaux: I think it has to be exciting because it is in such a visually stimulating site. There's a lot of ingenuity, a lot of three-dimensional ingenuity and Rubik's-Cubing all of this into this tiny block, a Manhattan kind of intelligence, although it really doesn't come across in images. With all that contextual complexity to mirror and manage, Ryan conceded, the building doesn't always avoid, "confusion but I like the windows here, it's fun to look out and see people busying around."

SOM Journal 10 Submissions

22 Hanover Square
London, UK

All Aboard Florida
Miami, Florida

Beijing Tianqiao Preforming Arts District
Master Plan
Beijing, China

Changsha North Star Delta Tower
Changsha, China

Chicago Public Library, Chinatown Branch
Chicago, Illinois

Dubai Tower
Dubai, UAE

Future Home 2050

Guiyang Cultural Plaza Tower
Guiyang, China

Guohua Financial Tower
Ningbo, China

Halcon Mesa

Hexi Tower
Nanjing, China

Iris Tower
Paris, France

LAX Pedestrian Bridge Prototype
Los Angeles, California

Nozul
Doha, Qatar

Pertamina Energy Tower
Jakarta, Indonesia

Raffles American School
Iskandar, Malaysia

Subtractions, Additions, Enhancements

Timber Tower Fargo Block 9
Fargo, North Dakota

University of Conneticut Master Plan
Storrs, Connecticut

Al Ahmadi Cultural Center

Al Ahmadi, Kuwait
Designed 2013–14

The Al Ahmadi Cultural Center is one of a series of new cultural centers proposed by the National Council for Culture, Arts and Letters (NCCAL) in Kuwait. The client's vision for the Cultural Center is that it will promote art, music, theater, and dance, celebrate Kuwaiti Culture, and inspire young Kuwaitis to study the arts.

Al Ahmadi is located south of Kuwait City, in an oil-rich area that has always been an economic engine for the country. The project presents an opportunity to extend cultural awareness to this region typically devoid of cultural resources, and to act as an attractor, sparking development in a currently under-developed neighborhood.

The program consists of two 800-seat theaters, a 400-seat concert hall, a hybrid lecture hall/cinema, a conference center, a children's center, galleries for the fine arts and historic objects, and below-grade parking. These spaces were organized in a square plan with a courtyard in the center, recalling the inward focus of traditional Islamic architecture. The plan locates the four major assembly spaces in each of the four corners, with the gallery sequences beginning along the sides.

In response to Kuwait's severe climate, the building's envelope was designed to filter sunlight to usable levels for the display of sensitive historical artifacts, and provide thermal mass to reduce cooling loads. This is accomplished using a series of pre-cast light-diffusing modules that allows light into the space while keeping the source of the light concealed. The low window to wall ratio and the square form of the building naturally allows for the most thermally efficient enclosure possible.

The modules occur at different scales: the façade module and the clerestory module stack like bricks to create the building façade. At the roof level, there are ten monumental light monitors that illuminate the courtyard at the center of the 115-meter floor plate. Located at each corner of the courtyard, addressing the four cardinal directions, the large arching windows filter natural light through modern Mashrabiya screens. Altogether these light wells create an even 150 lux, optimal for viewing artwork and displays. In the lecture hall, the light is modulated so that it can be shut for lecture or film-screening purposes. In the two 800-seat theaters, the façade lighting serves as house lighting during intermissions.

The three-dimensionality of the façade is emphasized at night by the illumination coming from each of the modules. The light patterns generated recall textiles created using the traditional Kuwaiti Al-Sadu process, which are on view in the galleries.

<< 1 Aerial view showing site; Mahboula Region, south of Kuwait City
< 2 Exterior rendering showing the façade's three-dimensionality
3 Program sketch-diagram; courtyard as main organizational device
4 Site plan showing project's location among several unbuilt sites in the half-developed neighborhood

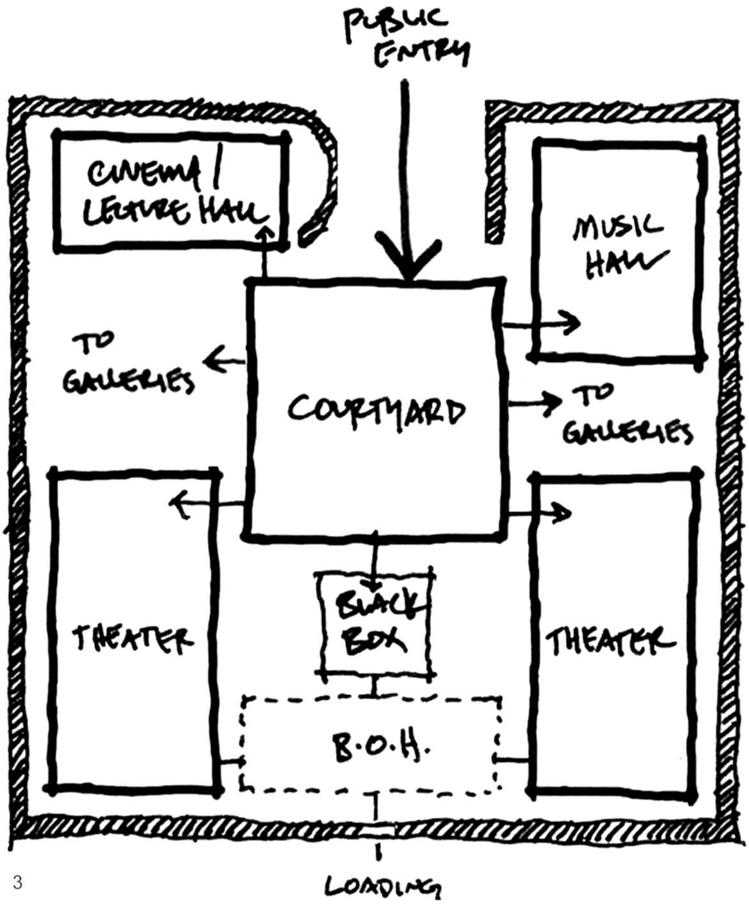

3

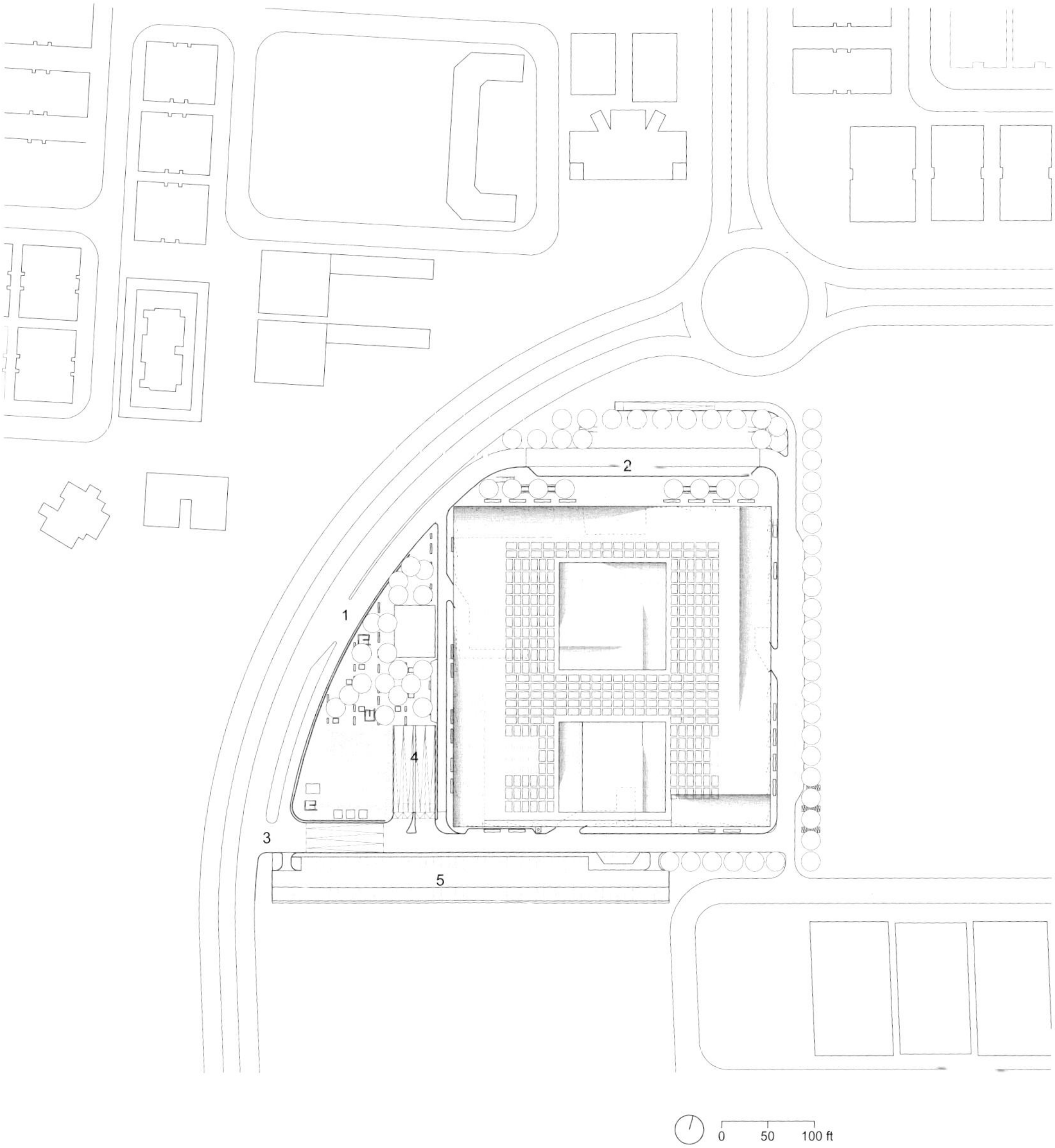

4

1 SITE ENTRY
2 DROP-OFF
3 SITE EXIT
4 TO PARKING BELOW GRADE
5 SURFACE PARKING

1 ENTRY
2 COURTYARD
3 CONCERT HALL (400 SEATS)
4 LECTURE HALL / CINEMA (250 SEATS)
5 THEATER A (800 SEATS)
6 THEATER B (800 SEATS)
7 BLACK BOX THEATER
8 BACKSTAGE
9 STAGE
10 CONCERT HALL LOBBY
11 RESTAURANT
12 LOBBY
13 LOBBY
14 PRAYER ROOMS
15 ELEVATORS
16 PERFORMERS LOUNGE
17 LOADING DOCK
18 INFORMATION DESK
19 DRESSING ROOMS
20 SCENE SHOP
21 PARKING
22 THEATER A LOBBY
23 THEATER B LOBBY
24 BLACK BOX THEATER LOBBY
25 LECTURE HALL / CINEMA LOBBY
26 GREEN ROOM
27 VIP LOUNGE
28 CHILDREN'S CENTER
29 FINE ART GALLERY
30 HERITAGE GALLERY

5 Building section, north-south
6 Ground floor plan

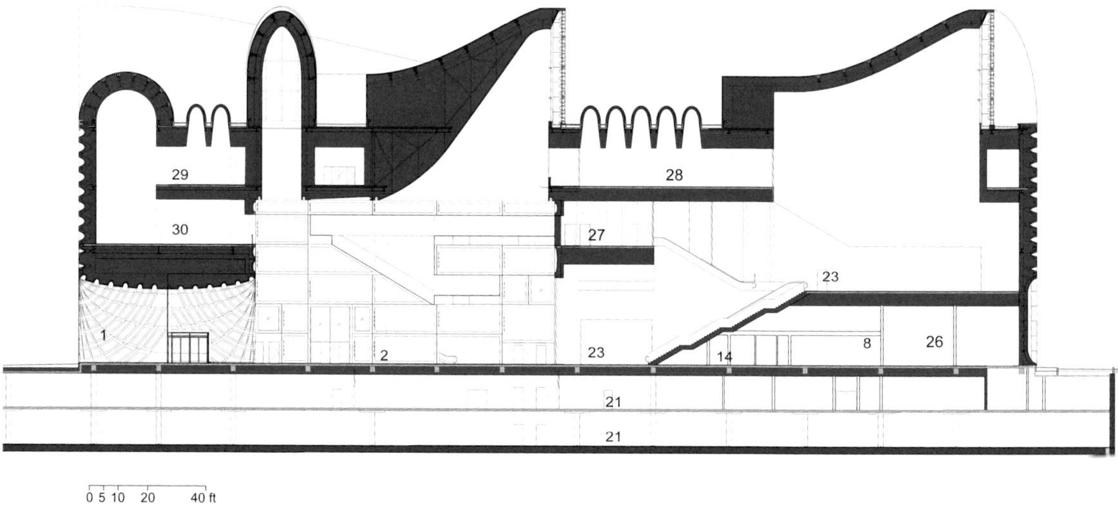

5

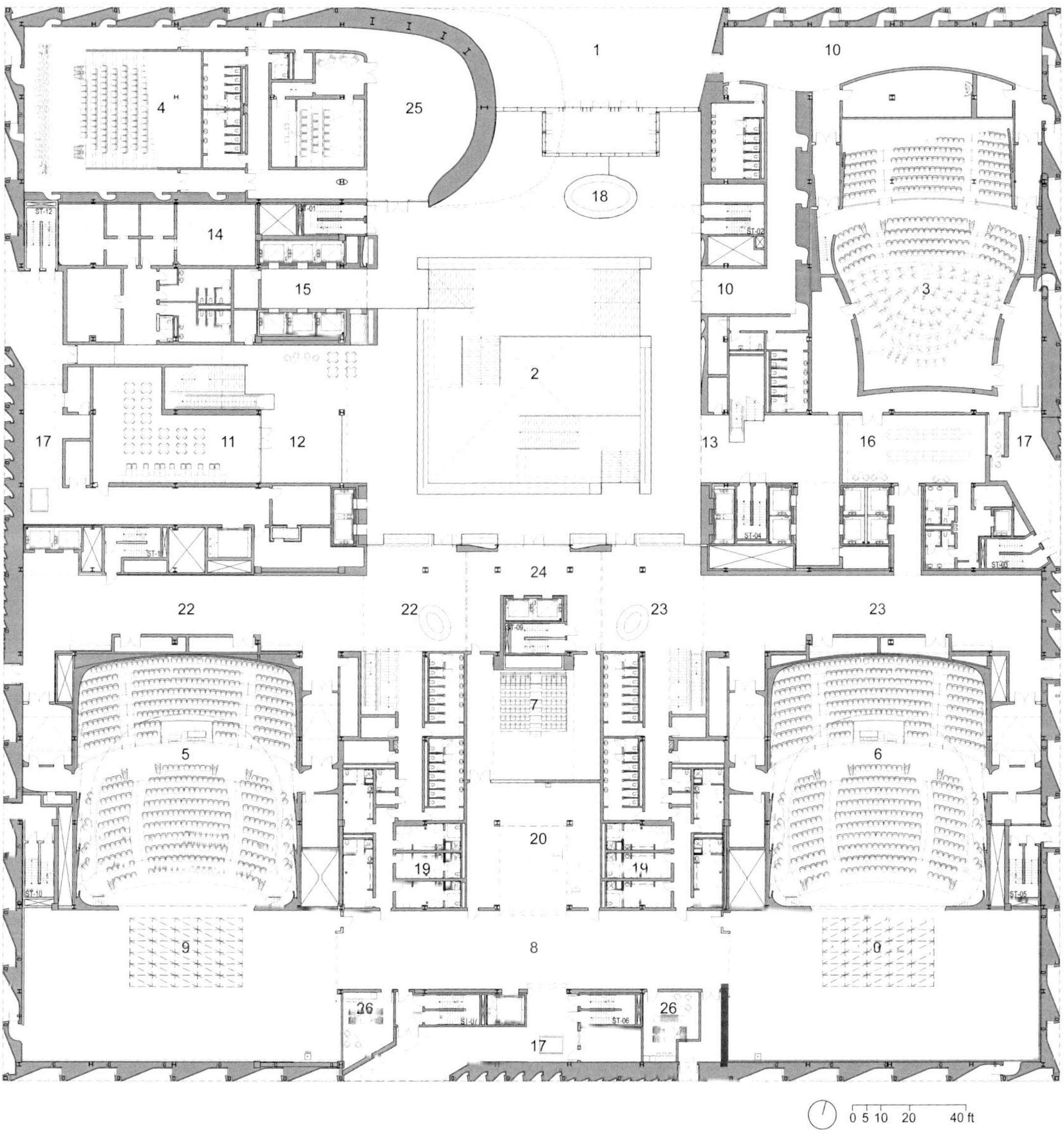
1
2
3
4
5
6
7
8
9
0
10
11
12
13
14
15
16
17
18
19
20
22
23
24
25
26
0 5 10 20 40 ft

6

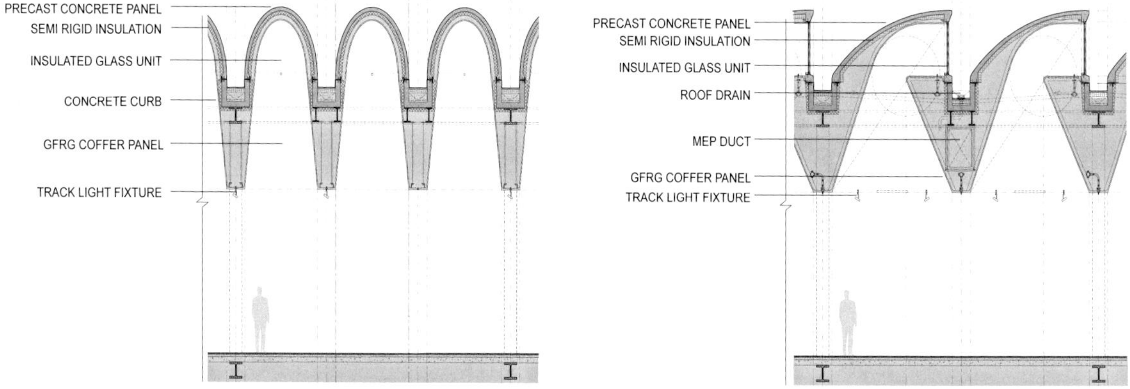

7

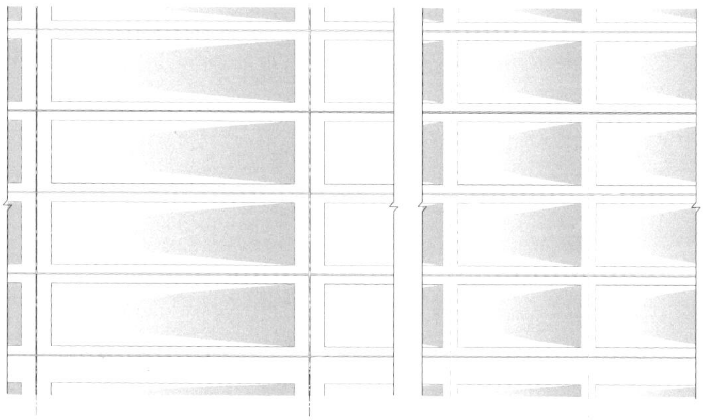

ENLARGED ELEVATION

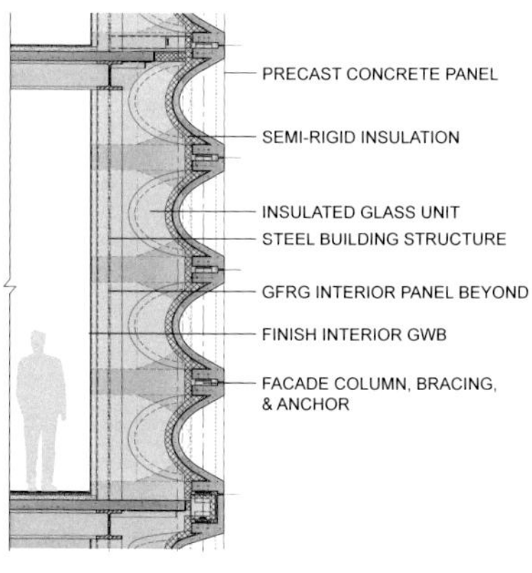

WALL SECTION

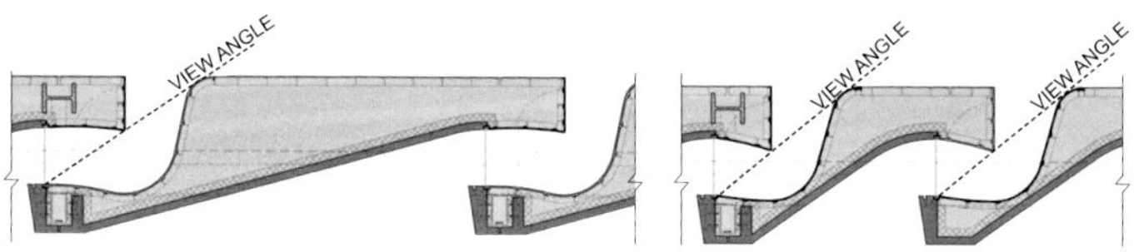

PLAN DETAIL

8

7 Enlarged section through clerestory light diffusing modules at gallery roof
8 Enlarged elevation, section, and plan detail of façade precast concrete light-monitoring modules
9 Precast concrete façade panel mockup
10 Axonometric view of exterior wall assembly
11 Interior daylight-study model

9

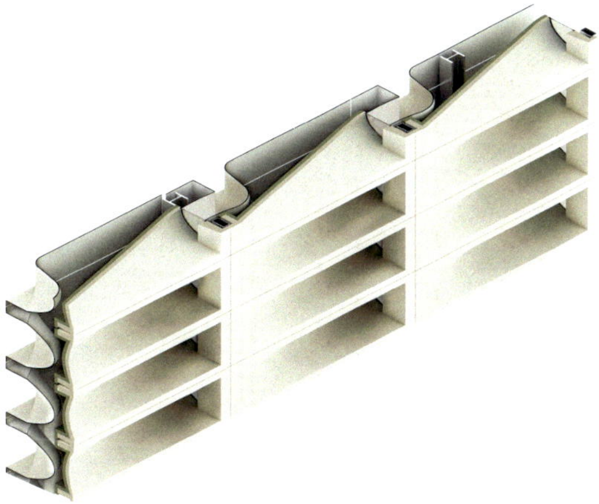

10

11

12

13

12 Theater lobby and conference center rendering; monumental light monitors filter natural light and animate the space
13 Fine arts gallery rendering; clerestory façade light diffusing modules filter daylight to create an even 150 LUX, ideal for artwork display

14

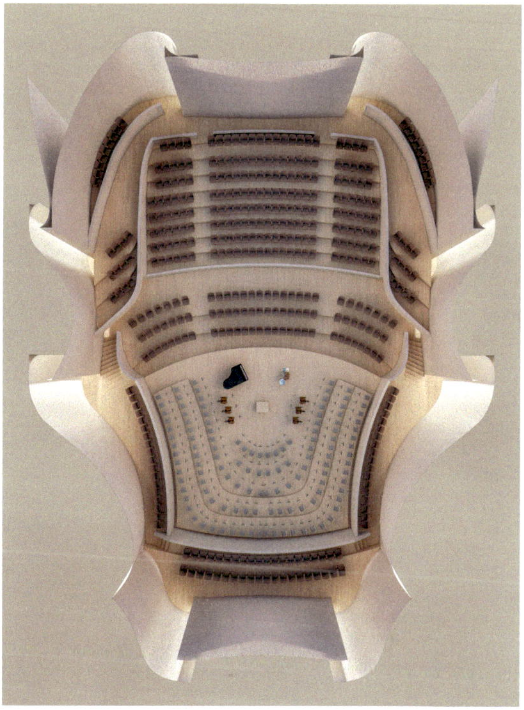

15

14 Concert hall interior rendering; the façade creates a dramatic backdrop for traditional music

15 Concert hall plan rendering; the hall's unique shape was fine-tuned to improve acoustics

Chhatrapati Shivaji International Airport Terminal 2

Mumbai, India
Designed 2007–14

The design for the new Chhatrapati Shivaji International Airport Terminal 2 adds 4.4 million square feet of new space to accommodate 40 million passengers per year while operating twenty-four hours a day. The terminal combines international and domestic passenger services under one roof, optimizing terminal operations and reducing passenger-walking distances. Inspired by the form of traditional Indian pavilions, the new four-story terminal stacks a grand headhouse, or central processing podium, on top of highly adaptable and modular concourses below. Rather than compartmentalizing terminal functions, all concourses radiate outward from a central processing core and are easily reconfigured to "swing" between serving domestic or international flights.

The prominent location of the airport bestows it with a strong presence within a portion of the city that is experiencing rapid growth and redevelopment. Terminal 2 is a significant part of this renaissance serving as an infrastructural anchor for the neighborhood. By integrating into the existing transportation system and by furthering connectivity through the simultaneous development of a new road network to service the airport, the terminal helps connect the historic heart of Mumbai to the south with the city's burgeoning peripheries to the east and north.

A key feature of the terminal design is a long-span roof covering 70,000 square meters, making it one of the world's largest roofs without an expansion joint. The roof is supported by thirty massive columns spaced at sixty-four meters north to south and at thirty-four meters east to west. SOM increased the depth of the trusses near the columns, and ran trusses in both an orthogonal grid and a forty-five-degree grid, resulting in generous spacing and cantilevers of 40 meters along the perimeter.

Due to the many site constraints—such as the presence of the Mithi River and nearby designated historical spaces—the terminal's elongated X-shape plan could both mold around existing structures and incorporate modular designs to accommodate rapid and phased construction. The X-plan came about not as a figure imposed on the site, but as a response to the necessity to "create" more airside for gates, remote stands, and taxi lanes.

Mr. Sanjay Reddy, Managing Director of MIAL, stated his goals very succinctly—the terminal must embody "the heritage of India and the spirit of Mumbai" with a modern, efficient, functional, and yet unmistakably Indian terminal. India is known for its hospitality, vibrant colors, and rich cultural heritage. The design sought to provide a sense of warmth through the application of wood ceilings, natural stones, and intimate lighting. There are many design features that allude to traditional Indian architecture, arts, and crafts such as the coffered ceiling of the main high roof, the jali screens, the strong colonnade of piers, and the back-lighted *diya* lamp wall in the immigration hall.

Departing travelers enter a warm, light-filled chamber, sheltered underneath a long-span roof supported by an array of thirty multi-story mushrooming columns that call to mind the airy pavilions of traditional regional architecture. At points in the lower-level arrivals hall and baggage reclaim, passengers can look up through openings around each column and see the roof above. Likewise, departing passengers can look down into these arrivals spaces. Small disks of colorful glass recessed within the canopy's coffers speckle the hall below with colored light that references the peacock, the national bird of India, and the symbol of the airport.

The retail hub is a common space that allows passengers to shop, eat, and watch planes take off through expansive, floor-to-ceiling windows. Within these spaces and throughout the concourses, culturally referential fixtures and details, such as custom chandeliers inspired by the lotus flower and traditional mirror mosaic work created by local artists ground the traveler to a community and culture beyond the airport. The prevalence of local art and culture, coupled with the use of warm colors and elegant accents, elevate the ambience of the terminal beyond the typical, often unimaginative airport experience.

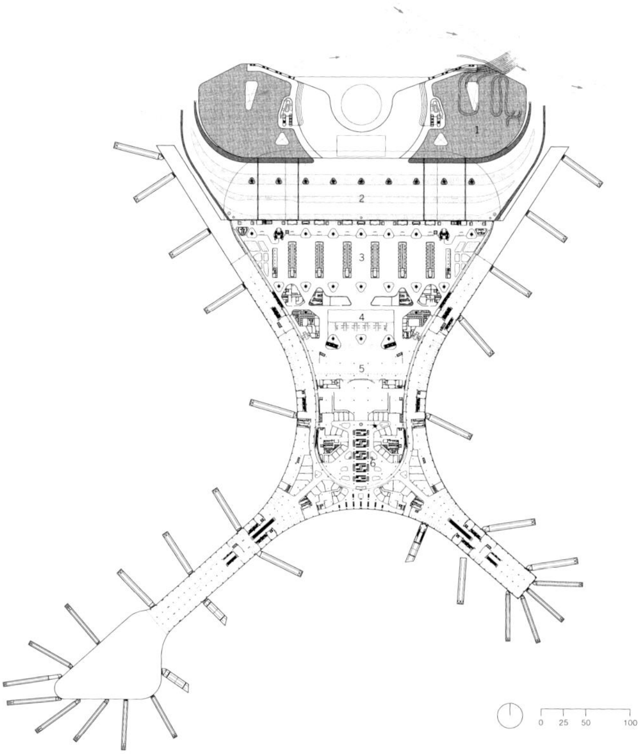

3

1 PARKING
2 DEPARTURES CURB
3 CHECK-IN HALL
4 SECURITY
5 OUTBOUND IMMIGRATION
6 RETAIL

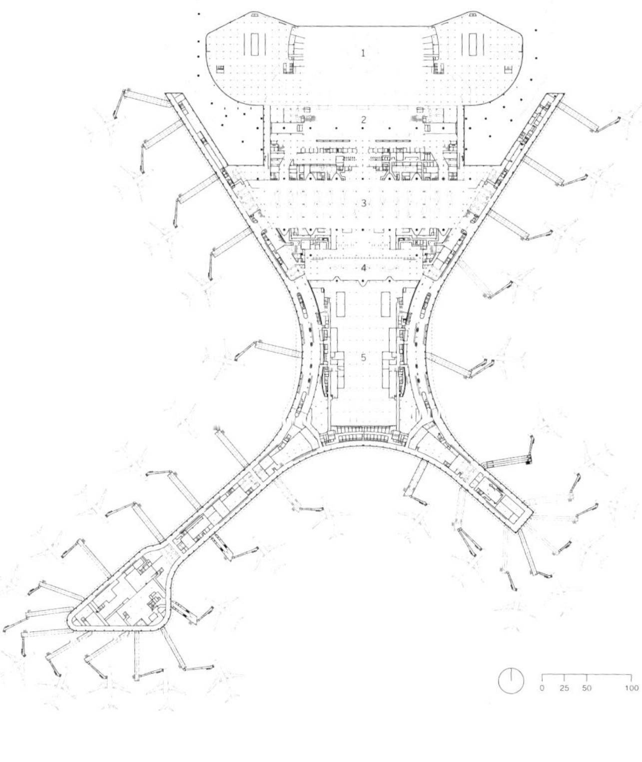

4

1 ARRIVALS PLAZA
2 ARRIVALS HALL
3 BAGGAGE CLAIM
4 INBOUND IMMIGRATION
5 ARRIVALS CORRIDOR

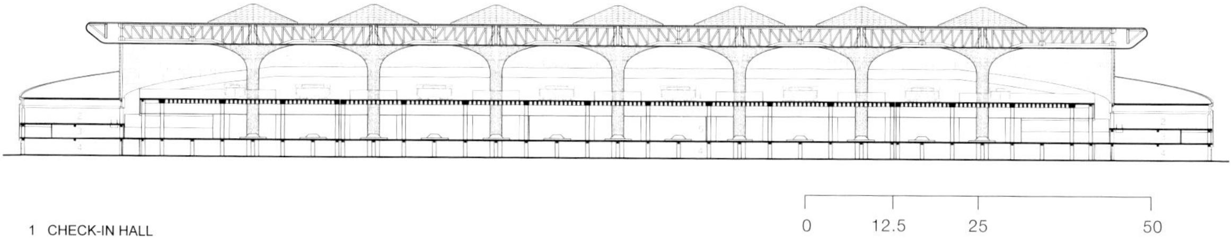

1 CHECK-IN HALL
2 DEPARTURES GATES
3 ARRIVALS
4 SERVICE
5 BAGGAGE CLAIM

5

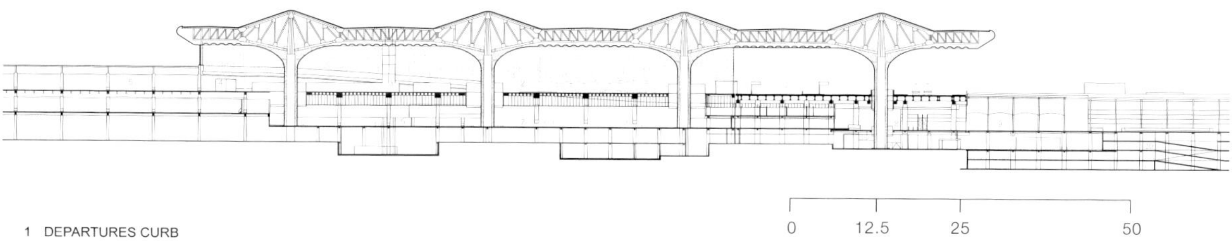

1 DEPARTURES CURB
2 CHECK-IN HALL
3 SECURITY
4 OUTBOUND IMMIGRATION
5 RETAIL
6 INBOUND IMMIGRATION
7 BAGGAGE CLAIM
8 ARRIVALS HALL
9 ARRIVALS PLAZA
10 PARKING

6

<< 1 Aerial view of the site after completion of phase one
< 2 View looking south at terminal headhouse just prior to opening
3 Fourth floor departures plan
4 Second floor arrivals plan
5 East-west section of terminal headhouse
6 North-south section of terminal headhouse

7 Rendered site plan
8 Construction phasing diagrams
9 Diagram of existing terminal, site constraints, and new terminal plan
10 Organizational flow for departing passengers

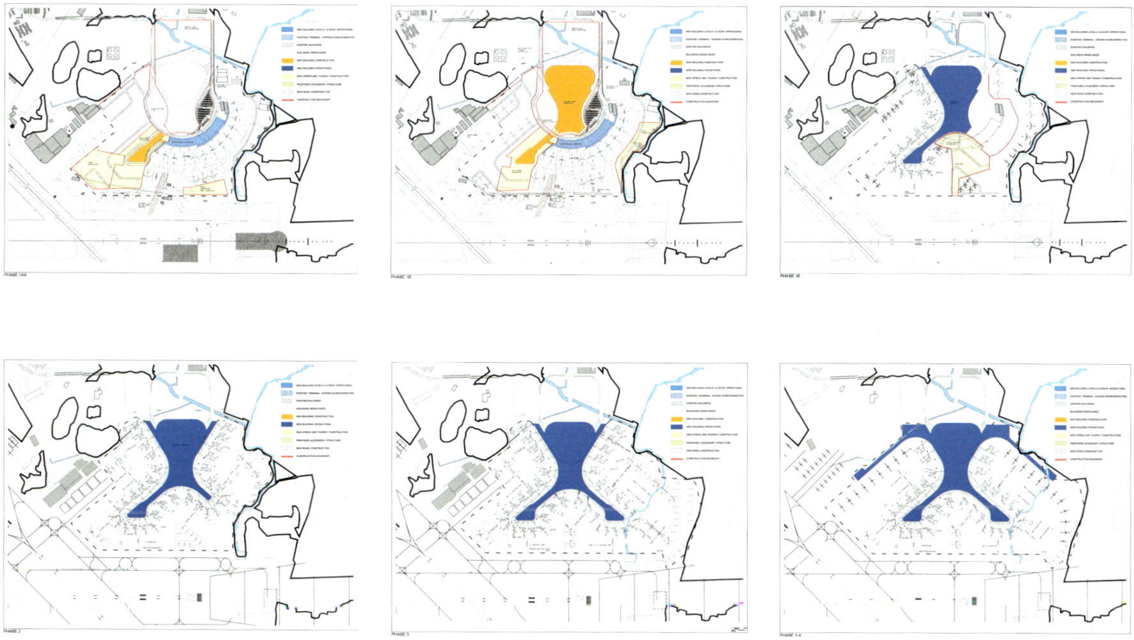

8

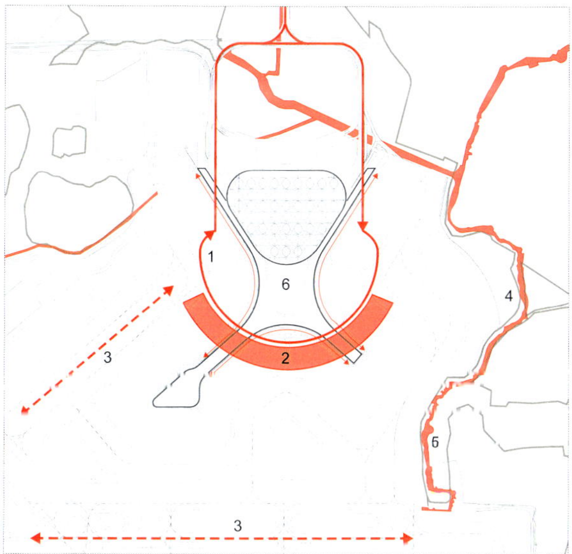

9

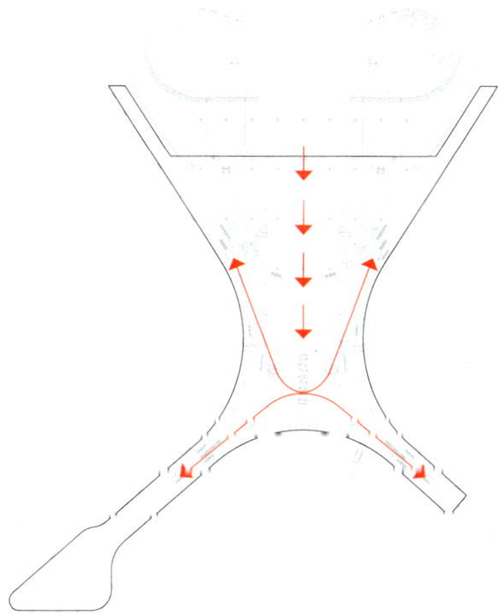

10

1 EXISTING DROP OFF LOOP
2 EXISTING TERMINAL
3 EXISTING TAXI/RUNWAYS
4 MITHI RIVER
5 HISTORIC VILLAGES
6 X - FORM

11

12

13

14

11 Departures Lounge with lotus chandeliers
12 Gate in Departures Lounge
13 Diya wall in Immigration Hall
14 Escalator opening from Ticketing Hall

15

16

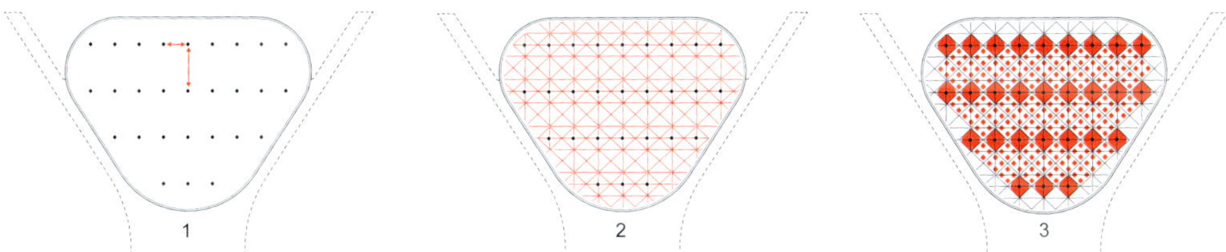

17

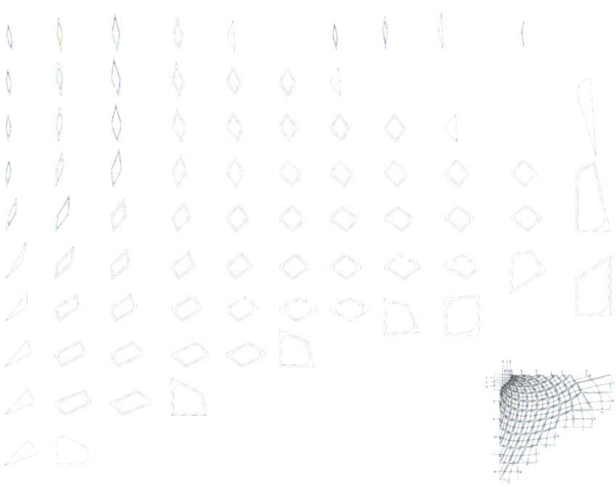

18

15 Detail view of exterior column top
16 Study model of feature column
17 Headhouse column diagrams
18 Unrolled coffer panel drawing
>19 Ticketing Hall just after completion

F

CITIC Financial Center

Shenzhen, China
Designed 2014 – ongoing

Positioned in a prime location with exceptional access to waterfront parks and rapid transit in the city's new Shenzhen Bay Super Headquarters district, CITIC Financial Center aims to be a new landmark for the city and a model of innovative sustainable development for all of China. As the foundational development of the district and the most convenient to the modern subway system, the project will be both the center of CITIC Securities and a nexus of public activity, connecting the urban environment with the landscape and the waterfront park by the bay. Through the integration of architecture, landscape, and engineering with a culturally sensitive urban strategy, the CITIC design seeks to advance the legacy of SOM and the firm's progressive implementation of applied research methods.

Only thirty-five years ago Shenzhen became the first Chinese city designated as a special economic zone, catalyzing its transformation from a rural fishing village to the dense urban metropolis it is today. In this context, the CITIC Financial Center will be a demonstration of SOM's research-based process and integrated practice, combining the firm's expertise in high-performance structural and environmental design with new research on best practices in Chinese urban planning and systems-based landscape design.

The project proposes a pair of towers to house a mix of office, condominium, and hotel areas, with a podium connected to the smaller hotel tower (Tower 2) for hotel amenities, conference centers, a ballroom, restaurants, and retail spaces. The project includes an adjacent park with below-grade retail connected on multiple levels to the main program spaces, to a new public transit metro line, and to the waterfront park.

The form and integral structural concept for the 312-meter and 212-meter towers are directly informed by climatic and geographic parameters specific to the project site. The towers are designed to resist primary lateral forces that affect the structure differently at the base and in the upper zones. Shenzhen is located in a seismic zone with moderate intensity, dictating structural design requirements at the base, while the height of the towers subjects them to lateral wind forces that define the metrics at the top. The global transformation of the form, from a solid square base to a circular geometry at the top, is driven by these performance measures, but also relates to Chinese cultural symbols. The geometry of the perimeter frame is inspired by SOM research on optimal discrete truss geometries and minimizes the structural material required. Based on the eponymous Mitchell truss, the similar but distinct brace geometry of each tower morphs from the bottom to the top, creating continuous variation in the brace angles over the height of the building to maximize the rigidity of the overall structure. Within the macro-structure of the diagrid, a fine-grain system of environmental façade details gives the towers a performance-driven texture.

Pulling the structure to the exterior simplifies interior layouts with column-free interiors, allows operable shades to pass cleanly behind the diagrid, and improves the performance of the building envelope by reducing glazing-incident solar radiation. An optimized light shelf and shading fin results not only in a preservation of views, but also a reduction in electric lighting use, with the knock-on effect of further reducing cooling loads and improving the thermal performance of the tower.

Connected directly to the shorter tower, the podium is conceived as an extension of the adjacent park, connecting indoor and outdoor spaces to generate public activity on all levels. The large ballroom space is formally distinguished as a cantilevered volume oriented toward the bay, while the south-west corner is eroded in contrast. The terraces created by this erosion suggest a formal relationship with the park and provide extensive outdoor seating areas for visitors to enjoy the warm weather of the sub-tropical Shenzhen climate. A dramatic central atrium and carefully stacked circulation system allow for accessible program spaces throughout. Every level of the podium is an accessible, landscaped open space with various program possibilities.

2

< 1 Aerial view showing site
2 Rendering of area between towers showing connecting bridge, pedestrian area, and lobby entrances
3 Project rendering looking south of the two towers and waterfront activity at dusk

4 Map showing project's waterfront site and convenient location for business and travel
5 Roof plan showing connections to parks and future waterfront amenities

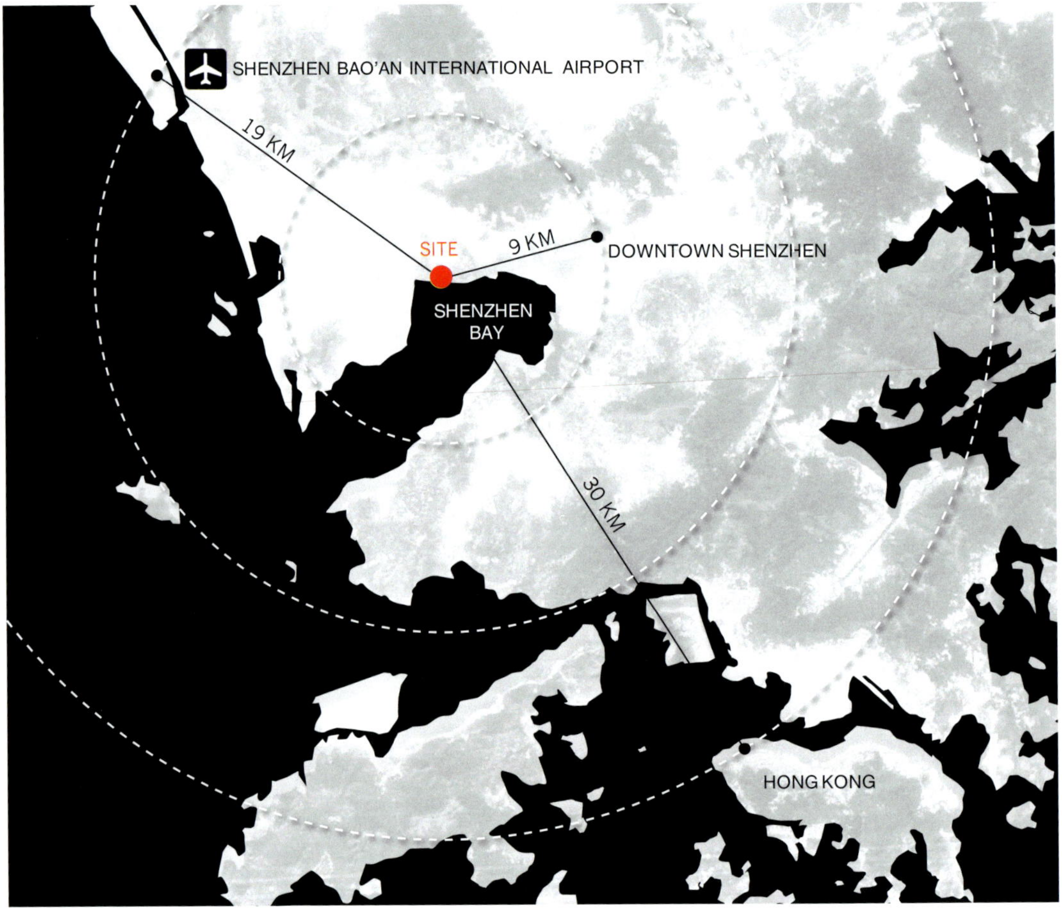

4

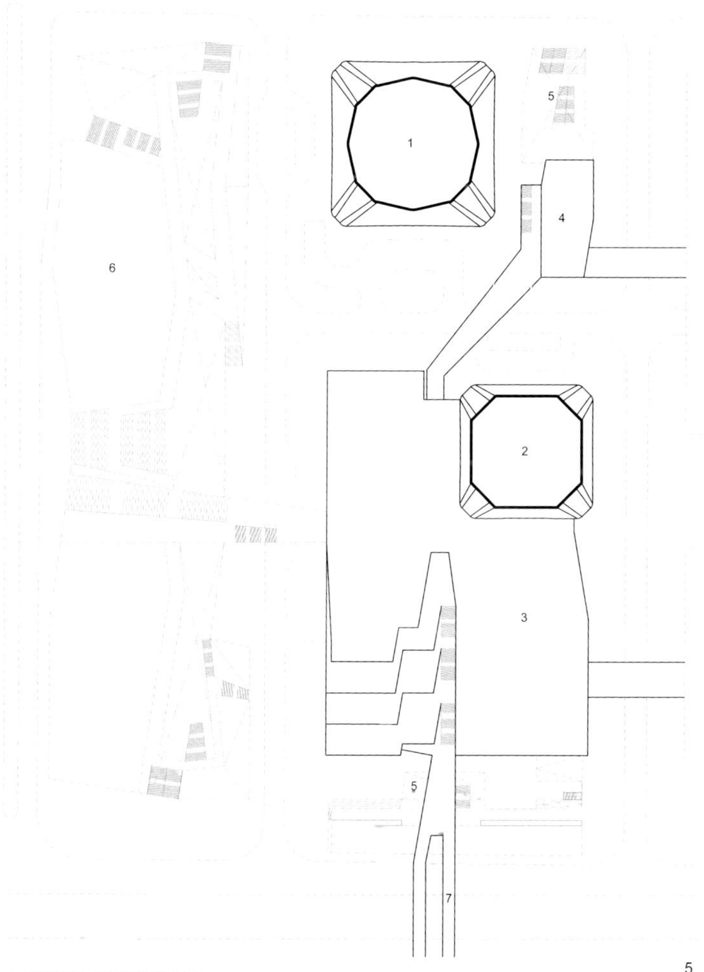

1 TOWER 1 - OFFICE/CONDO
2 TOWER 2 - HOTEL/SOHO
3 PODIUM - CONVENTION/BALLROOM/RETAIL
4 RETAIL PAVILION
5 SUNKEN PLAZA
6 PHASE 2 PARK
7 FUTURE CONNECTION TO WATERFRONT PARK

6 North-south section of tower one, with elevation of tower two
7 Tower one: 63rd residential floor plan
8 Tower one: 28th residential floor plan

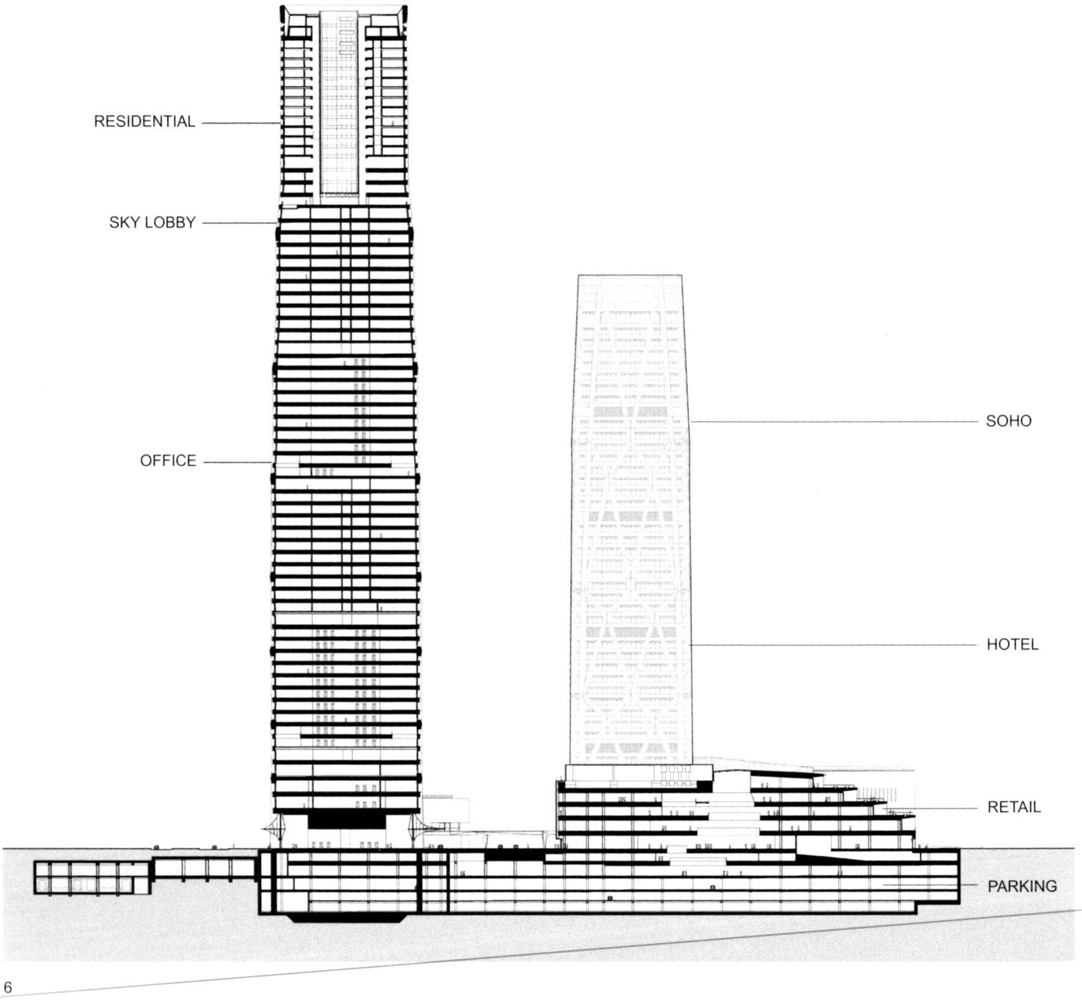

6

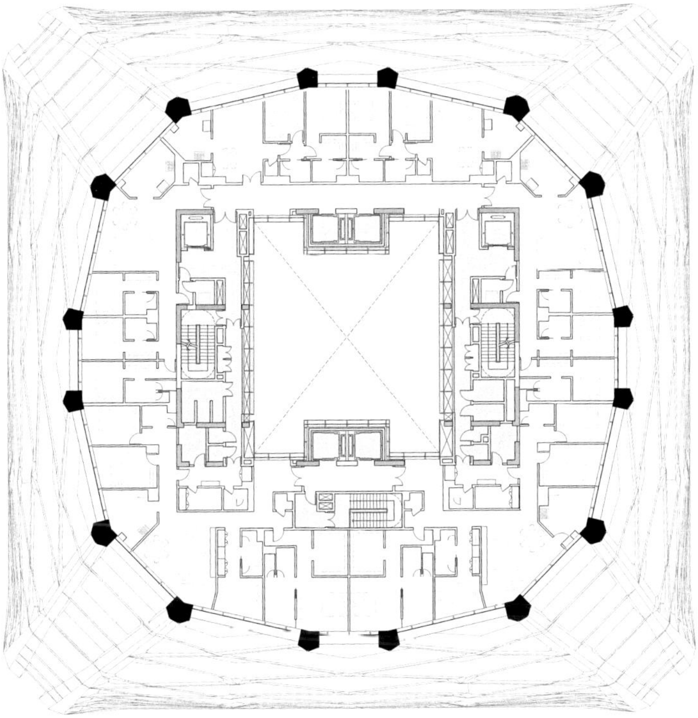

7

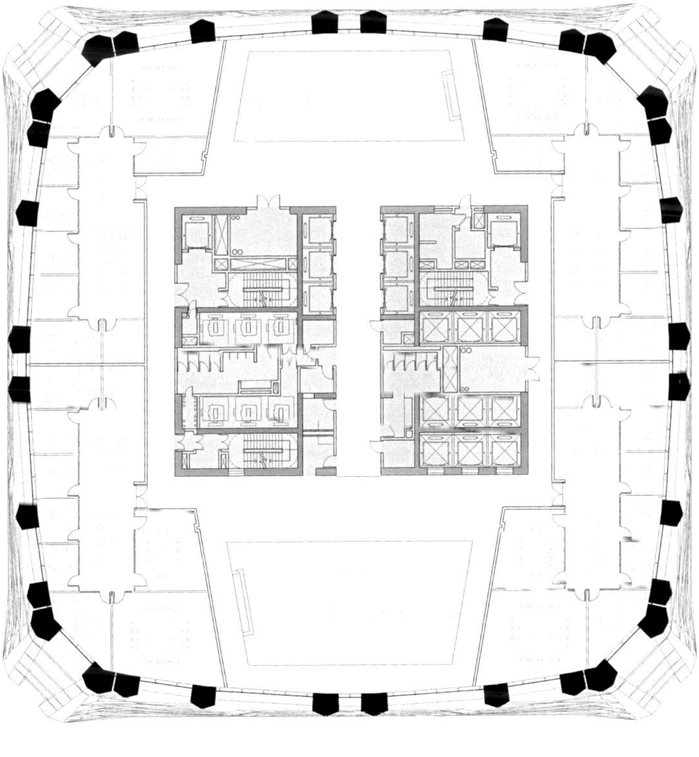

8

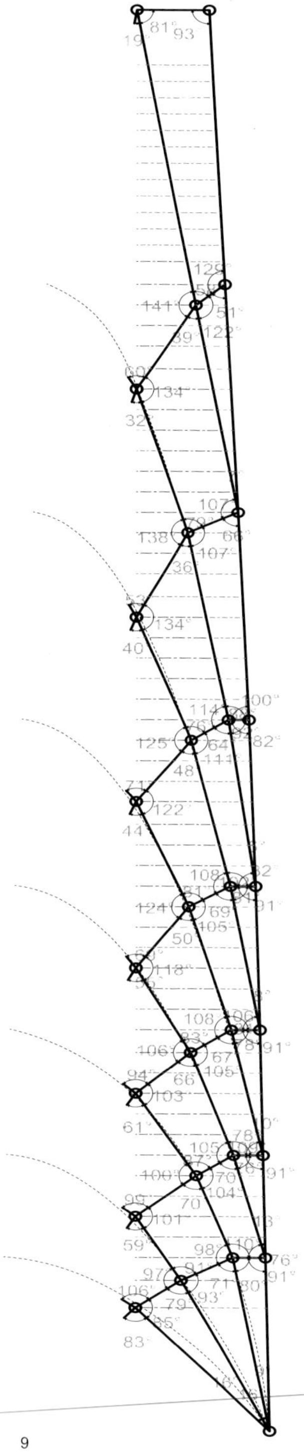

9

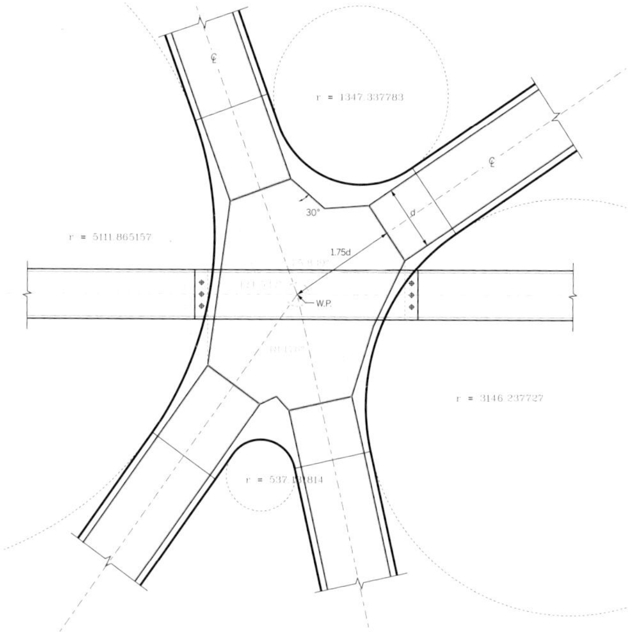

10

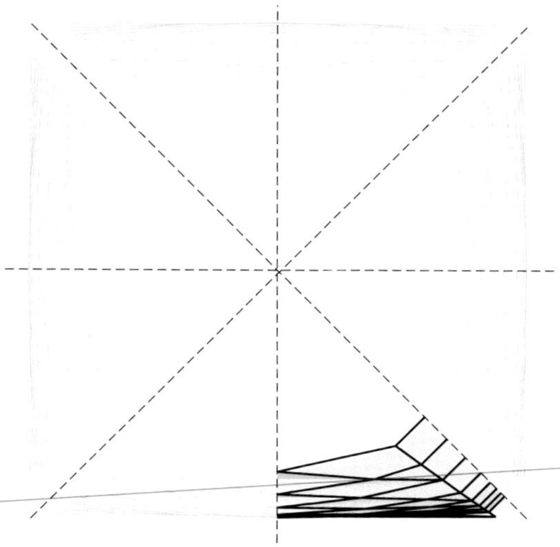

11

12

9 Half elevation showing structural connection locations
10 Typical node diagram
11 Plan showing symmetry axes
12 Detail of structural system and curtain wall

13 Diagram showing evolution of truss geometries to final structural design
14 Structural concept showing how truss design changes to mitigate effects of seismic and wind forces

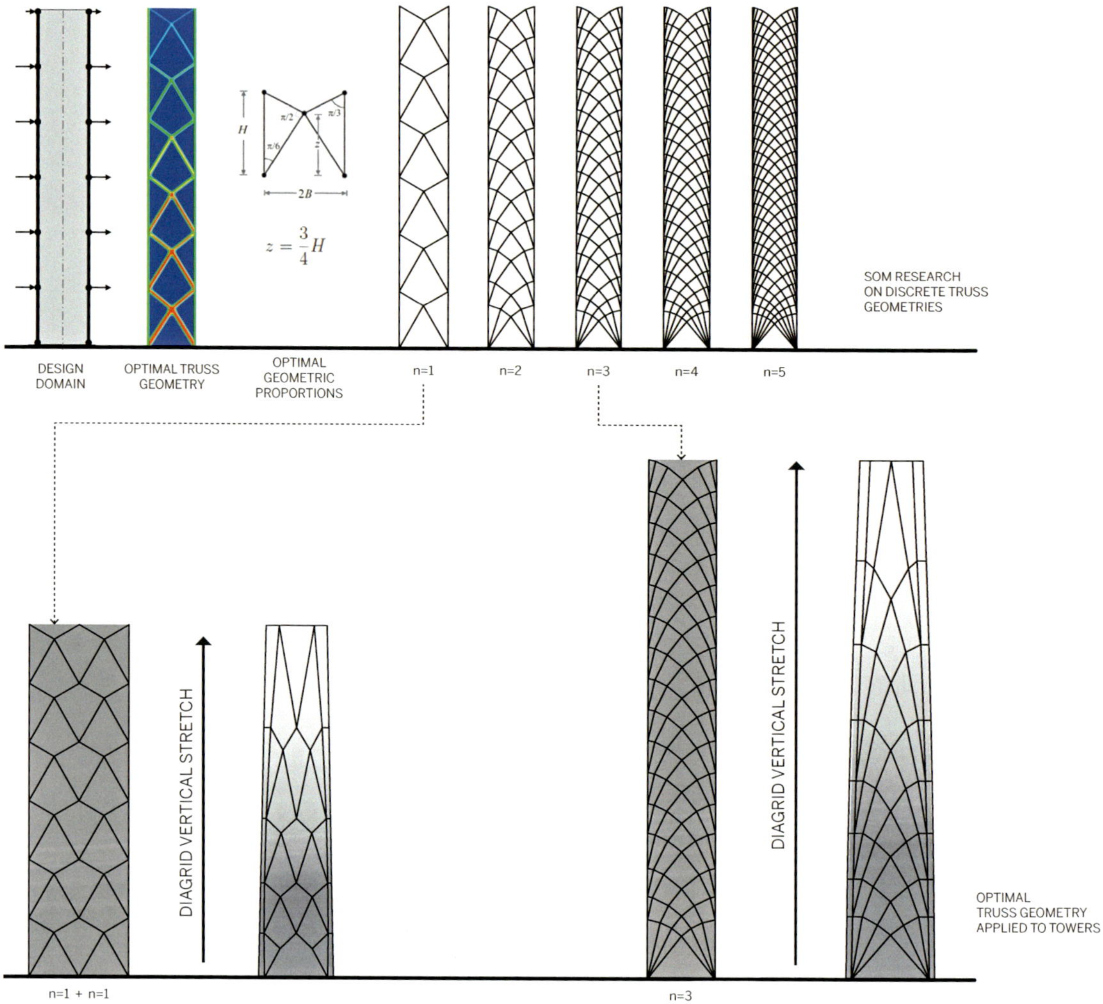

13

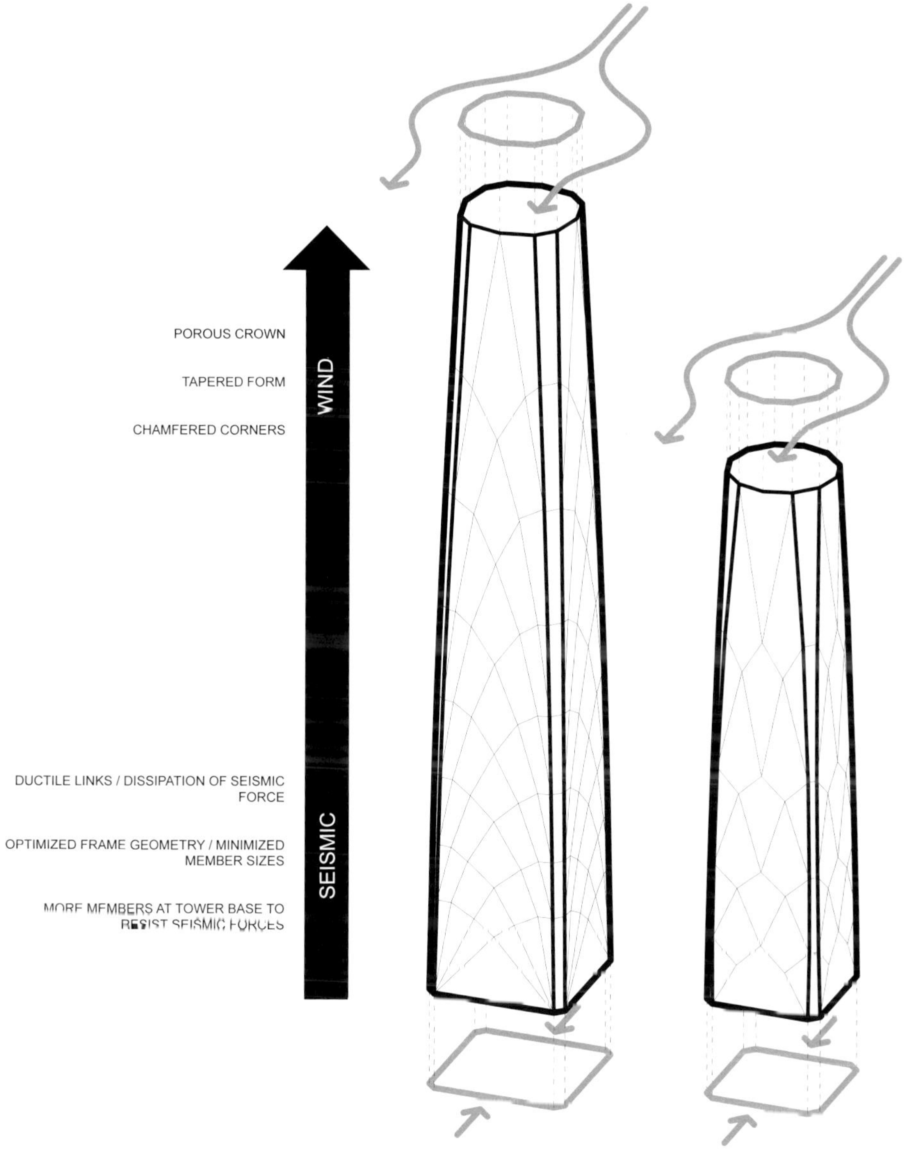
POROUS CROWN
TAPERED FORM
CHAMFERED CORNERS
WIND
DUCTILE LINKS / DISSIPATION OF SEISMIC FORCE
OPTIMIZED FRAME GEOMETRY / MINIMIZED MEMBER SIZES
MORE MEMBERS AT TOWER BASE TO RESIST SEISMIC FORCES
SEISMIC

14

15 Aerial rendering showing project site and close relation to waterfront access
16 View looking up at tower one (right) and tower two (left)
17 Project rendering showing structural bracing at main entrance

16

17

Closed Cavity Façade

Designed 2009-14

The innovative Closed Cavity Façade system was developed as a unitized curtain wall system responding to the requirements of European Energy Directives and the Swiss Minergie sustainability rating. The CCF system was researched and developed with Josef Gartner GmbH, during an era of growing skepticism over the future and sustainability of all glass curtain wall systems for offices. This double façade system builds upon SOM's decades-long history of developing innovative curtain wall solutions and building envelope technologies and represents one of the best performing all glass façade systems in SOM's history.

Both European regulations and the Minergie Standard aim to reduce energy demand significantly by introducing criteria for façades of all new buildings. The prescriptive requirements suggest that the façade system should achieve the stringent G-value (solar energy transmission) of maximum 0.10 (summer); minimum 0.40 (winter) while the performative requirements suggest a U-value (heat loss parameter) of maximum 1.0 $W/m^2 K$.

Working within these performance requirements, SOM sought to develop a façade system that maintained the visual qualities of an all-glass façade design (panoramic views, abundant daylighting, and refined aesthetics) while responding to the demands of seasonally changing external climatic conditions. The CCF system prioritizes occupant comfort while reducing the whole building's energy demand and carbon emissions.

The CCF system consists of triple glazing on the inner layer and single glazing on the outer, forming a cavity with a fabric roller blind in between. The panels are sealed and equipped with a pressurized supply of filtered and dehumidified air in order to avoid condensation and heat build-up inside the cavity. The air circulation is controlled by a small engine that is connected to each individual cavity. Triple glazing together with low-emissivity insulating coatings achieves the low U-value ensuring comfortable conditions for workspaces located near the glazing even in winter time and in the evening. The selection of low-iron glass improves color rendering and achieves neutral tones of reflection.

The glazing for the Closed Cavity Façade was carefully selected to achieve both aesthetic and performance aspirations. The outer layer glazing of the panel is typically a single 10mm (or laminated 2x6mm) low-iron glass pane with a reflective solar control coating on the inner face. This provides the panel with solar gain protection, and gives it a clear and silver-reflecting appearance to the outside. The inner layer glazing is made up of a triple-glazed insulated unit; the innermost glass pane is laminated for safety purposes.

All mullions and transoms are made from extruded aluminum with a robust natural anodized finish. These act as the structural components for the façade system as well as the decorative weave of the quilted skin. The outer layer glass is bonded to the mullions with structural silicone to keep the fascia visually pure and geometrical.

During the research and development process, as proof of concept, the CCF system underwent extensive testing of large-scale mock-ups. The quilted design and glass selection was tested and refined with several visual prototypes. Air and weather tightness were tested on typical full-scale panels and all corner conditions to prove the effectiveness of the sealed cavity and dehumidified air supply in preventing condensation build-up. The motorized roller blinds were subjected to many thousands of up and down cycles at high temperatures in order to demonstrate their durability in the harshest anticipated cavity conditions.

During concept development, close attention was paid to the likely maintenance requirements through a building's lifetime. A glass replacement methodology was developed allowing the facetted outer panel of the façade (comprising two triangular glass panes bonded to a lightweight aluminum "carrier frame," at 3 meters wide x 4.2 meters high) to be lifted off completely using the rooftop Building Maintenance Unit, giving unobstructed access for cleaning, maintenance, and repair.

3

< 1 Façade system exterior photograph
2 View of applied system from pedestrian bridge
3 JTI Headquarters with Closed Cavity Façade system

4 Typical bay module
5 Paper model
6 Detail through vertical mullion
7 Diagram of typical module

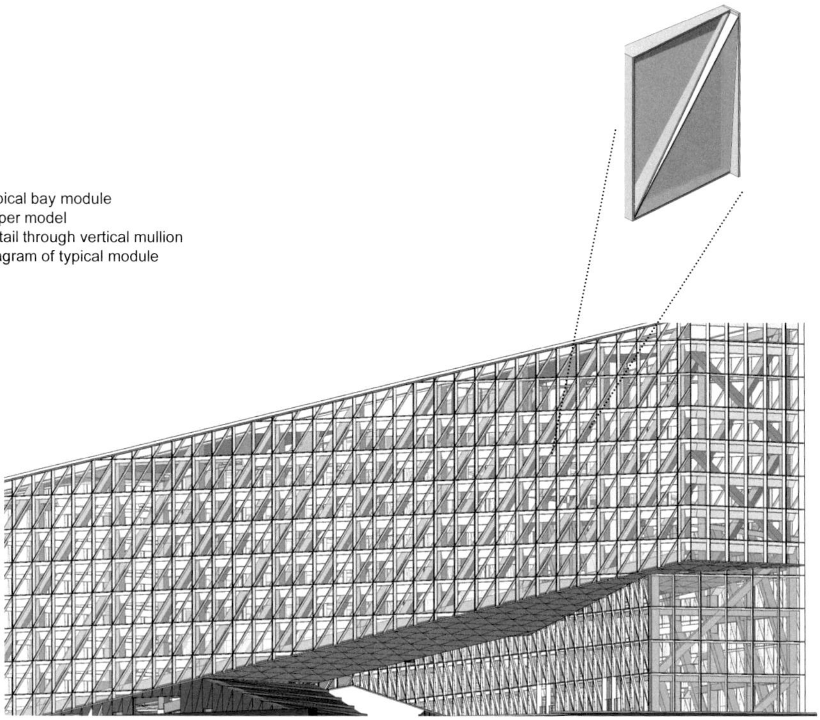

4

5

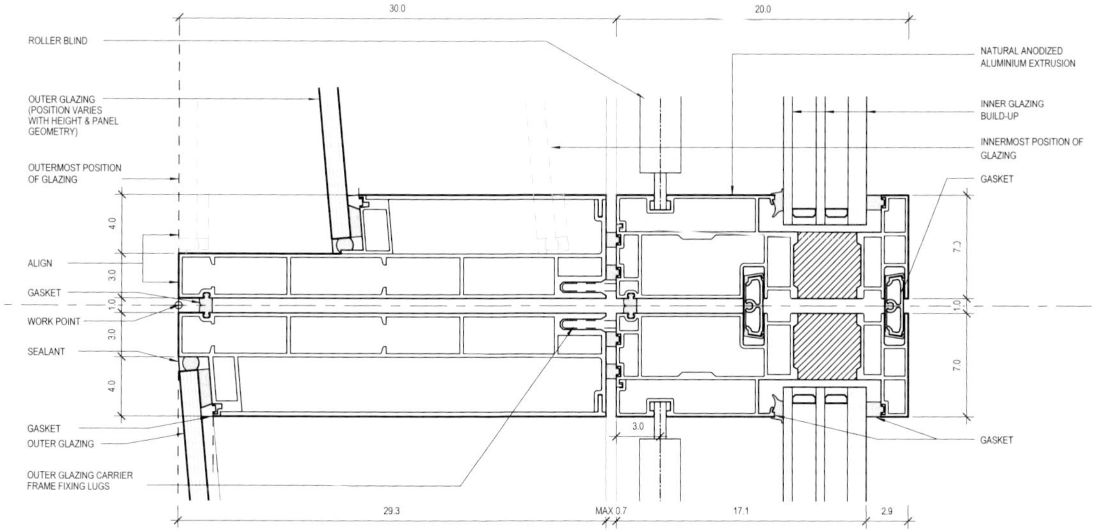

6

Roller blind cover:
Natural anodized aluminum extrusion

Spandrel panel:
Natural anodized aluminum sheet

Inner pane glass:
Low-iron triple glazed insulated unit with low emissivity coating for increased overall insulation value

Roller blind:
Fabric type 'Thermoveil 1519' with a grey internal colour to maximise the visibility to the outside.

The blind is highly reflective to the outside to increase reflectance and reduce heat absorption

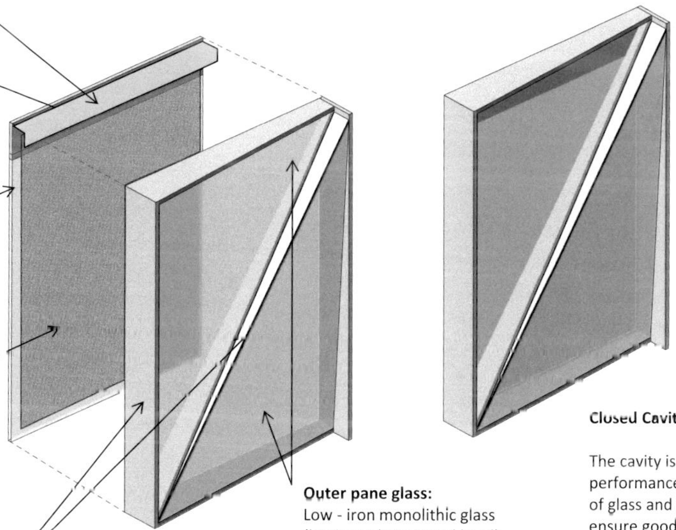

Mullions & transoms:
Natural anodized aluminum extrusions

Outer pane glass:
Low - iron monolithic glass (laminated at ground level)

The solar coating, ipasol bright, reduces solar energy entering the cavity and makes the facade reflect its surroundings

Closed Cavity Facade system

The cavity is sealed and the performance of inner and outer layers of glass and the blinds is balanced to ensure good conditions in summer and winter.

- High performance
- Less frequent cleaning
- Shading device is less prone to damage

7

9

10

8 View through top floor restaurant
9 Construction photograph showing module installation
10 Perception varying from quilted to glazed

Denver Union Station

Denver, Colorado
Designed 2006-14

The Regional Transportation District (RTD) FasTracks Program is a multi-billion dollar comprehensive transit expansion plan to build 122 miles of new commuter and light-rail, eighteen miles of bus rapid transit, 21,000 new light rail and bus station parking spaces, and enhanced bus service for easy, convenient bus-to-rail connections across the eight-county district. The centerpiece of this public/private transit project is Denver Union Station (DUS). The $500 million Denver Union Station redevelopment elevates not just its immediate surroundings, but an entire city and region. By connecting Metro Denver with the rest of the state and the country DUS has transformed a once vacant neighborhood.

Since its initial phases opened in 2014, the project has succeeded as its stakeholders envisioned, integrating disparate urban elements into a cohesive, uniting urban center. Some nineteen-and-a-half acres of new office, retail, and residential development surround the freshly renovated station, in which multiple modes of transportation converge upon new rail facilities and comfortably integrate with shops, restaurants, a boutique hotel, and inviting public spaces.

As originally conceived, DUS was quite large in scale—encompassing over a half-dozen city blocks. Early in the design process a solution was devised that brought the light rail and commuter rail stations to grade, spread them apart by two blocks, and linked them together via the underground bus station. This allowed for the creation of a transit backbone rather than a singular intermodal building, leading to a superior passenger experience, better orientation, enhanced connections to the local modes, and—most importantly—the integration of transit into what has become known as the Transit District. This sense of district, its scale, and clear functionality are reinforced by the mannered but bold architectural pieces which culminate at the commuter rail terminal and historic station. The open design blurs the boundary between pure transportation spaces and general public circulation areas and encourages a range of character for individual spaces—from dynamic and highly programmable to quiet and neighborhood-oriented.

The train hall is the focal point of Denver Union Station and was conceived as an efficient and formally expressive means of clear-spanning across multiple tracks. The primary structural system consists of eleven steel "arch trusses" extending nearly 180 feet, from a single large-diameter pin connection atop eighteen-foot-tall arched column supports. The arch-trusses behave as their name implies: in part like a truss and in part like an arch. Each truss is stabilized by bracing struts between trusses. In the central region of the train hall, the arch-trusses are replaced by cantilevered trusses. Together these support a tensioned PTFE fabric chosen due to its flexibility and ability to allow diffuse natural light to permeate, taking advantage of Denver's three-hundred plus days of sun annually.

The profile of the commuter train hall canopy rises seventy feet at the head-end platform, descends in a dynamic sweep to twenty-two feet at the center, and then rises again at the far end. This form allows the structure to protect the platforms of the station, while remaining clear of the view corridor established by zoning to protect views of the historic station from the west along the axis of 17th Street. This large center oculus serves as the iconic focal point to the district and results in what some call "Denver's living room."

Nine types of transportation converge in the hub and showcase downtown Denver's first commuter bike station, offering lockers and bike racks, as well as memberships for daily commuters. Additionally the hub features an improved regional bus system centered around a new depot underneath 17th Street, with twenty-two bus bays and an underground, enclosed passenger concourse awash with light from the skylights above.

The Denver Union Station project won the 2015 Global Award for Excellence by the Urban Land Institute, which recognizes real estate projects that achieve a high standard of excellence in design, construction, economics, planning, and management.

UNION STATION
TRAVEL by TRAIN
UNION STATION

TRACK 5

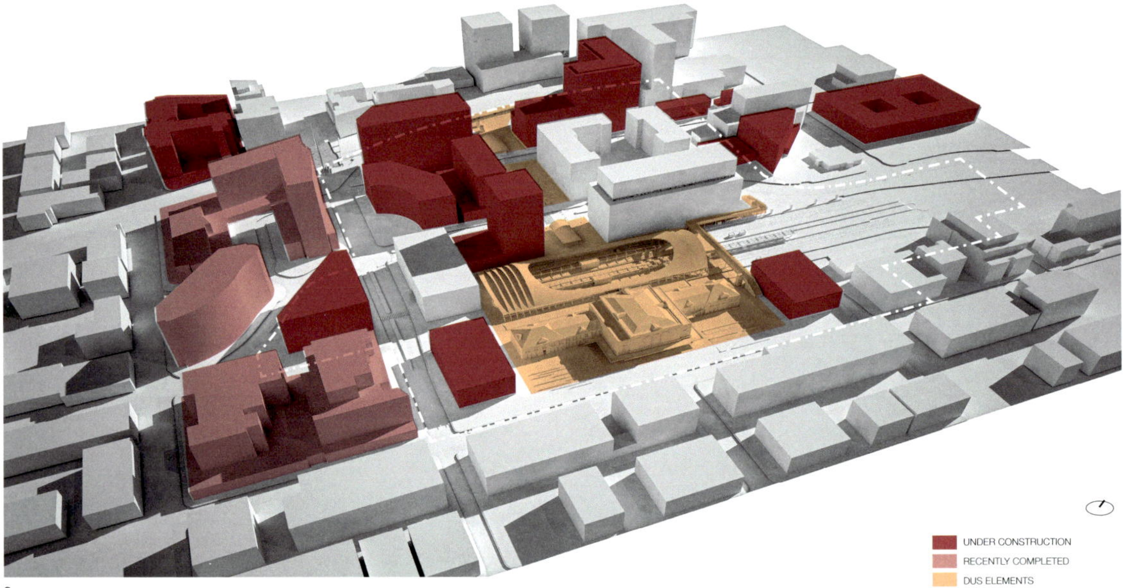

3

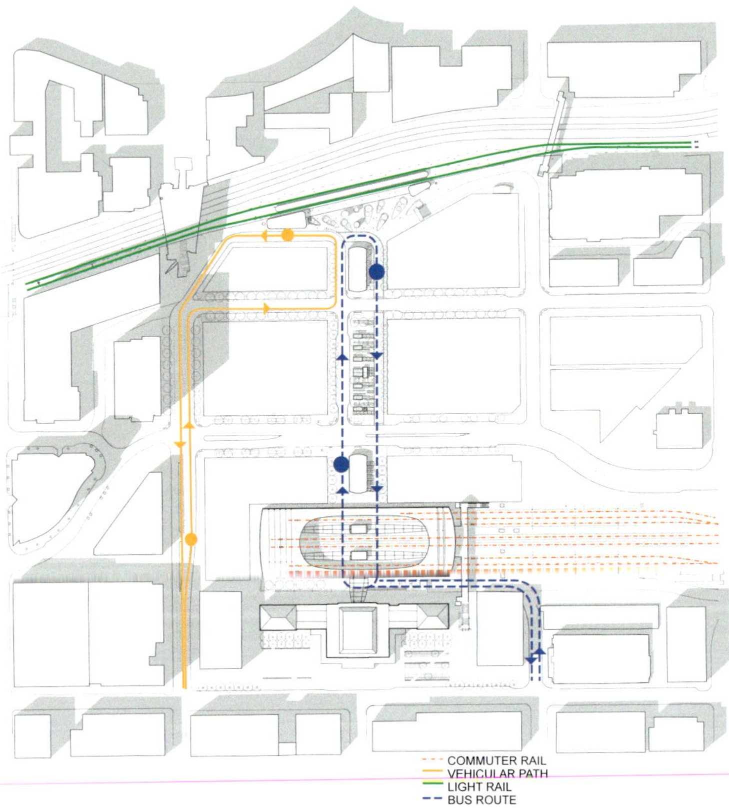

4

<< 1 Aerial view of site
< 2 Evening view from inside canopy
3 Master plan development diagram
4 Transit backbone diagram
5 Site plan

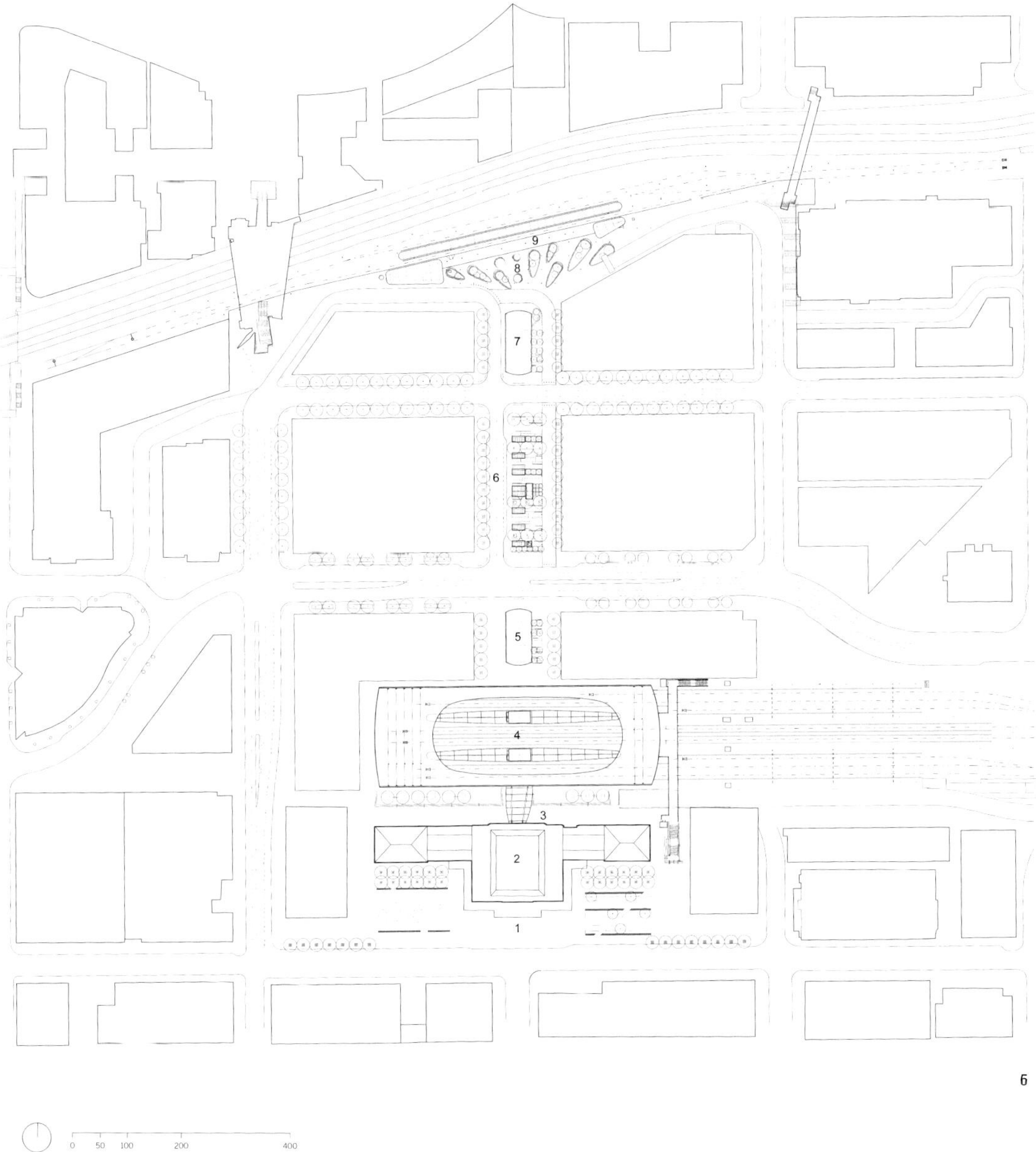

6

LEGEND

1 WYNKOOP PLAZA
2 HISTORIC DENVER UNION STATION
3 DUS CANOPY
4 C.R.T. (COMMUTER RAIL TERMINAL)
5 WEWATTA PAVILION
6 17TH STREET SKYLIGHTS
7 CHESTNUT PAVILION
8 VENT STACKS
9 LIGHT RAIL STATION

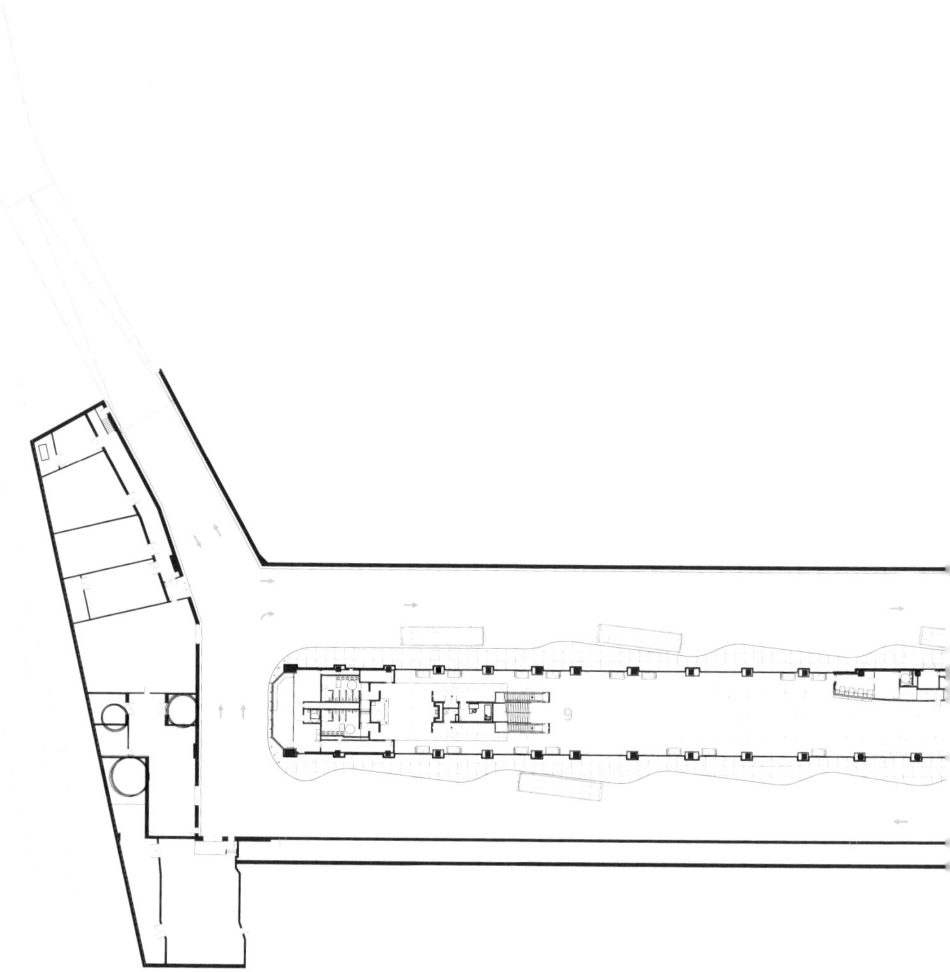

1 WYNKOOP PLAZA
2 HISTORIC DENVER UNION STATION
3 DUS CANOPY
4 C.R.T. (COMMUTER RAIL TERMINAL)
5 WEWATTA PAVILION
6 17TH STREET SKYLIGHTS
7 CHESTNUT PAVILION
8 VENT STACKS
9 LIGHT RAIL STATION
10 VENT STACKS
11 LIGHT RAIL STATION

6 Bus concourse plan
7 East-west site section

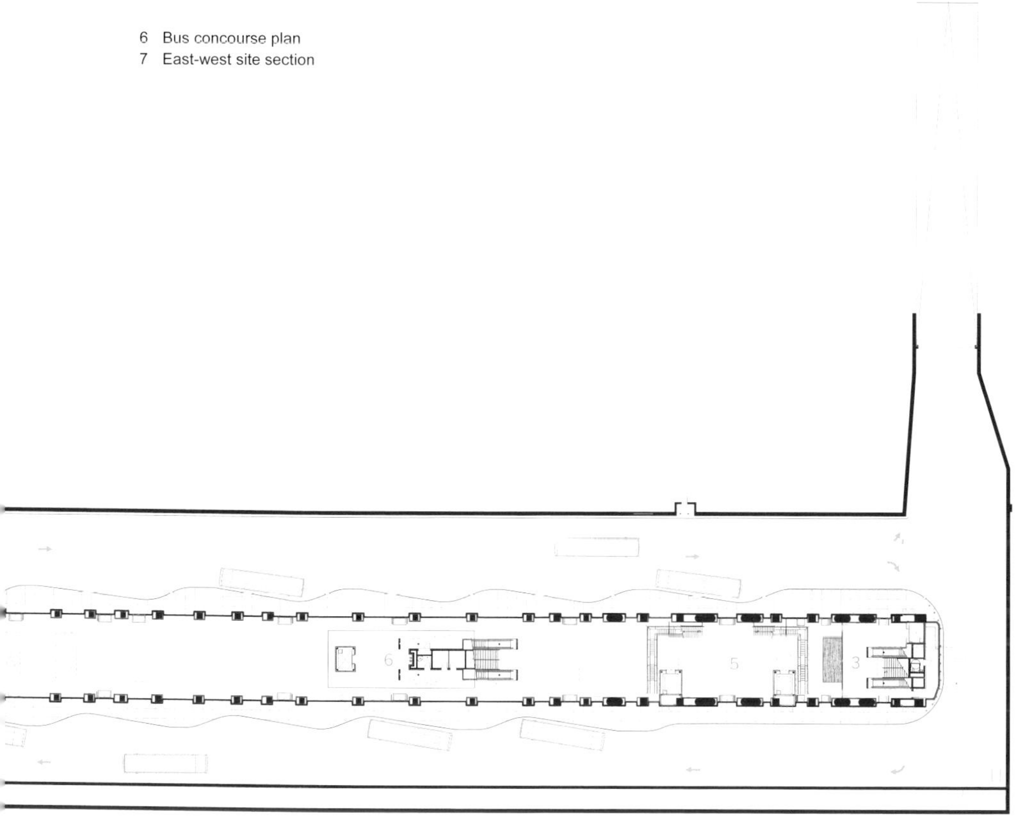

6

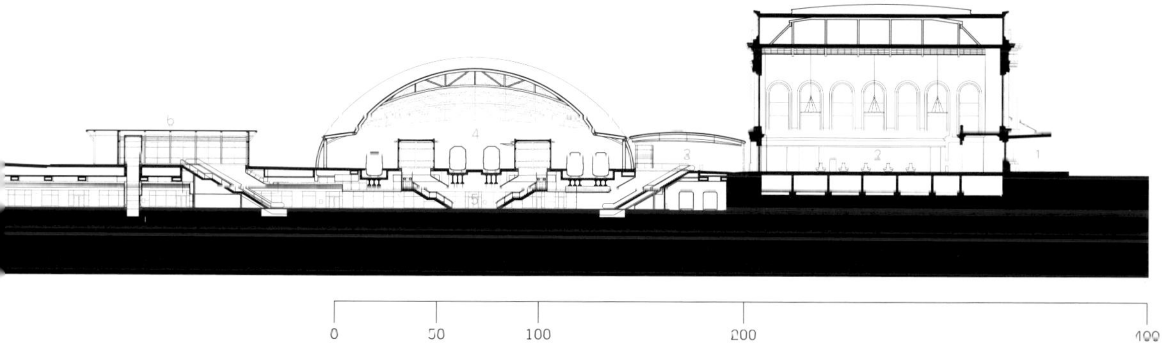

7

8

8 Canopy at night
9 Image of truss detail

10

11

10 Entrance to Chestnut Pavilion
11 Underground bus concourse
12 Bus concourse stairs
> 13 Train hall

12

Shenzhen Rural Commercial Bank Headquarters

Shenzhen, China
Designed 2012–14

The Shenzhen Rural Commercial Bank Headquarters (SRCB) is a 150-meter tower located prominently on a public park that fronts the Pacific Ocean. The tower will be an owner-occupied headquarters, with the flagship public bank at the ground floor. Shenzhen is one of the most progressive cities in China, with close economic ties to Hong Kong, and approximately 15 million inhabitants. Shenzhen was the first Chinese city to be named a "Special Economic Zone"—a designation that allows for economic governance more aligned with a free-market approach. SOM's client, the Shenzhen Rural Commercial Bank, was formed in that context and has grown from a bank with primarily agrarian roots to be one of the largest banks in Southern China with diverse holdings in multiple markets.

There were three core ideas that helped drive the overall concept for the bank headquarters. The first was an interior that would provide flexible workspace that considered potential future changes needed by the client. SOM took this opportunity to update one of the core structural partis in SOM's design legacy—the external diagrid. The exterior structure's primary job is to handle the gravity loads for the building while the core absorbs the building's lateral loads. With a substantial portion of the steel pulled away from the façade, there is more room for dramatic, column-free interior office space. This means that even in a high seismic activity-zone like Shenzhen, the diagrid structure can still provide more structural efficiency compared to a traditional column and beam building. The diagrid's repeating criss-cross pattern on the façade also adds a signature presence to the skyline and the adjacent park and seaside.

SOM envisaged this project as an opportunity to develop several next generation sustainability technologies, which became the second core idea for the overall building concept. The building's diagrid structure was designed as a fundamental device in reducing heat-gain. The external grid provides a shading to the interior without losing the long views over the park and sea. Additionally, by orienting the atrium to the east and west, the amount of occupied floor area experiencing low angle sun is considerably reduced. The atrium can also be utilized as a "lung" for the building—a dilating air shaft that can be used for natural ventilation on days with good external air quality, and for return air distribution on days when it makes more sense to use conditioned air, thus improving the mechanical performance of the building and reducing energy costs.

The Shenzhen Planning Bureau, the governmental oversight board responsible for overseeing and planning all new large-scale construction, envisioned the park and surrounding neighborhood to be a new center for Shenzhen. Along this park will be cultural amenities and major architectural landmarks. SRCB Tower will be the first new tower built on the park, due to its status as a trusted institution in Shenzhen. The building is on a corner lot, and the atrium is oriented so that every visitor will get to look out onto the park upon arrival at each floor.

The design concept takes advantage of the tower's rural location by implementing natural elements into the experience and function of the building. Water is integrated into the arrival experience on the ground floor and the banking interior through a dramatic cascading wall of water that flows over the full height of the lobby windows. The sound of the water creates a calming effect and makes the microclimate more comfortable by evaporative cooling in the city's hot climate.

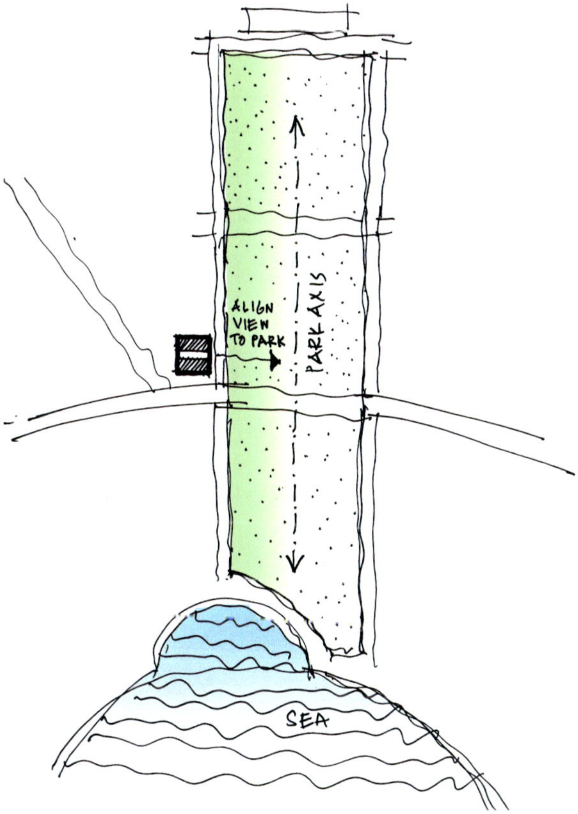

3

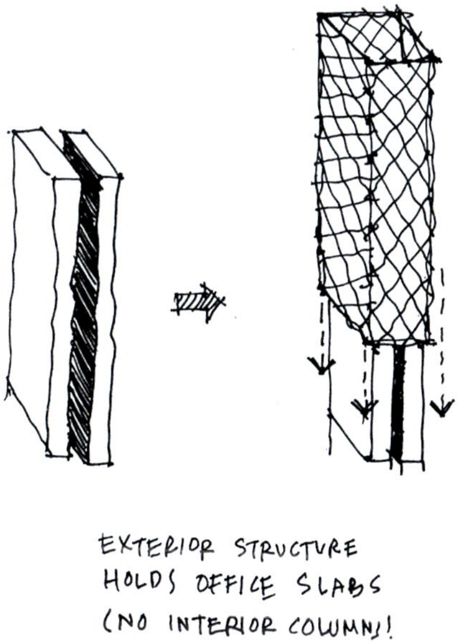

4

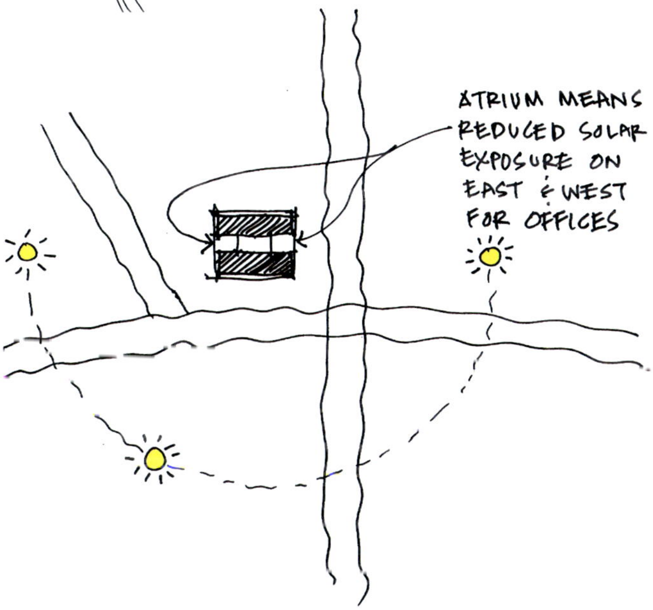

5

< 1 Aerial view of the site
2 East elevation rendering
3 Site diagram showing proximity to sea and park
4 Structure concept
5 Solar path diagram

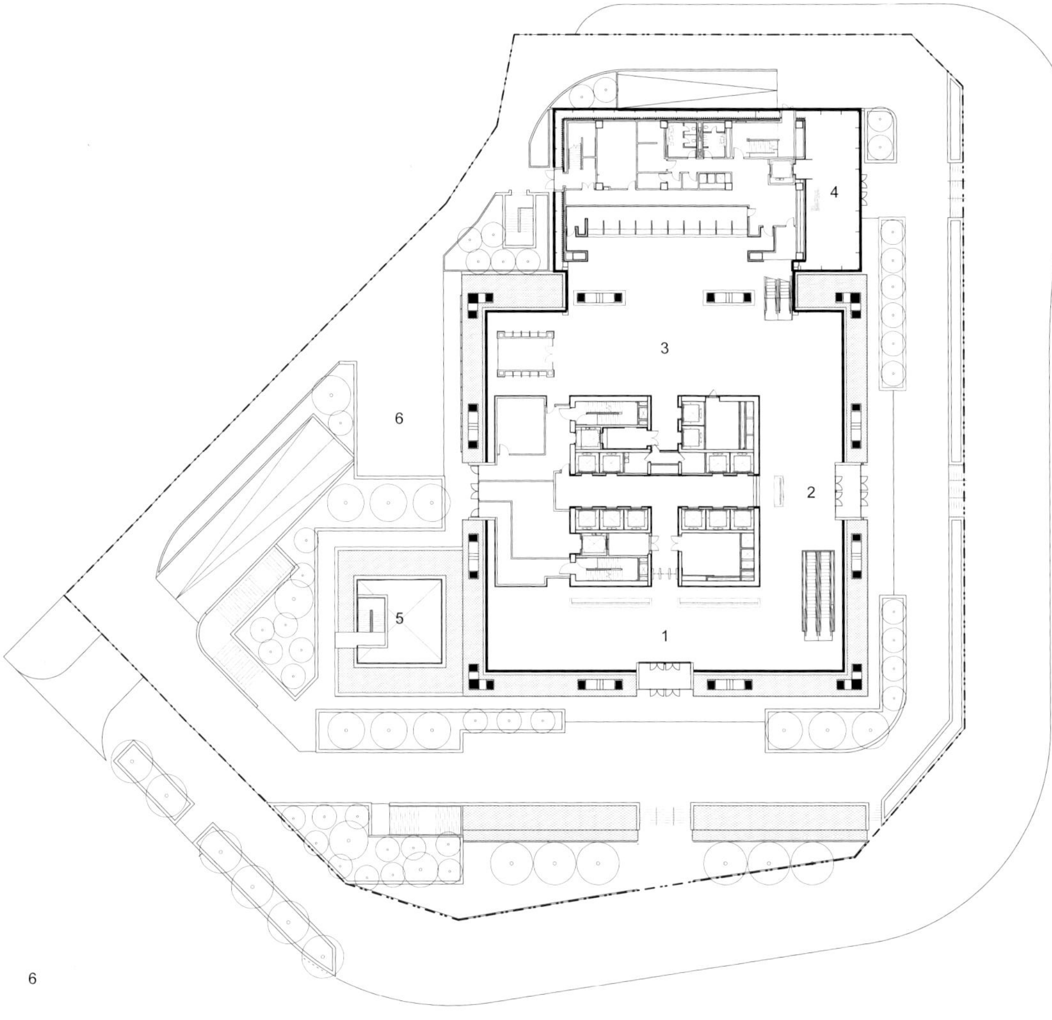

1 OFFICE LOBBY
2 PUBLIC LOBBY
3 BANKING HALL
4 VIP BANKING LOBBY
5 SUNKEN COURTYARD
6 VIP OFFICE ENTRANCE

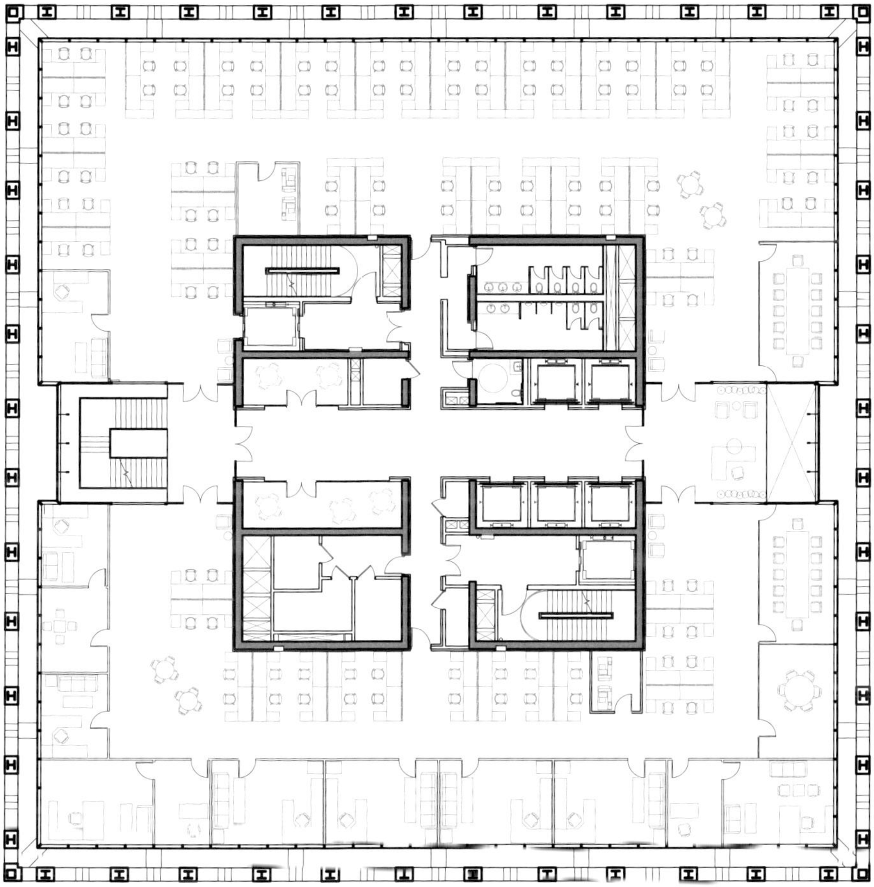

7

6 Site plan; gray areas indicate water features
7 Typical floor plan showing office relationship to atria

8

8 Rendering of diagrid structure connection to curtain wall
9 Cross-section rendering of atrium
10 3D node diagrams
11 Diagram showing east-west air flow in open louver zones
12 Diagram showing stack effect air flow

9

10

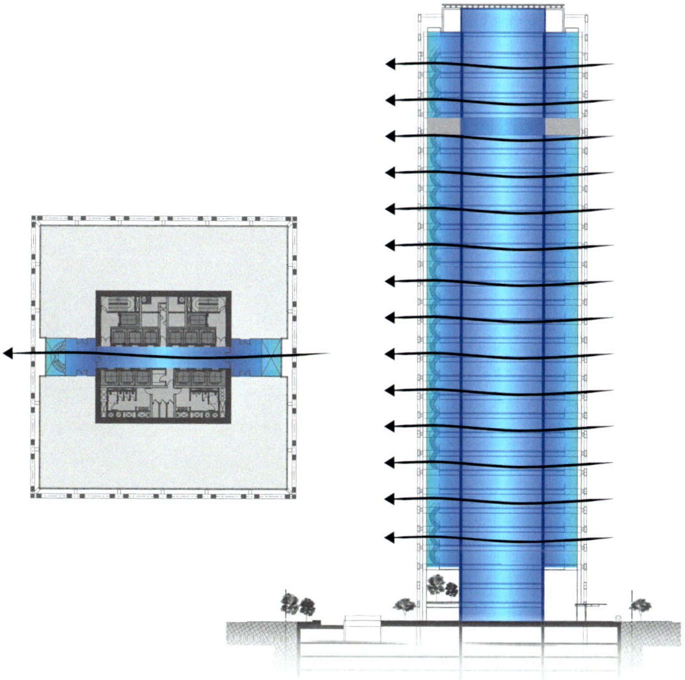

11

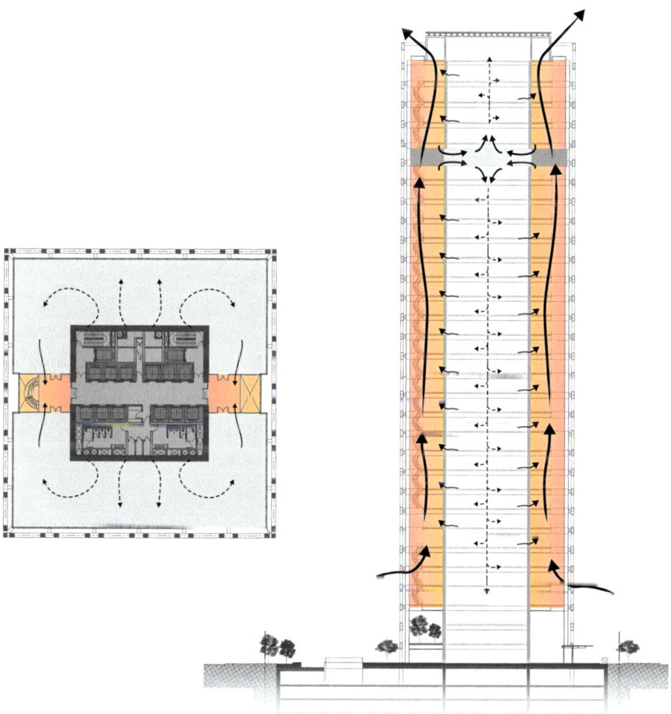

12

13

14

13 Office space rendering
14 Rendering of communicating stairs
15 Base temperature vs. base with diagrid shading
> 16 Lobby rendering showing waterwall
> 17 Lobby rendering
> 18 Rendering of entrance at exterior

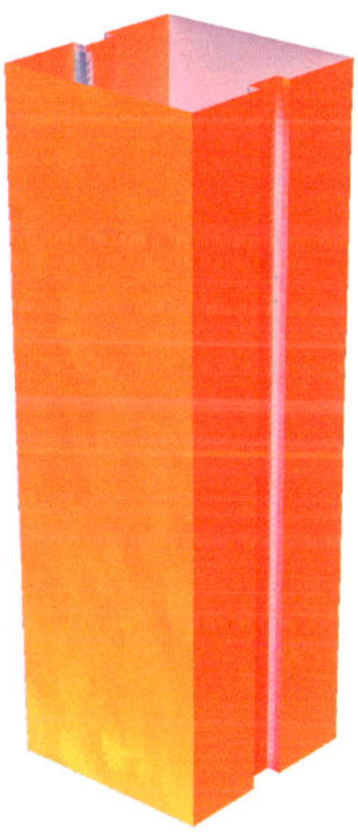

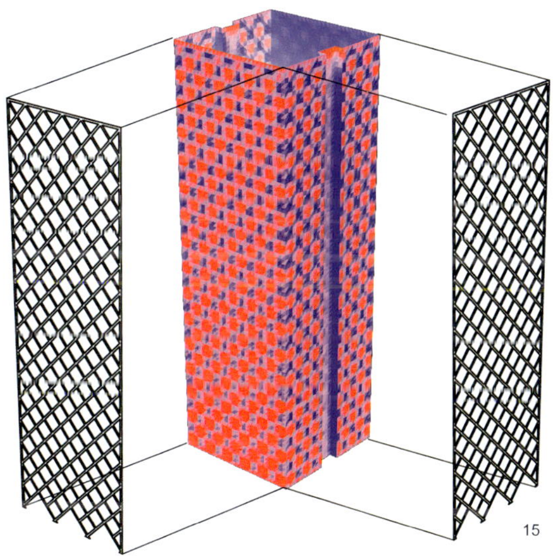

15

16

17

18

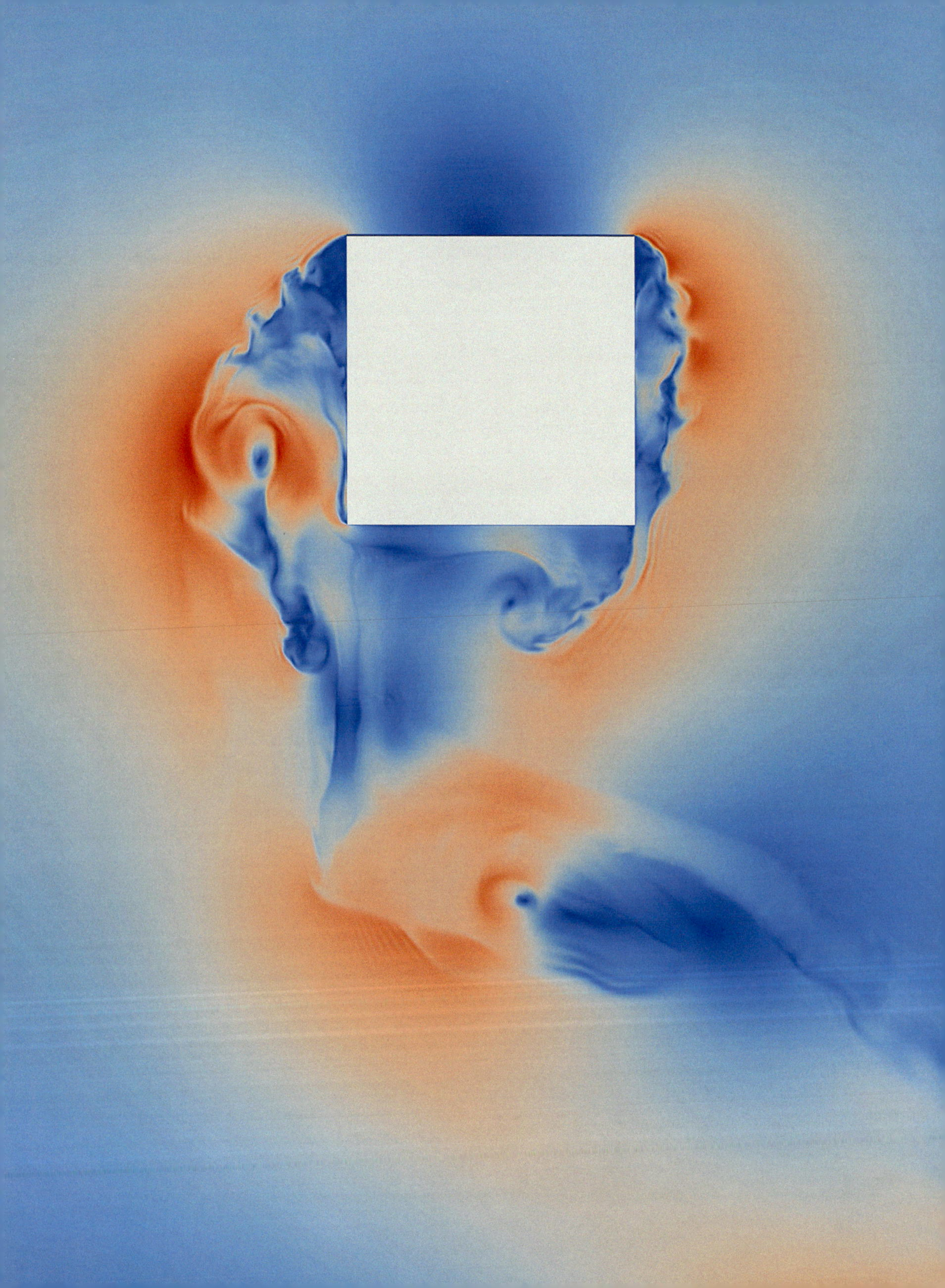

SOM Tools
SOM HPD Methodology + SOM Wind Tunnel 260

Chicago, IL
Designed 2011–ongoing

The SOM High Performance Design (HPD) Methodology and the SOM Wind Tunnel 260, are internally generated initiatives meant to inform multiple aspects of work across the firm. It is anticipated that together, these initiatives will have lasting impacts on not only the quality of future design solutions but on their process of discovery, evolution, refinement, and, ultimately, data collection and the establishment of reference standards.

The HPD portal is a web-based interface that was developed as a design and project management tool that informs and tracks a project's environmental performance throughout an iterative design process and after construction and operation. The ultimate goal of the HPD portal is to allow firm-wide knowledge sharing across cities, program typologies, and climate zones.

The SOM Wind Tunnel is a controlled, in-house wind-testing environment that furthers our research and empirical understanding of building shaping and performance while assembling a database of knowledge with the goal of creating more efficient buildings.

The iterative nature of SOM's design process remains, at its essence, a constant. What has changed over time is the speed and accuracy to generate, document, evaluate, edit, and refine solutions that emerge from this process. The advent of computational tools whose accelerating efficacy, reduced cost and logarithmic capabilities increase in performance throughout the second half of the twentieth century has had remarkable impacts on both the formal complexity and sophistication of these solutions, but also on the ability to create and extract data from them. Both of these tools seek to further this line of inquiry: the portal, by rigorously collating, analyzing, and archiving performance data, and the wind tunnel, by shortening the duration and accelerating the responses. Conventionally, wind tunnel testing is a very formal and often protracted process due to the relatively few full-scale wind tunnels in North America, where even short analyses must be booked months in advance.

The HPD Methodology is implemented at the commencement of every new project. This portal facilitates data mining across offices, projects, and locations for both environmental technologies and innovation transfer between project teams in different offices. The tool allows scheduling and tracking of project goals, client decisions, and project milestones to maintain (and direct) achievable performance standards for each project. All future projects will include a Performance Label identifying anticipated energy, carbon, and water use. These metrics are tracked continuously through the different phases of a project and are charted on the dashboard to ensure project team awareness of specific performance metrics (i.e., what is the impact on energy when making design adjustments?) Beta testing of this tool began in 2011 and firm wide roll-out occurred in 2012.

There is an arsenal of environmental design techniques that we can deploy to improve the quality of our projects. We aimed to learn how to leverage this into higher and better performing projects that move beyond green-washing to break new ground in markets with regulatory barriers and diverse client groups. To address these concerns and to continue to value quality in design across our entire portfolio we have developed baseline energy, carbon, and water performance metrics, among others, to be applied to all SOM projects with incremental increases over time—targeting the goal of net zero consumption in the future. These metrics guide project teams and benchmark stringent standards for the firm to uphold.

With wind forces having a high level of importance and significant impact in tall building design, the SOM WT 260 gives our multidisciplinary teams the ease and capability to explore several iterations of multiple shapes and configurations of a tall building at the conceptual stages of the design process.

This project was initially inspired by a strong desire to enhance collaboration between the structural and architectural design teams and further our combined knowledge of tall building shaping and design. Bolstered by many historic photographs of pioneering work in wind tunnels and aeronautical design, we set out to develop a portable, modular wind tunnel. A large team from multiple disciplines was assembled—Structural, Architectural Design, MEP, Sustainable Design, Interior Design, and the Technical Group—to derive an object that would have an aesthetic presence, meet our needs and embody our design ethos. The SOM wind tunnel fills an entire room on the second floor of the Daniel Burnham Railroad Exchange Building, where SOM's Chicago offices are located, and is highly visible to the public.

The SOM wind tunnel itself consists of four equal modules. It is transparent on one side with operable, sliding acrylic panels allowing visual and physical access throughout the length of the tunnel. Each module is framed by steel profiles and is supported on solid "I" shaped legs. At the opening of the tunnel, the air is straightened and organized through an in-house, custom-made grid made of aluminum composite panels.

Powered by six fans creating airflow drawn in through an air straightening grid that serves to establish a uniform and laminar flow. Beyond the grid, the airflow is accelerated to the desired velocity by the gradually reduced cross-section of the wind tunnel. Before the air enters the measuring section, the air distribution over the height of the wind tunnel has to be changed from constant to a layered distribution as found in nature, called the boundary layer. Selection of the boundary layer depth in turn defines both the geometry of the spires, which are triangular shaped blades, and their distance from the model as well as the configuration in the roughness area at bottom of the tunnel.

The building model, typically made out of high density lightweight foam, sits on top of a load cell in the measuring section. This is mounted on a rotatable stand isolated from the wind tunnel and the floor to minimize transmission of vibration. The load cell is used in the High Frequency Force Balance technique to track shear forces in two directions and moments in three directions at its base, while the air flows around the testing model.

The layout of the fans and the tunnel dimensions were considered to establish an internal average wind speed of 8.0 m/s (~18 mph). As a typical wind tunnel has a rectangular cross-section in landscape orientation, SOM engineers decided for portrait orientation as most explored projects will be high-rise buildings. The scale of the building model is defined by both the physical dimensions of the wind tunnel and the selection of a boundary-layer depth as well as minimizing the blockage to less than five percent of the tunnel cross-section. Considering these conditions SOM is capable of testing a tower 600 meters tall at a scale of 1:800 in the tunnel with a slenderness ratio of 1:8.

The wind tunnel gives SOM the capability to explore various geometric configurations of a building in a highly iterative manner. An example of the impact the shaping of the tower can have can be seen in the diagram monitoring the crosswind base overturning moment spectra. These plots help to find the best performing configuration, from both a serviceability and strength design point of view. Combined with an in-house model shop, the wind tunnel provides another component of the iterative design practice at SOM and enables refined design within reduced time frames.

< 1 Plan view modelling of wind forces on building model
2 SOM Structural Engineering Partner, Bill Baker discussing a tower model in the wind tunnel

2

3 Development of boundary layer chart
4 Section diagram of Wind Tunnel 260

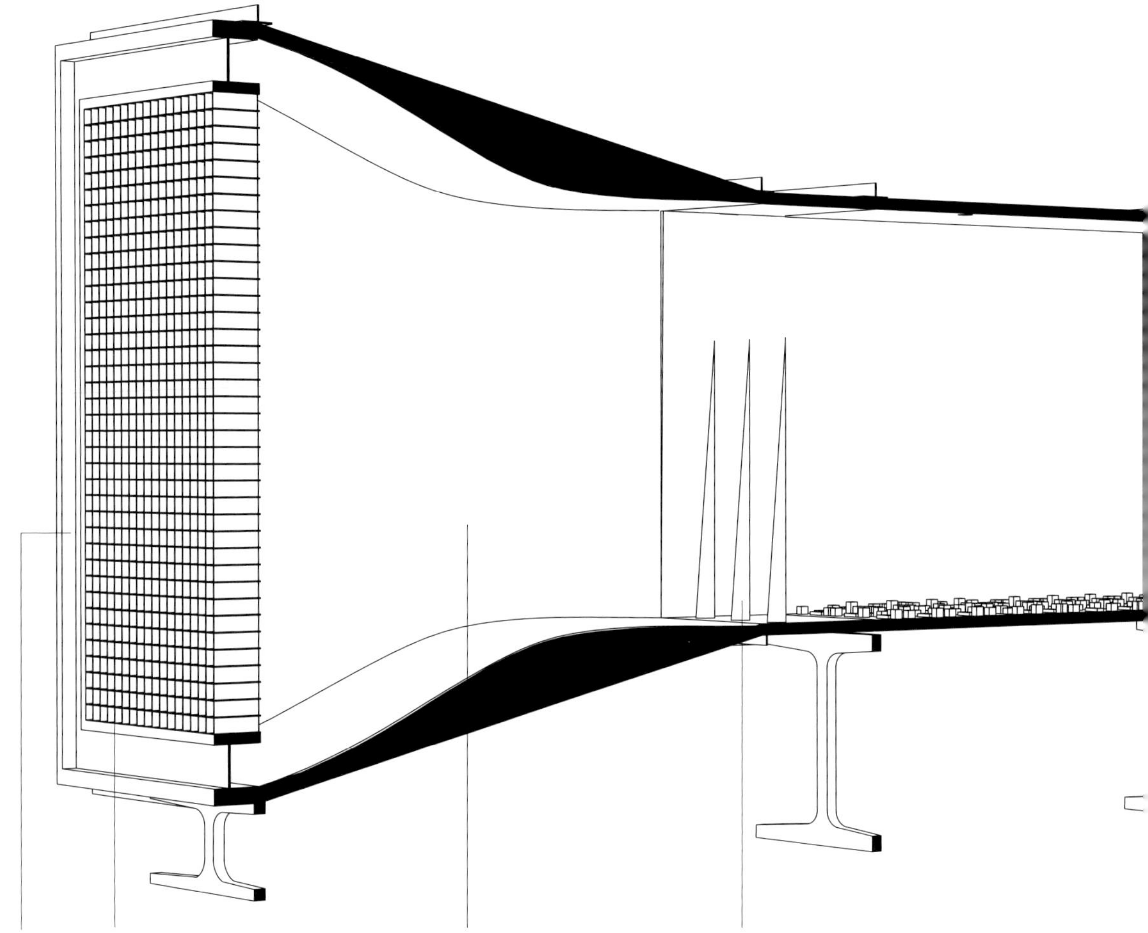

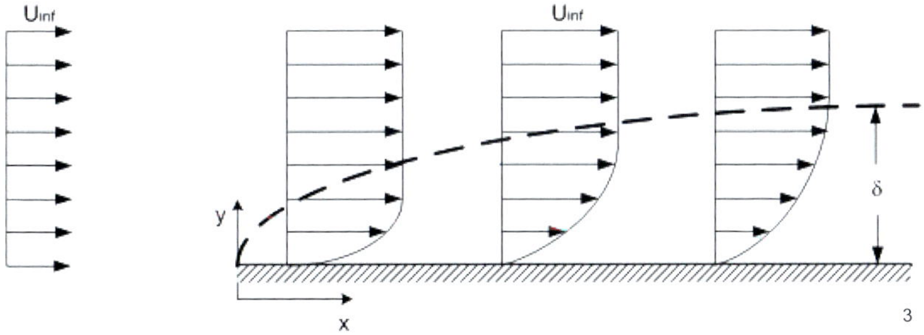

Uinf
Uinf
y
x
δ

3

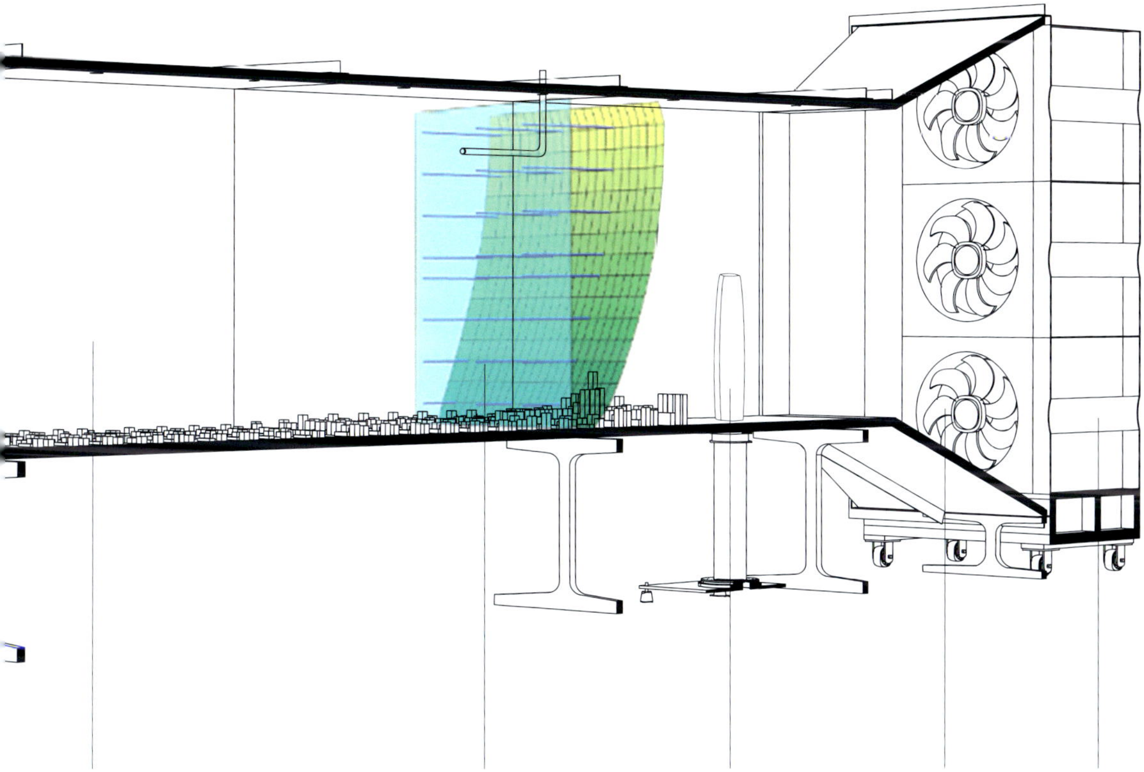

ROUGHNESS AREA
STABILIZE BOUNDARY AREA
WIND SPEED VERIFICATION
MEASURE WIND SPEED
MODEL PLATFORM
MEASURING SECTION
WITH PITOT TUBE
LOAD CELL
FANS
INITIALIZE
WITH TURN TABLE
& AIR FLOW
EXHAUST
DOWNSGTREAM
OF MODEL

4

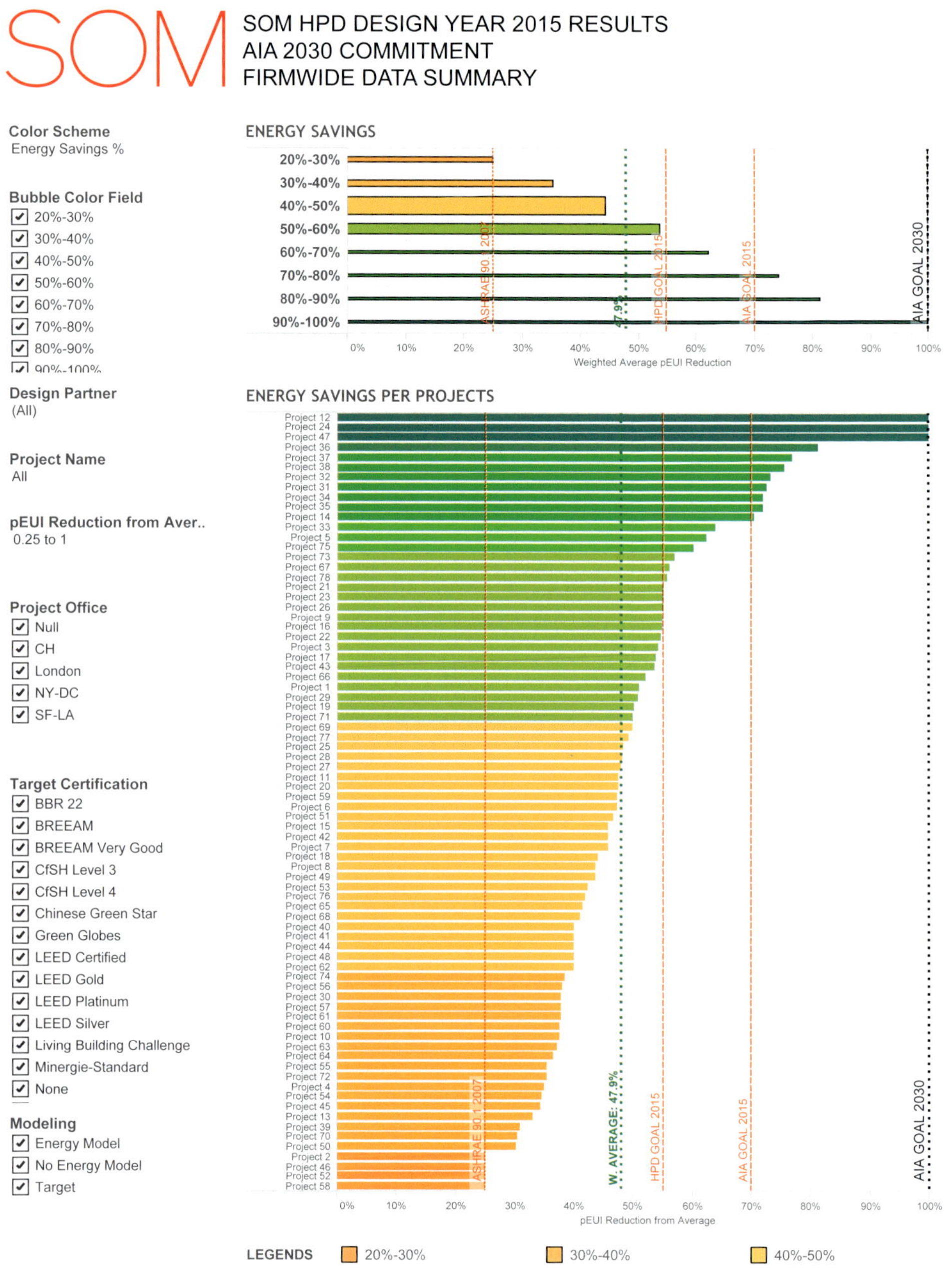

5 HPD Portal firmwide energy reduction comparison chart

PROJECTS LOCATION

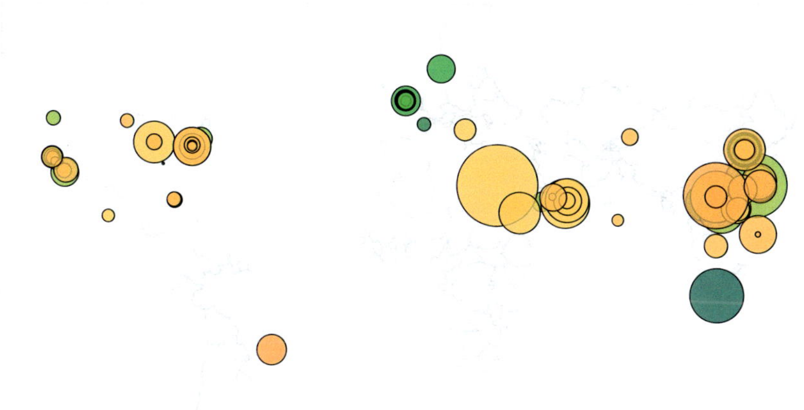

PROJECTS % GSF

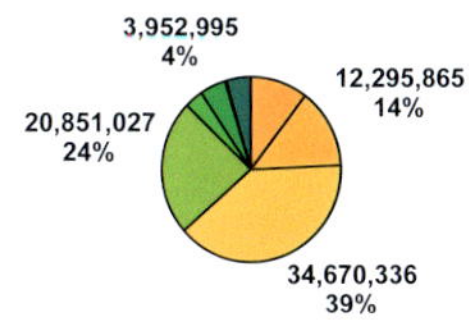

PROJECTS COUNT

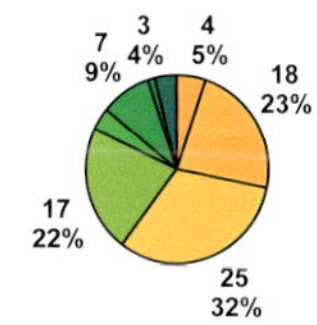

OFFICES DESIGN PERFORMANCE

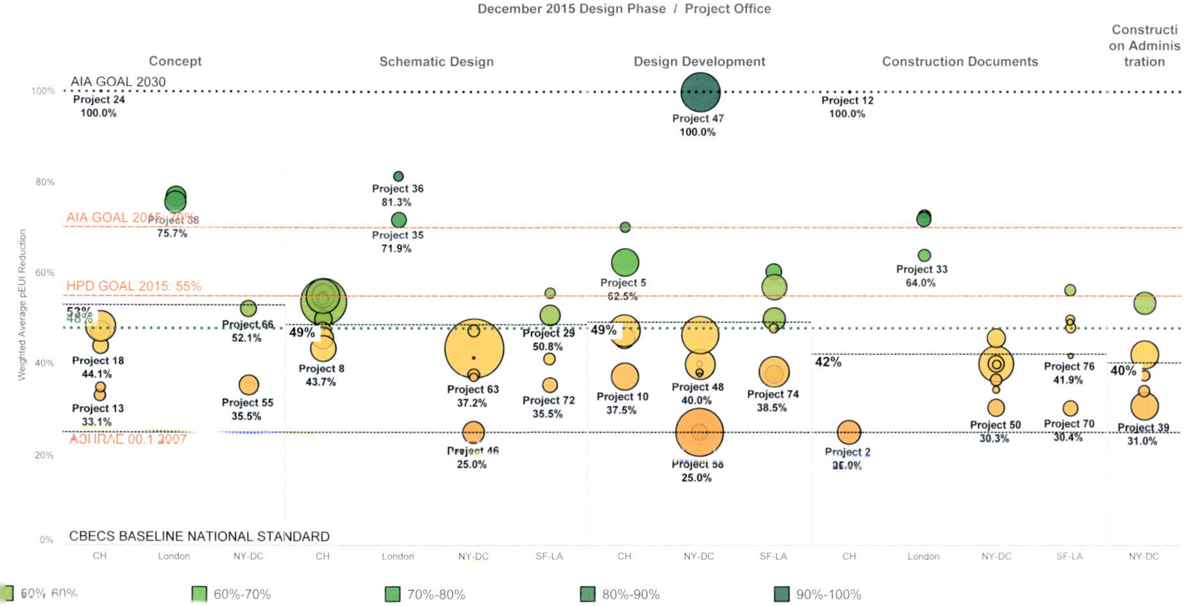

The University Center at The New School

New York, New York
Designed 2005–13

A slow aggregation of schools and buildings left The New School with a fundamental problem: seven schools scattered around the city. The unique way the university had grown resulted in a balkanized institution with significant inefficiencies and a lack of communication across divisions. Internally, the question posed by the administration was how could they reinvigorate their university and spur innovative thinking by softening the boundaries between disciplines. The charge from university President Bob Kerrey was to create a campus that would break down the barriers between the schools and bring The New School together in a pioneering way—to utilize architecture as a catalyst for informal communication, school integration, interdisciplinary collaboration, individual creativity, and, ultimately, a unified identity.

Acting as the "heart" of The New School, the sixteen-story University Center provides space for all aspects of a traditional campus, with 200,000 square feet of academic space on the first seven floors and 150,000 square feet for a 600-bed dormitory on the levels above.

Rather than create a building that stacks each element of the program and limits interaction, the design comingles the teaching spaces with key amenities, ensuring that appealing destinations will animate each floor. These spaces are staggered in section, tied together by the unraveled fire stair, and clad in glass to act as small-scale meeting spaces where the diverse populations of the seven schools can casually meet and exchange ideas. At the center of the building on the 6th and 7th floors is the Central Library, which acts as the apex of the cascading interactive spaces of the academic floors and the base of the residential floors above. Its placement reinforces the library as a crossroads for students from each of The New School's seven divisions. Below, between these activated meeting zones are long, loft-style spaces which house 50,000 square feet of design studios, classrooms, and computing labs. These spaces are flexible and can be reconfigured with no impact on power, data, or lighting. These spaces dedicated to making were kept intentionally raw—the structure and building services are exposed and the façade is clad in two horizontal strip windows. These spaces signal to the students and faculty that they are meant for creating.

A new type of stair was invented for the University Center, one that combines an egress stair with a communicating stair, to provide additional circulation while also transforming a required piece of infrastructure into an amenity. This new stair type creates two very different experiences; the communicating stair is open to the interior spaces, and moving between floors is a much more open, social experience. The egress stair has full-height glass to the exterior allowing views into classrooms and other spaces. To achieve this new stair typology, the traditional egress stair had to be reinvented. Located against the exterior, glazed wall of the building a detail was developed to firestop the stair against the curtain wall. A system of fire shutters was developed to break down the building into double height zones in the event of a fire. To achieve the effect of the stairs moving weightlessly through the interior spaces, a system of supports was devised where the landings are either supported by posts or hung with hangers, with the stair runs spanning the landings. At the exterior wall, the stair landings are cantilevered from the façade truss, which is also used for lateral support for the building. The geometry of the exterior façades are derived from the code strictures which determine the integer of the fire stair.

The University Center is LEED Gold, making it one of the most sustainable academic buildings in the United States. The building uses low- and high-tech energy-saving solutions. One such solution is an ice storage system, which uses electricity from the power grid during off-peak times to freeze water in a series of chambers. This ice melts during the day, producing electricity and reducing consumption during peak times. The project also employs heat-recovery wheels that retrieve heat from exhaust air, which aids in heating supply air. A green roof captures water and mitigates heat-island effect. Stormwater capturing and gray- and black-water treatment facilities in the building reduce water consumption.

THE NEW SCHOOL
THE NEW SCHOOL
UNIVERSITY CENTER

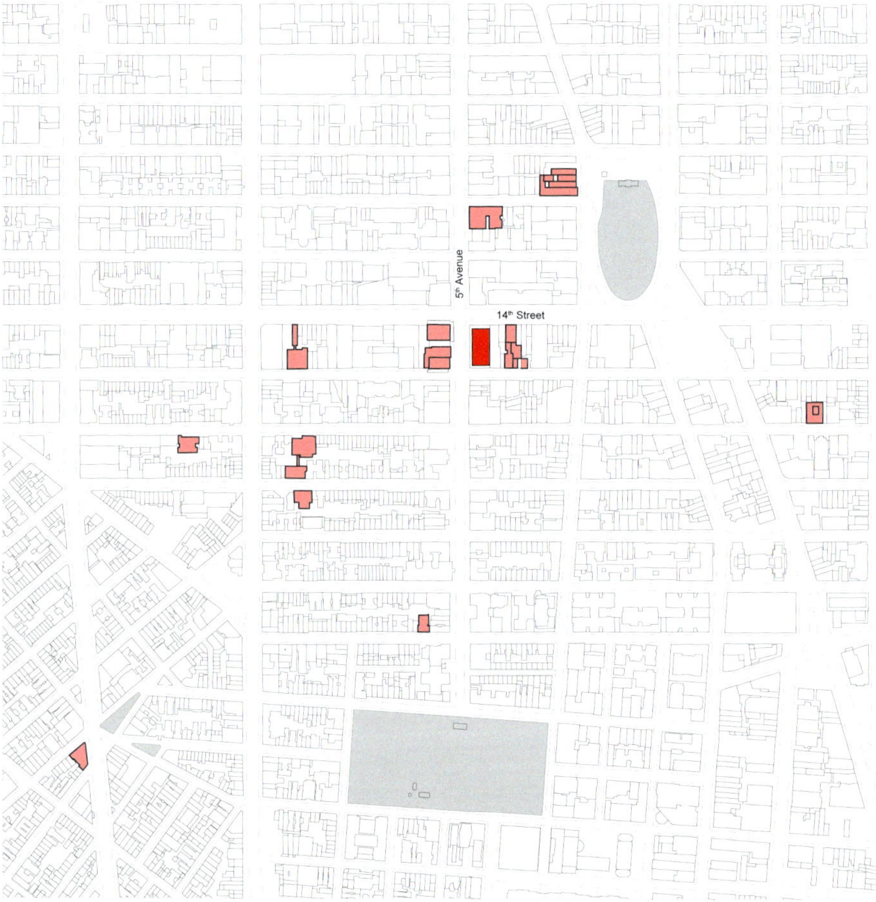

3

<<1 Aerial view of site
<2 The University Center main entrance on Fifth Avenue
3 Map showing campus buildings around city (pink), and new campus location (red)
4 Ground floor plan

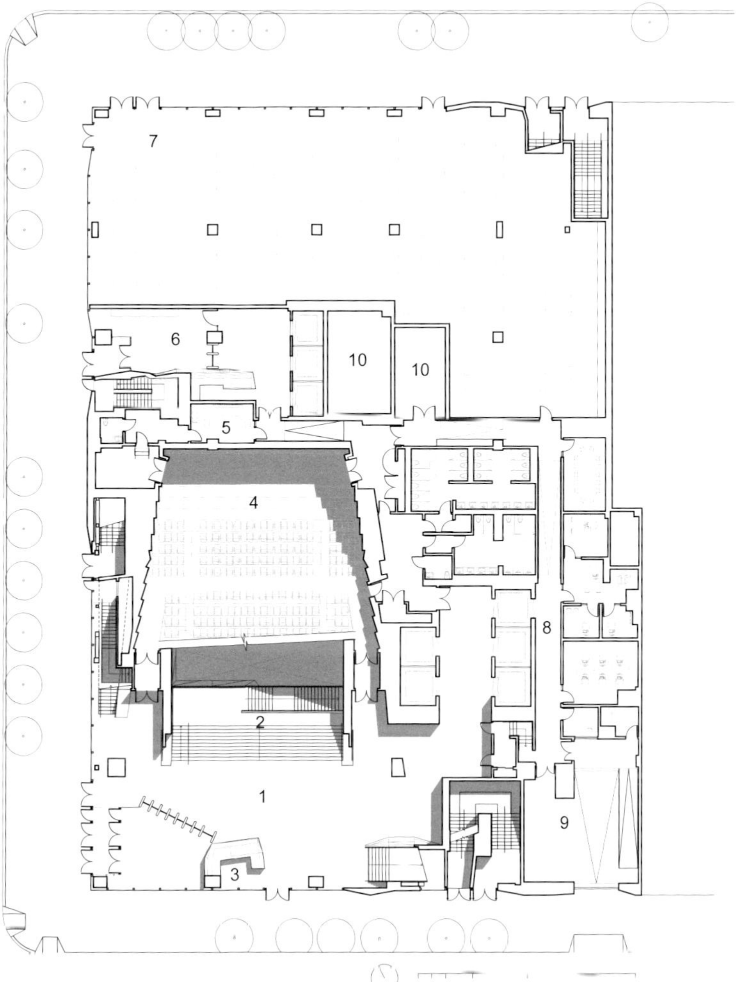

4

1 ACADEMIC LOBBY
2 EVENT SPACE
3 SECURITY DESK
4 AUDITORIUM
5 GREEN ROOM
6 RESIDENCE LOBBY
7 RETAIL
8 FACILITIES OFFICE
9 LOADING DOCK
10 MECHANICAL

5 Second floor plan
6 Fifth floor plan
7 Vertical campus diagram, showing common areas in green
8 Fifth Avenue elevation
9 Section through auditorium

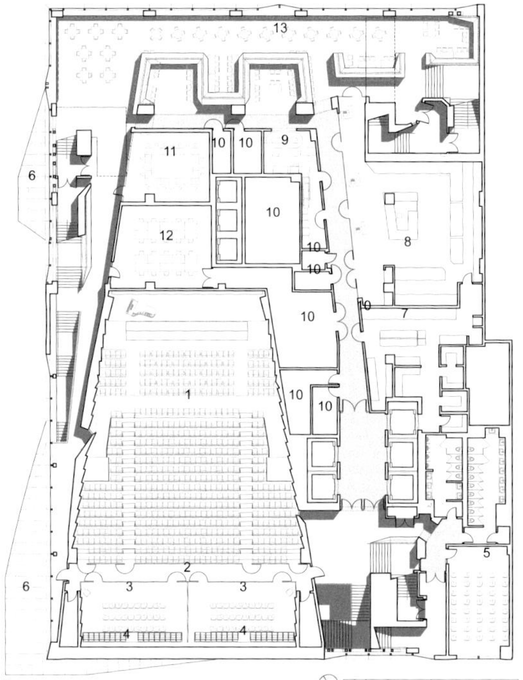

5

1 AUDITORIUM
2 MOVABLE PARTITIONS
3 TEMPORARY CLASSROOM
4 TELESCOPING SEATING
5 CLASSROOM
6 CANOPY
7 KITCHEN
8 SERVERY
9 DISH WASHING
10 MECHANICAL
11 FASHION DRAWING STUDIO
12 FASHION CONSTRUCTION STUDIO
13 CAFETERIA

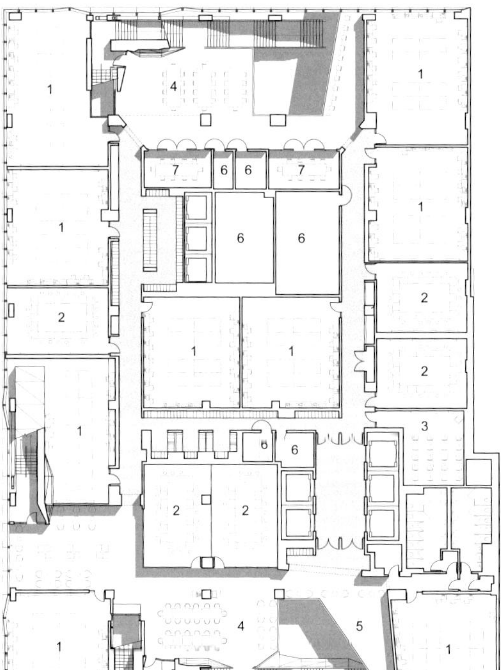

6

1 FASHION CONSTRUCTION STUDIO
2 FASHION DRAWING STUDIO
3 CLASSROOM
4 STUDY SPACE
5 LOUNGE
6 MECHANICAL
7 GROUP WORK ROOM

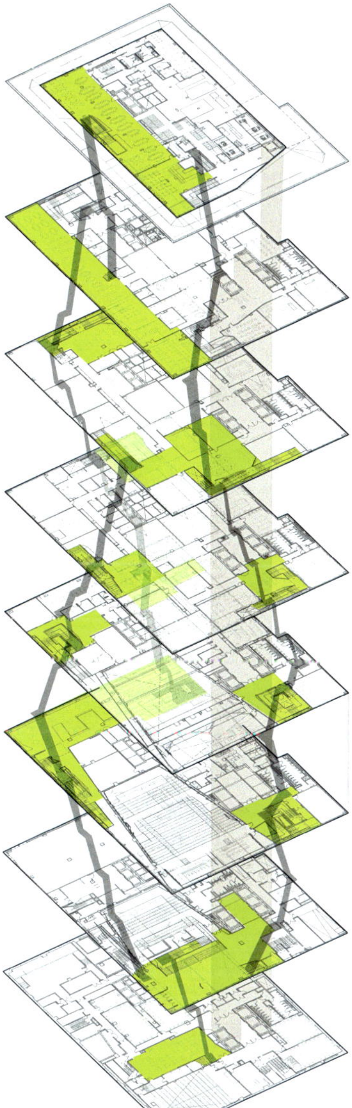

7

1 AUDITORIUM
2 LOBBY
3 EVENT CAFE
4 EVENT SPACE
5 COMPUTING CLASSROOM
6 BACK OF HOUSE
7 GREEN ROOM
8 RETAIL
9 RETAIL STORAGE
10 CAFETERIA
11 CLASSROOM
12 FASHION CONSTRUCTION STUDIO
13 FACULTY RESOURCE CENTER
14 LOUNGE
15 STUDY SPACE
16 LIBRARY BOOKSTORE
17 LIBRARY STUDY SPACE
18 OFFICE
19 STUDENT RESIDENCE
20 MECHANICAL PENTHOUSE

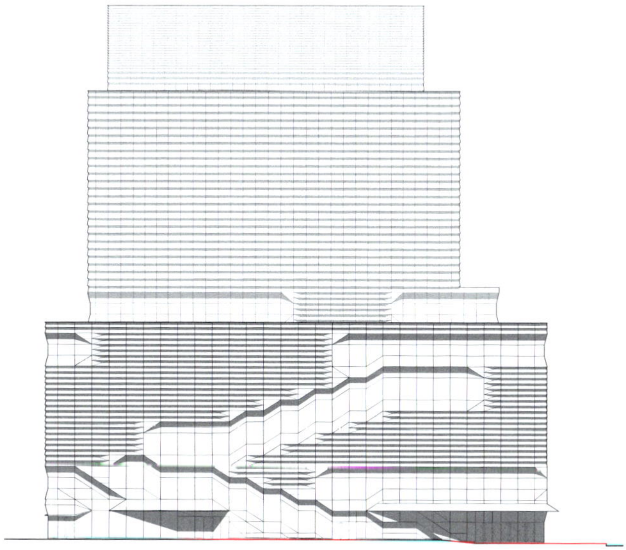

8

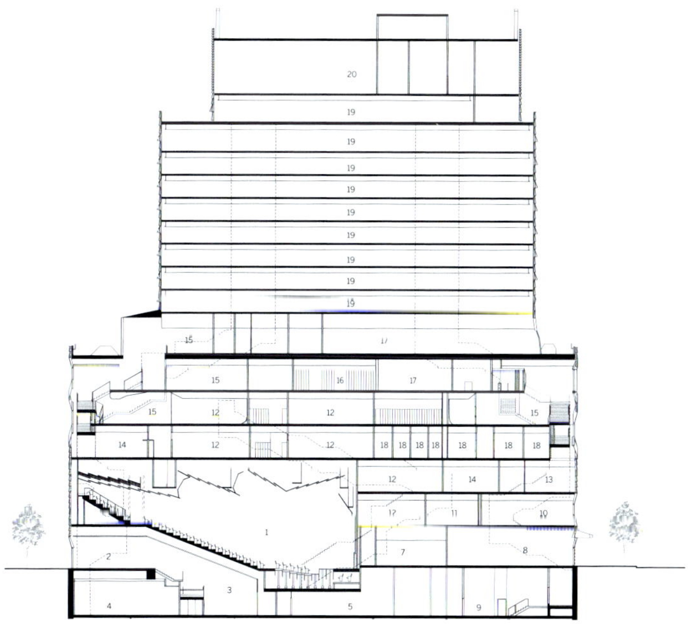

9

10

n or apart from them, No more
tireless, and cannot be shaken away.

11

12

10 Detail of Glenn Ligon's neon work, *Comrades and Lovers*
11 Student at event cafe seating space with Ligon work beyond
12 Signage by Ruedi Baur at stairwell ceiling

Bells and Whistles, a pentagonal brass profile, takes its dimensions largely from its function as the egress stair pressurization duct. Spanning six floors and over 530 feet long, the work weaves in and out of classrooms and communal spaces, creating an episodic presence throughout the visual journey of the building. As each space is unique, the ducts resist standardization; rather, consistent with the building's infrastructure, the ducts' profile changes, twisting and turning to resolve each obstacle.

From a close collaboration with Skidmore, Owings & Merrill and an early engagement with the design process of The University Center at The New School, Rita McBride has realized what she calls a "dream public artwork." Her sculptures and installations are often prompted by the struggle between serving and served space—a struggle central to modernism—the open, inhabited, and transparent areas versus the dark, concealed, mechanical spaces. In earlier installations entitled *Servants and Slaves,* McBride addressed the relationship of art and architecture by highlighting buildings' mechanical programs. *Bells and Whistles* employs the same brass material as the University Center's facade, but is formed by another set of functions, the essential but hidden mechanical life of the building.

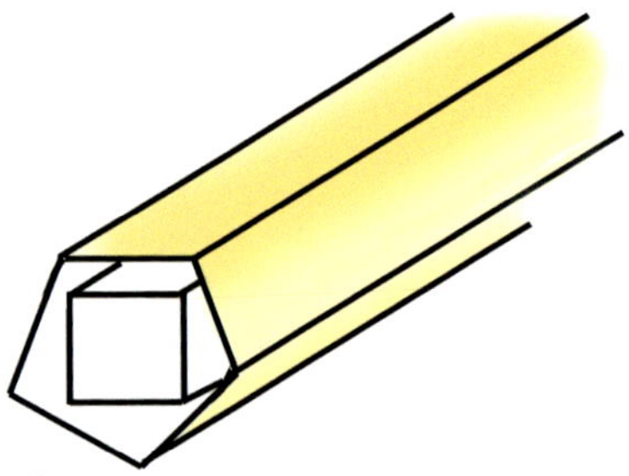

13

13 Rita McBride's detail of *Bells and Whistles*
14 Axonometric diagram of *Bells and Whistles* ductwork throughout the campus building
15 Photo of second level common area with a portion of the artwork

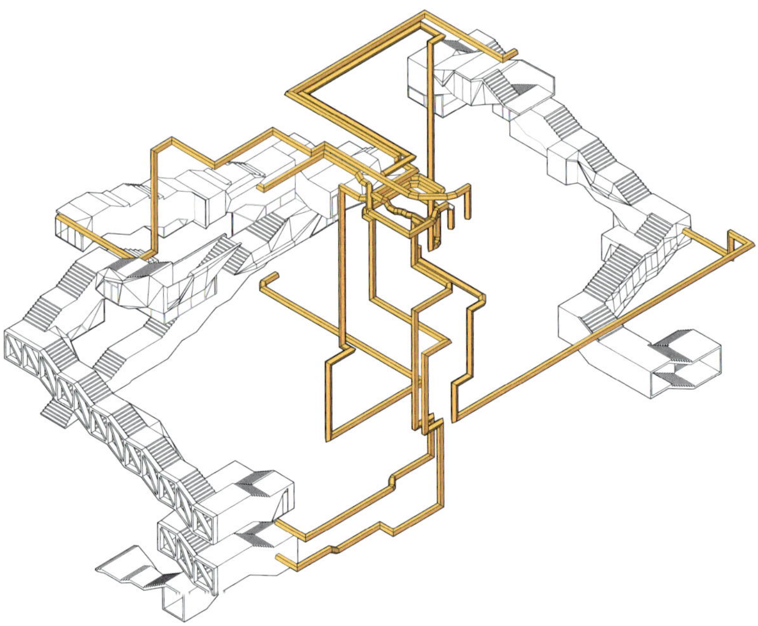

14

OPEN FOR DISCUSSION
DIGITIZING HUMANITIES
EXPLODING WITH IDEAS
ASKING WHY DESIGNING HOW
CHANGING THE RULES
IMAGINING TOMORROW
GREEN

17

18

19

16 Students in the Fifth Avenue windows
17 Communicating stair
18 Parsons Fashion corridors
19 Parsons Fashion corridor

TWA Terminal by Eero Saarinen, 1962

When Mid-Century Met Modernism

Karrie Jacobs

If you ask Google—and why should this inquiry be different than any other?—it will tell you the term "mid-century modernism" or "mid-century modern" came into regular use during the last two decades of the twentieth century. Because the Ngram viewer, the Google device that charts the appearance of phrases over time, doesn't show results beyond 2008, it's impossible to say if that use has crested or if we're in the midst of peak mid-century modernism.

However, it is possible to pinpoint the beginning of the upswing. It clearly started with the 1984 publication of a book titled *Mid-Century Modern: Furniture of the 1950s*, written by design maven Cara Greenberg, once a familiar byline in magazines like *Metropolitan Home*. The book, a cavalcade of Eames chairs, George Nelson storage systems, with a little Saarinen and Jacobsen thrown in, codified and popularized a trend that was just rising to the surface. The odd thing is that, while the word "modern" is generously sprinkled throughout the book, and the term "mid-century" comes up now and then, the title phrase doesn't show up until page 48, in a section entitled "The End of an Era." "Mid-Century Modern's golden age was over," Greenberg wrote, arguing that the era of furniture that truly embodied new manufacturing techniques, unorthodox use of materials, and form driven by a cheerful approach to functionalism began in 1947 and ended in 1957. She blames the downfall of the movement on a plague of bad knockoffs and a fickle public, for whom modernism was just another style, like Italianate or chinoiserie.

What Greenberg's book made obvious was that the 1950s, despite the decade's reputation for conformity and kitsch, was a wildly innovative time. During World War II, architects like Eero Saarinen and Arne Jacobsen had few buildings to design, so they turned their attention to furniture that embraced new forms and materials. Then, in the postwar years, pent up demand drove furniture sales, and a new aesthetic—stripped down and emphatically non-traditional—was embraced by the general public. Even my own parents, who were not the least bit interested in design, picked up a shockingly minimalist sofa and arm chair for our TV room in a style that was called Danish Modern. The pieces, I'm fairly certain, had not come from anywhere near Scandinavia, and were bought at a discount store along a New Jersey highway. That presence of even a whiff of Danish chic in my childhood home suggests to me that the mid-century was a moment when we shed traditions easily, without necessarily being aware we were doing so.

Generally, mid-century modern is a term we use today without thinking too much about it. Say it and Case Study Houses or a George Nelson clock ringed by colorful balls comes to mind. It's an easy way of codifying a certain stylistic lightness, a proclivity for making materials perform new tricks: bent plywood, glass walls, strong plastic. Unlike the prewar modernism of the Bauhaus, De Stijl, and other largely European movements, mid-century modernism implies an American joie de vivre. It was less about engineering a machine for living and more about establishing an aesthetic that expressed the insouciance of this country after the war. (Note that when we refer to mid-century modernism, we don't generally mean certain other works from the same period, such as the Pruitt Igoe Houses [1954], which became the symbol of the bad kind of modernism, the kind that was shorthand for the dumb imposition of bureaucratic power, a strain of modernism that we prefer to associate with the 1970s.)

So where did the notion of mid-century modern come from? Greenberg, who still writes about residential interiors, believes she coined the term. When I suggest that she might not have been the first to use it, she bristles. But when I searched the *New York Times* archives, a prior use of the term instantly came up in a 1953 article headlined “Modern Furniture is Getting Fancier.” The story, a brief one, concerns a line of furniture on sale at Wanamaker’s department store: “Practically none of today’s popular motifs and materials have been omitted from a new collection … Called ‘Mid-Century Modern’ the group is by J. Stuart Clingman.” According to the article, Clingman was mainly known for his traditional furniture, but he turns out to be a rather interesting designer, lost to history or, at least, to the readers of Greenberg’s account of the era. He was a second-generation furniture maker and worked out of that Athens of home furnishings, Grand Rapids, Michigan, where he was design director for John Widdicomb Co. His pieces, lean and eccentric, still turn up in online marketplaces like eBay.

I found it remarkable that right smack in the middle of the century, Clingman was self-aware enough to coin a term that positioned his work in its moment. Though maybe that wasn’t so unusual after all: according to lexicographer Jesse Sheidlower, formerly an editor at the Oxford English Dictionary, “People in the 1950s were definitely aware of being mid-century.” However, Sheidlower cautions, “That doesn’t mean that ‘mid-century modern’ then means what it does now.” Sheidlower’s words make me question whether “mid-century” circa 1953 actually implies the cloudless optimism I associate with it, or whether the notion of “mid-century” also incorporates the looming threat of the bomb, much as the idea of the Millennium, a half century later, carried with it a hint of apocalypse.

Whatever the term “mid-century modern” evoked in 1953, Clingman’s bright idea failed to catch on. Other pre-Greenberg uses show up, a rate of one or two per decade. For example, the lead sentence of a *Washington Post* article previewing a 1975 furniture exhibition at the Smithsonian’s Renwick Gallery says, “Mid-century modern as a style may be said to have arrived.” And, given that the exhibition involved pieces produced by Knoll and Herman Miller, the expression meant to the *Post* reporter exactly what it did to Greenberg nine years later. “I didn’t know about that show,” Greenberg insists.

Eventually I found my way to Clark Malcolm, who’s spent the past thirty-three years working as an in-house writer and editor at Herman Miller, the furniture maker that produced all those iconic George Nelson designs, the “voice and soul of rational, elegant design” in Greenberg’s estimation. His first response to my query about how the term “mid-century modern” was applied at a company where it should have meant a great deal, was short and sweet: it wasn’t. Malcolm attributed the phrase to Greenberg and explained that, in the 1980s, when her book was published, “Herman Miller had little enthusiasm for the people and products it describes. It was exactly that year that George Nelson visited Ann Arbor on four occasions to lecture at the school of architecture and no one from Herman Miller had time to take him to dinner. We had discontinued many of his and the Eameses’ products, and would discontinue more before the taste pendulum began to swing in the other direction.”

When you think about it, the fact that mid-century modernism was not a part of Herman Miller corporate culture in the 1980s is not so surprising. The 1980s is when I first began to navigate design culture and, at the time, critics and theorists mostly talked about modernism as something we’d finally—finally!—transcended. All the deep thinking was about postmodernism. I devoured essay collections like *The Anti-Aesthetic: Essays on Postmodern Culture* (1983) edited by Hal Foster and *Design After Modernism: Beyond the Object* (1988) edited by John Thackara. The message in these books was that modernism, as a powerful force in contemporary life had expired because a) it had been reduced to a mere style and b) it was no longer a radical, anti-authoritarian movement but rather, the default way authority presented itself. Modernism was boring. It was uncool. It was over. A typical sentiment from Thackara’s compilation can be found in an essay by architect and author Nigel Coates: “By the mid-sixties, when the old ideological crusades of modernism actually seemed to have been won, the architectural visions of this century finally took shape identically in suburbs from London to Moscow. The home in particular had become a formula, capable of being repeated, labeled and stacked … .”

And so it was in the 1980s. Modernism was passé. We had moved on. Which made the 1990s resurgence of everything from Brasilia to East German Plattenbau apartment blocks to New York’s long detested Pan Am building both entirely predictable and a complete

Heydar Aliyev Center by Zaha Hadid, 2012

Inaugural issue of *Wallpaper* magazine, October 1996

surprise. This swelling of interest in mid-century design was lucratively advanced by *Wallpaper* magazine, which launched in 1996. The publication initially embraced mid-century style because, as its founder, Tyler Brûlé, recently told me, it was what people his age (he was twenty-eight at the time) had grown up with. "There was a familiarity to it," Brûlé says. "These were the tables that helped you take your first steps." In other words, *Wallpaper*'s role in reviving modernism as an architectural style was sparked by nostalgia for the furniture, specifically Danish modern, perhaps the same bargain basement version my parents brought home. From there, the magazine's editors began to develop a taste for the architecture, seeking out and publishing modernist buildings, often ones like those in Canberra or Yokohama, that would appear exotic and alluring to readers in London or New York.

So, a decade after the architectural profession declared an end to modernism, substituting hothouse variants such as deconstructivism, *Wallpaper* took great pleasure in showcasing mid-century buildings and populating them with cool, expressionless models. Brûlé claims the magazine was motivated, in part, by a preservationist urge, "racing against the clock to chronicle places that we know probably wouldn't be with us much longer." But really, *Wallpaper* transformed architecture into a fashion. And once that happened, mid-century modernism became a lingua franca, transmutable, easy to reference, and subject to revival upon revival.

Today, the icons of the postwar decades, whether we're talking George Nelson's Marshmallow Sofa or Eero Saarinen's TWA Terminal are so universally beloved that it is often difficult, in this country, to think about modernism without its familiar modifier. And this is a problem, historically and philosophically. The popular enthusiasm for mid-century modernism, arguably, is the death of Modernism—with a capital M—because the adjective undercuts the meaning of the noun.

Greenberg can tell you why: "The word modern always means the same thing. It means of the moment, as I understand it." Accepting her definition of modern—which is also what the Random House Dictionary says—and coupling the word with a historic period turns it into a paradox. If Modernism was "of the moment" some sixty years ago, what is it now?

Even though I was writing regularly about architecture for most of the 1990s, I didn't give much thought to the notion of mid-century modernism until I started working on the 2000 start-up of *Dwell*, a magazine launched specifically to champion modern residential architecture and design. One of the things that happens when you work on a start up, is that you spend a lot of time explaining what you're doing. And my well-worn spiel on the nascent magazine was often greeted with the same vexing question: Are you going to publish just *mid-century* houses? The answer—obvious, I thought—was no. And initially, at least, I didn't understand why anyone would even think that.

At the time, the one US magazine that focused on modern homes was completely devoted to houses built from the 1940s through the 1960s. Many of them, like those erected by the pioneering California developer Joseph Eichler or the ones conjured up for experimental postwar subdivisions like Gregory Ain and Garret Eckbo's Mar Vista Tract, were quite wonderful, innovative in their flexible use of space, their blurred barriers between indoors and outdoors and their structural simplicity. It was easy to understand why homeowners cherished and obsessively restored their mid-century landmarks.

But that wasn't what we, at *Dwell*, were interested in. I came to realize that I had to find a way to make it impeccably clear that what we meant by modernism was different: we were not planning to look backward. So I did what any respectable Modernist would do, I wrote a manifesto. In the magazine's first issue we declared: "Rather than being an historical movement from the first half of the 20th century, left over and reheated, we think of modernism as a frame of mind. To us the M word connotes an honesty and curiosity about methods and materials, a belief that mass production and beauty are not mutually exclusive, and a certain optimism not just about the future, but about the present."

It was so obvious; modernism is not something that happened once, and came to an end. Rather, it is a way of looking at the world. It is a constantly changing set of technologies and opportunities, a method for integrating a ceaseless pageant of radical breakthroughs into our mundane routines. Modernism is a technique for taking the explosive forces that are constantly reshaping the human environment and domesticating them. For that reason, modernism is infinitely, endlessly relevant.

Except that it's not.

Because there's another problem, one that is not so easily dispatched. Even if you detach it from "mid-century," the word "modernism" itself is redolent of the past. In our present moment, "modern" sounds oddly quaint, the signifier of a future that didn't quite pan out. But it seems wrong to jettison the word unless we know how to replace it.

Except that we can't.

As far as I can tell, it's almost impossible to pinpoint the moment we're in right now. What word do we use to describe it? A composer friend suggests "contemporary," which works to an extent in music and the fine arts, but carries its own troublesome baggage when you're talking about architecture, where it's often a euphemism for modernism-lite. All the defining terms that anyone comes up with are either too narrow or have no legs. Remember the Information Age? In architecture nothing has the sweep or grandeur of modernism: postmodernism, deconstructivism, blobism, parametrics, passive design, sustainable architecture. None of it is broad enough. Or visionary enough. Or simple enough.

Sheidlower points out that "modern," when it became an -ism took on the same baggage as "catholic" did when it became The Church. "This is a common problem when you have words that theoretically have a broad application, but come refer to something specific—the general sense gets skunked by the specific one," he explains.

So we wind up talking about post-postmodernism or meta-modernism. (Meta-modernism even has its own manifesto: it has something to do with oscillation.) Brûlé, for his part, talks about the present by employing the prefix "re-" as in, "I feel that we're in this period of renewal and relaunching."

Probably the broadest current trend in architecture is form that is generated by an astonishing level of function, buildings that brilliantly advance a societal goal: net zero or carbon neutrality or improved health. But what is this very au courant data-driven type of building if not modernism? Today's office complexes and apartment towers are, quite literally, machines for living. Le Corbusier would be gobsmacked. Modernism has never been more vital; it's a way of thinking that could easily carry us to the middle of a newer century. Except that that modernism is solidly a century old which means that, by definition, it's over.

Chapel window view looking west from entrance, Chapel House 1957

"You Young Men Are So Sure": Architectural Ethos at J. Walter Severinghaus' Chapel House

Nicholas Adams

Architecture, as every artistic discipline, requires the forming power of a great tradition and sufficient vitality to insure the adaption of that tradition to current interests... i.e. to the temper and functional requirements of a technical age.

—Reinhold Niebuhr, "Tradition and Today's Ethos," *Architectural Forum,* December 1953

"Well, it looks to me very much like a greenhouse, but you young men are so sure that it is the right way to do it that we'll go ahead."

— Genevieve Ludlow Griscom, patron of Chapel House, in conversation with its principal designer, J. Walter Severinghaus, Kenneth W. Morgan, and Everett Case, 1957

1. The Spaces in Between

"A gyroscope spin sending forth glowing structures ... tumbling from the charred pinwheel spokes in an awful rush of terrifying violence." That is how, in the opening pages of his autobiography, *The Spaces In Between: An Architect's Journey* (1973), Nathaniel A. Owings (1903–1984) describes a troubled Fourth of July nightmare. In place of rockets fizzing out into the night sky from a pinwheel, he sees the major buildings of Skidmore, Owings & Merrill; he awakes with terrible questions of self-doubt. "Was this evidence of forty years of designing constructs simply detritus? What parts were relevant? What was their place? For me, these designs were intended to be 'form-givers,' for purposes deeper than mere shelter—but had they turned out that way?"[1]

Owings' nightmare presents a disturbing picture of SOM as seen by one of its founders nearing the end of his career.[2] The dream suggests a fear that the compulsions that had given meaning to his life now signified nothing, and SOM itself just a centrifugal imperative, a whirling dynamo. As Owings awakes, he wonders: is there any logic to hold that achievement together? Where are the centripetal forces to resist this seeming splintering energy? The answer, of course, is in one's hands. Ostensibly an autobiography, *The Spaces in Between* was Owings' best effort to map out a new vision for the firm he had founded almost forty years earlier. It reflected Owings' continuing confidence in the firm's durable version of modern design but it also told of his newly-awakened awe for the collective power of nature and the environment, for community and social life, for family and the small (and often unremarked) victories achieved by architects.

The Spaces in Between was, assuredly, an old man's book, the work of a veteran reviewing old campaigns and reborn into a wider understanding of the world. But while the book was an effort at legacy, its concerns resonate prophetically today. The darkest interpretation of Owings' dream would be of the body of work as flaming out in sound and fury, without pointing to anything beyond or within itself. The brightest interpretation would be of that pinwheel as a kind of propulsion device: an energy that could be harvested and sustained today to find and extend common denominators, identify and nurture convergent forces and principles in design. Owings' nightmare had its birth in the recognition that forces beyond any one person's control—institutional, conventional, social, cultural, and more—shaped the firm's practice as much or more than the individual or collective intent of its designers. In retirement, as a kind of insider-turned-outsider, all Owings could do was write a book, pointing what he thought should be the way forward; it is probably no surprise that his former colleagues largely ignored his message—or at least the built and written record shows them uninflected by his particular doubts. He was not a popular man among the partners at this point, his writing skills had their limits, and feeding the beast, keeping money flowing through the pipeline was, then as now, a constant condition. In any event, establishing the parameters of a practice, defining the spirit of a place, was probably not something someone on the outside, even Owings' privileged kind of outside, could ever do.

Owings' concern was, arguably, with ethos: which is part of what happens in the spaces in between, often unarticulated but deeply communicated. SOM was of course characterized from the beginning as a collective or corporate construction of design authorship, a counterpoint to the would-be heroic Modern Masters. But ethos, while dependent on, is different from, a "house style": it's a kind of belief, often unstated, that lends confidence, that amounts to assuredness—to whatever it is that makes you sure enough of a design decision. Given the all-encompassing nature of an ethos when applied to an architectural firm, to the variably collaborative processes within it, how does a historian understand practice as it took place fifty years ago? So much of what defines a practice is what doesn't have to be said—and unspoken rules are by definition, not part of historiography, and are hard to tease out from the past. It's similarly hard to prove a counterfactual: visual evidence about the design paths untaken, to pick one example, is only rarely available. As a result we tend to focus on what we see. And even there, we struggle. Today, an observer might like to establish a historical ethos by calling out projects: "it's Lever House, or the John Hancock Center, or the Alcoa Building." But there is something unbearably static in identifying a specific building or a group of buildings with an ethos—with a dynamic of continuous communication and adjustment. We would also have to take into account the critical role of Owings' earlier parti for Lever House (1952); of Graham's temper at Hancock sticking one tower on top of another (1965); or Goldsmith's influence on Bassett's design at Alcoa (1964). Those events are not systematic, but neither are they really eccentric—and in that sense they are part of an ethos. Alternatively, we could identify the work of Gordon Bunshaft, or Bruce Graham, or Myron Goldsmith, as exemplary of an ethos, after all, their work individually changes over time just as the ethos changes. Even so, there is something overly personalized in identifying an ethos with one individual—or even three people or practices that were so different from one another. Discerning an ethos is rich in paradox: because it expresses itself in dynamic processes of communication, decision, and transformation, whatever is essential to those processes is also mutable—and as soon as we define it, it may redefine itself.

Looking from the outside, perhaps we come a little closer to the ethos of a period and practice when we can't distinguish who did what. A colleague recalls a New York hospital visit in which she found herself looking at an unidentified building across the street and slowly, through the post-operative haze, becoming aware that the windows and mullions she could see from her window could only have been designed by someone at SOM. They called to mind other buildings by SOM she knew—perhaps, like George Kubler's "linked series," forming a chain of facade solutions. The effect is more associative than attributable: an early article on interiors designed by SOM's Chicago office in the January 1959 issue of the magazine *Interiors*, asserted a distinctive "Chicago" style of interior design. But the Chicago designs look all but indistinguishable from the New York designs. Was there, at the time at SOM, an architectural ethos—dependent on, but also transcendent of, an architectural style or a definite authorial attribution?[3] I'd nominate the Inland Steel Building in Chicago (1958) as an effective representative of the ethos at that time precisely because the question of authorship can't properly be settled between Graham, Walter Netsch, and my candidate for the critical impact, Gordon Bunshaft. It is pure ethos inasmuch as each contributor appears to have worked towards an unstated goal that was understood by all participants. Finding buildings that carry that quality is instructive, an assembly of the package of qualities that makes up the ethos of a particular time and place. Might we find a single building, maybe precisely an uncelebrated building, in which this ethos is above all to be found?

If we suspect that the ethos of today's SOM is wholly or partially stored in an understanding of its historical work of the mid-twentieth century, perhaps we should seek among that work an uncelebrated building; a building in which elements of style are apparent but not rigidly enforced; a building that is unattributed or attributed to a notably unprolific designer; and a building whose own program was explicitly concerned with the relationship between the tangible and ineffable. A building like Chapel House (1958–59) at Colgate University in Hamilton, New York.

2. The Ethos in Chapel House

I approached Chapel House for the first time after finding it on a list of SOM buildings. Puzzled by the name, I made a detour there a half a dozen years ago after a visit to the architectural remnants of the utopian Oneida Community nearby in upstate New York. It was High Summer and the campus was deserted; the building, set well apart from the academic buildings, was open to visitors, welcoming and peaceful but entirely empty. I wandered through, wondering who or what part of SOM had produced it. It had not appeared in the *Architecture of Skidmore Owings & Merrill 1950–1962* (1963), and had not registered in the architectural press of the day. No one at SOM seemed to have a record of the designer and there was no explanation available at Colgate on a summer's afternoon. Yet it spoke so eloquently as an SOM building from the 1950s that I revisited it this spring to see if it had held up against my memory, and whether I could make more sense out of it. It turned out to be under restoration: a temporary state of transformation that allowed me to see it stripped and opened, waiting for its pieces to be reassembled for a new generation. In time I explored its history and met one of the sons of the first director (and the building's client), discussed it with the son of its designer and the granddaughter of the woman who conveyed the money to Colgate for its construction.

Chapel House was unusual for its day: a building dedicated to non-sectarian religion on a campus with Baptist roots. It was neither dedicated to worship in the university's way (for that there was the Memorial Chapel with compulsory weekday attendance in those years) nor was it dedicated to teaching the Protestant traditions of the school (which remained reflected in the core curriculum in which the departments of religion and philosophy played a significant role). Chapel House was designed to foster religion in the abstract and at a singular level. It was a place where anyone, from on or off campus might come and be alone with their thoughts, might read and think, might listen to music, look at religious art, meditate, contemplate, or pray. There were no regular services. It was a place for the personal exploration of all religions with special emphasis on the eastern religions poorly known in the United States.

The initiative for Chapel House came from the university chaplain and professor of religion, Kenneth W. Morgan (1908–2011).[4] After college he had enrolled in the Philosophy Department at Harvard University, before moving to the Divinity School where he received his Bachelor of Sacred Theology (1935). He was something of a seeker, fascinated with the ways different religions found God. His earliest religious experiences were in the Methodist Church but while in Cambridge, when time allowed, he made sure to visit Jewish and Catholic services as well as those of other Protestant denominations—and even some of the "strange sects advertised in local publications."[5] In 1934 he met Swami Nikhilananda (1895–1973), head of the Ramakrishna-Vivekananda Center in New York City and with his help he undertook a trip to India staying in Ramakrishna ashrams and studying Hindu practices (1935–36). After working with the Society of Friends and wartime service as a conscientious objector—he later joined the Society of Friends—Morgan went to Colgate University as Chaplain (1946). The experiences with Eastern religions returned and became the inspiration for his first book, an edited collection of studies of Hinduism by Indian authors (1953), a book that set a pattern for later books on Buddhism (1956) and Islam (1958).[6] Designed for students in an institutional or private setting the books generally drew praise as fair-minded and un-exotic, filling a long-recognized gap for English readers. It was Morgan's reputation as an even-handed presenter of different religions that led directly to the construction of Chapel House.

In early 1956, Genevieve Ludlow Griscom (1868–1958), an elderly and wealthy New Yorker, contacted Morgan, directed to him by a J. N. Spalding, a prominent English

View of Chapel House shortly after renovation, 2016

supporter of comparative religion. She revealed little of herself to Morgan but made it clear that she wished to find a way to advance the cause of Eastern religions and their relations with Christianity in the United States. How could she do that? With Morgan's help an introduction was made to the appropriate people at Harvard University and Griscom subsequently gave $500,000 to establish the Center for the Study of World Religions within the Divinity School.[7] She then spontaneously sent a check for $350,000 to Colgate with which Morgan was to apply to advancing the study of the great religions of the world there.[8] Spurred by this largesse (and possibly encouraged by her) Morgan put together a proposal that he sent to her for "a small building where a seeker could study how the religious beliefs and practices in all traditions have been presented in books, in recordings of religious music, and in reproductions and originals of religious arts." It would be "a place designed for anyone who wants to know more about worship, devotion, meditation, unselfishness and caring in the religions of the world." He imagined a chapel, a library, a music room, some bedrooms for overnight visitors, and a small kitchen and dining room. "It would be a place welcoming seekers from any religious tradition or none who wanted to know more about the religious paths followed by other seekers; about their personal devotional rituals, chanting, prayers, meditation, and what they have read."[9] Mrs. Griscom offered Morgan $600,000 for his meditation center (more than he had asked for) and had two requests: her name "was never to be mentioned, and she must approve the architectural plans."[10] Morgan persuaded the University to accept the gift and thereafter resigned as chaplain to become the center's first director. The senior designer at SOM was not one of the firm's prominent designers but J. Walter Severinghaus (1905–1987), a friend of Morgan's at Ohio Wesleyan University in Delaware, Ohio.[11]

Morgan left a number of accounts of his meetings with "the Lady," as he referred to her—or "Mrs. B." as he also called her. She was eighty-seven years old when they first met in 1956. They met first in her mansion, Fair Hill (now called "Fieldstone") on her estate, Chapel Farm, in Riverdale, New York, and though Morgan seems to have known relatively little about her life or at least does not report any knowledge of it, they must have talked extensively about religion. He knew that she had long-standing spiritual interests, particularly in Eastern spiritual traditions, and had money (not from her personal estate, she underlined) to give for educational purpose. He knew, too, that she was a theosophist and even participated in discussions of the terms of the gift to Harvard that she and her "friends" formulated.[12]

Though Morgan met her at Chapel Farm he does not report (and may not even have known) the full purpose of Fair Hill or Chapel Farm. In fact, Chapel Farm was home to a group called "The Outer Court of the Order of the Living Christ" (or simply, Order of the Living Christ) of which, by then, Mrs. Griscom was the oldest (if not the central) figure.

The Order of the Living Christ was all that remained of a splinter group of theosophists, based in New York City known as "The Theosophical Society" or "The Theosophical Society of America." Founded in 1894, as the theosophical movement broke apart following the death of their founder, Madame Helena Blavatsky (1831–1891) and disputes among her followers, they had been the major East Coast center for theosophy. They had, indeed, formed a group to study the spiritual texts of the Christian mystics and the major texts of Eastern religions, as she told Morgan, but they also held public lectures, seminars, retreats, annual conferences to promote theosophy and had sponsored an Episcopal mission on Horatio Street, the Chapel of the Comforter. There they installed a theosophically minded priest, Clarence C. Clark.[13] Episcopalianism was their exoteric face, theosophy their esoteric heart. In 1903 at Fair Hill, they started a magazine, *The Theosophical Quarterly,* which they published regularly until 1938. The house was a massive 14,000-square-foot mansion of local granite built in a modified French country style.[14] Fair Hill had been home to the *Quarterly* and many of its activities, and the cottages at Chapel Farm had been the home to many of the theosophists. Griscom herself had authored a regular column for *The Theosophical Quarterly* under the pseudonym "Cavé" (a reference to buried ancient knowledge) entitled "Fragments," and her essays had been collected in three small volumes called *Fragments*.[15] Although she and her husband, Clement A. Griscom (1868–1918), president of a prominent engineering firm, Griscom-Russell, that specialized in heat exchangers, were the primary support of The Theosophical Society they were far from alone. The leader of the group was the troubling Ernest Temple Hargrove (1870–1939). Hargrove's personal life had a rather seamy side as revealed in a court case following his death.[16] The key intellectual light was the Irish writer and editor Charles Johnston (1867–1931). A specialist in Russian as well as Sanskrit, he had translated the Bhagavad Gita, among other spiritual texts into English. He had also introduced the poet W. B. Yeats to Madame Blavatsky and was married to Blavatsky's niece, Vera. One of the most important members was Henry Bedinger Mitchell (1874–1956), who taught mathematics at Columbia University. Mitchell was editor of the *Quarterly* from 1903–1938 and everyone called him "the Professor." His brother John (1877–1956), a Wall Street lawyer, was also a member and probably the person who first made contact with Morgan. When Henry Mitchell died in July 1956 his estate, valued at $1.1 million, was left to Griscom as head of the Order of the Living Christ.[17] It was Mitchell's money (added to funds left by others) that became the foundation for Chapel House—one reason why she said that the money she gave to Colgate was not hers.

By 1956, however, the Theosophical Society no longer existed. In 1938 *The Theosophical Quarterly* had stopped publication. In a letter to subscribers, bound into the October 1938 issue but dated December 31, 1938, she wrote that the law of cycle "teaches us that outer activities, beneficial during one period, at another do more harm than good, and that spiritual progress can be achieved only by Indrawl." "Indrawl" was a neologism. It did not mean "giving up," as in a "withdrawal." It referred, instead, to a waiting period, a pause as the group looked forward to a more auspicious moment. "The *Quarterly*," the editors wrote, "has proved that it knows when and how to speak; now it is proving that it knows when to be silent."[18] Precisely what prompted the closing of the *Quarterly* is not clear—but evidently there was no second generation adequate to the work. Johnston died in 1931; Hargrove the following year and in 1938 Mrs. Griscom was seventy; Henry Bedinger Mitchell was sixty-four, his brother John sixty.

What those who remained did after closing *The Quarterly* (and, effectively, the Society) is not known. Presumably they attended to their own spiritual needs; they visited the Chapel of the Comforter (though that too folded into the church of St. John's, Waverly Place by 1950). The Order of the Living Christ was very well endowed and Griscom and Mitchell defended their interests—fighting a brutal New York Supreme Court case over Hargrove's will in 1941.[19] Perhaps they sought more public ways to advance their causes. Joanie Griscom, Mrs. Griscom's granddaughter, has described Fair Hill as a rather eerie place—one of Mrs. Griscom's sons (Ludlow) was deeply ashamed of his mother's religious activities; the other (Clement) was something of an eccentric. Of this Morgan probably knew little if anything. He describes a chauffeur driven car and immense formality; Joanie Griscom recalls her grandmother trailed by "the Professor" calling her "my lady."

After seeing Mrs. Griscom's very traditional house, Morgan's decision to call on his friend Walter Severinghaus and SOM was something of a risk. Morgan was clear that architectural symbolism would need to be muted: the building, he thought, "would have to speak for itself" and its inclusive ambitions meant that it could not employ common ecclesiastical symbolism: modern architecture was appropriate.[20] At one point, as plans were being drawn up, Morgan let Mrs. Griscom know that SOM were the architects and that an exhibition at the Museum of Modern Art (*Buildings for Business and Government*) would contain some of their works (the exhibition ran from February 26 to May 5, 1957). According to Morgan: "She immediately telephoned to say that she did not see how architects who would allow their work to be shown at the Museum of Modern Art could create anything she could approve, for that Museum had not shown anything she would go across the street to see." When Severinghaus, Morgan, and Colgate president Everett Case brought a model and plans to her a few weeks later they did so with some trepidation. "She listened without comment to the detailed explanation of the plans, then remained silent a long time, looking at the model, and finally said, "Well, it looks to me very much like a greenhouse, but you young men are so sure that it is the right way to do it that we'll go ahead."[21]

Set at the western edge of Colgate's campus, Chapel House consists of two linked rectangles set at right angles to form an "L" on an open grassy shelf, like an open hand, overlooking Lake Moraine and the valley beyond. On construction the views were breathtaking but today trees form a dense curtain to the west. One arrives along a steep tree-flanked minor road to find the open "L" of Chapel House and its glass corridor: the building embraced by the trees in a modernized version of one of Andrew Jackson Downing's rural settings. The site forms a natural amphitheater, a unique piece of scenic landscaping on a campus that offers otherwise little breathing space: tall pines to the west and south; lilacs, euonymus, and viburnum above the retaining walls to the south; a line of spruce trees (originally dogwoods) along the stone path to the entrance on the north; birch trees set on the lawn.[22] To the south is the chapel, a thirty-five-seat rectangular box resting on a concrete pass and fronted with orange German cathedral glass and marked by four white wide-flanged beams at the corners supporting an extended flat roof.[23] The double layer of glass bathes the interior of the chapel with an even golden light and a mosaic reredos echoes its colors. At night with the Chapel lit from the inside it becomes a Chinese lantern, glowing orange in the dark. A suspended gable ceiling, though thoroughly modern by mid-twentieth-century norms, also recalls traditional nave forms or the folded interior of a tent. The chairs have arms, cushions and straight backs, to facilitate peaceful sitting. At the back of the chapel are private wooden seating chambers called "oratories" by Morgan, but recalling Catholic confessionals—with the proviso that there is no room for a priest. These have curtains that can be drawn for privacy. In front of the oratories is a wooden frame seating area with a row of six chairs separated by partitions, where persons can sit facing forward without seeing others to left or right. Other chairs can be arranged as wanted. Though a curtain can close it off, a cross on the altar wall seems out of place given the goal of the building to serve all religions.[24] At either end of the exterior of the chapel are richly colored granite walls (with stone brought from Yonkers) laid in an irregular sawn-cut pattern. Morgan persuaded Severinghaus not to stack the stones in equal courses; in that case, the recollection of Chapel Farm would have been lost.[25]

The second wing employs the granite wall as the major façade device. Inside is daily living; in effect, the house: a library, music room, director and administrative offices, dining room, and kitchen. The spaces are simple and originally had white walls and a white plaster ceiling. Inset panels in the dining area contained religious sculptures and elsewhere the walls were hung with eclectic religious art collected by Morgan. The contemporary photographs by Ezra Stoller emphasize the domestic simplicity of the spaces and the restrained presentation of the art recalls the success SOM had in the placement of art within office buildings and hotels. Chairs in the common living room have high extended and angled wings to emphasize privacy. These are silent spaces for inward focus. Students, faculty, and visitors (from the community and beyond) are welcome. Downstairs are seven small guest rooms for overnight visitors much in the manner of a convent or a monastery or even the ashrams Morgan had known on his travels in India. Visitors come for a period—two days at a minimum—to read from the religious literature in the library, listen to music (on headphones), meditate, or walk in the woods. There may be a resident from the campus or from elsewhere who can answer questions or offer suggestions, but there is no spiritual agenda, no direction, no agenda. It is a place to find quiet and invite your soul. Talking is sanctioned only at mealtimes. At one time there were views over the Chenango Valley—and these have been reemphasized in the current restoration. Originally the valley-facing windows were small and the trees below had been allowed to grow to reduce sound from traffic in the valley. Nothing suggests that the view of nature was ever intended to be dominant. If anything, it was the reverse. One of the most poignant of spaces is on the south side of the chapel where the retaining walls meet and a bench (added later) allows a visitor to sit with the chapel on its podium and its white beams, like modernized totem poles, on one's right hand. Trees shelter the site giving one a surprising sense of oasis-like isolation, a quiet and restful spot in a formal park. (Some of that has been undone by the restoration, which has strengthened the link to the outside, south of the glass connector.)

3. The Young Men in their Time

J. Walter Severinghaus was one of the earliest employees brought in to the New York office by Louis Skidmore. He had worked with Adams & Prentice after graduation—perhaps working on the Yale *Daily News* Building (1932) with them. He started work at SOM in 1938, the year after Gordon Bunshaft. Owings called Severinghaus "the conscience and the worrier, the ultimate guarantor of credibility … ." Deliberate in speech and action, Severinghaus was the one, Owings said, who met the wildest of ideas "with a tempered logic and reason."[26] In photographs he sometimes looks more like a lawyer or a family doctor than an architect. He served as the representative for the New York office on the partners' committee and as a project manager, noted for his efficiency and appreciated for the care with which he dealt with problems for Gordon Bunshaft at Chase Manhattan (1961) and Michael McCarthy at the Texaco Headquarters (1973) and many others.[27] Severinghaus, however, was not noted for design—and Chapel House, the commission from his college classmate, may be the only design work of his maturity.[28] Still, from a historical point of view if one were to look for people who represented the continuity of SOM's practice, it would be in people like Severinghaus, who put the pieces together, who were ready to meet with the clients, who adjudicated disputes, ran the partners' committees, and who stood, for the most part, in the background.[29] Were they, possibly, the ones who defined the ethos of their day?

When it came time to design Chapel House, Severinghaus looked hard at contemporary design. Simple flat-roofed and abstracted formalism was something that SOM did—at Connecticut General (1955) and at the United States Post Graduate Technical School, Carmel, California (1955), as well as at elementary schools such as Grout Creek, Schenectady, New York (1954), among others. Chapel House, however, is somewhat looser in feeling. The two part cranked plan recalls a characteristic binuclear plan by Marcel Breuer, something like the

Chapel interior

Geller House (1947), the McComb House (1951), or Ferry House (1952), or even harks back to Frank Lloyd Wright's Unity Temple (1908). The granite walls, too, grounded in similarly detailed pavers in the entry court, are a favorite Breuer motif.[30] They are, however, a surprise when paired with white wide-flange members that, columns outboard of and laminar to the beams they support, recall Mies van der Rohe's Farnsworth House in Plano, Illinois (1951), on which Myron Goldsmith (1918–1986), then up-and-coming with SOM in San Francisco, had worked. Here the beams recall Japanese temples, Buddhist shrines, or even the simplest of primitive huts, even the tent figured in Le Corbusier's "Primitive Temple," from *Vers Une Architecture* (1923). There are also reminiscences of Eero Saarinen's MIT Chapel (1955) in the binuclear plan, the golden palette of the chapel interior, and the simple glass corridor (as originally constructed) connecting the two wings with its shifted-vertical-rectangle pattern of the mullions. Using quite different means, Severinghaus,' mosaic wall even captures something of the evanescent shower of Harry Bertoia's altar-screen sculpture at the MIT Chapel.

Chapel House was a significant contribution to modern religious building at a time of crisis in the typology. The theologian Reinhold Niebuhr had argued in an influential article entitled "Religious Building: Tradition and Today's Ethos" in *Architectural Record* (1953) that modern efforts to adapt Gothic architecture to the modern age had suffered from "archaism," thus proving that there was "insufficient vitality in the religious or architectural tradition to adjust and apply the tradition to contemporary interests."[31] A year later, Walter Netsch's mechanized gothic Chapel for the Air Force Academy (1954) would face that argument head on.[32] Certainly in religious circles, the architecture of Rudolf Schwarz (1897–1961) was to be preferred over the architecture of chapels such Mies van der Rohe's Robert F. Carr Chapel (1952), which though initially sponsored by the Episcopal Church, became a non-denominational "god box." Chapel House, with its eccentric religious program followed another path, closer to the principles then being articulated by the Belgian Roman Catholic Frédéric Debuyst (b. 1922). For him, and his American Protestant follower Edward Sövik (1918–2014), church should be a kind of "living room for celebration marked by aesthetic exaltation and graciousness." It should be designed for hospitality and comfort creating a domestic ambience. Enriching the spaces with art created a "calm, recollected and transparent celebration."[33] Later, Sövik visited Japan where he found the teahouse—the tea ceremony providing a useful model for a building that combined the domestic and the spiritual.[34] Severinghaus had, as it were, already been there. Colgate's "ashram," with sleeping, dining, and domestic spaces for meditation and prayer and an annexed chapel for modest exaltation offered comparable effects for the original program.

Whether Morgan and Severinghaus reflected any of Griscom's theosophical ideas at Chapel House is harder to say. The choice of the name "Chapel House" was an obvious echo of Chapel Farm. The specification of the stone patterns (not to mention the source of the stone) could also be an acknowledgement of Griscom's Fair Hill. Above Fair Hill, in the rocky landscape behind the house was a cross. Placing a cross on the reredos in the chapel may also have recalled Morgan's recollection of his patron's house. In the end, however, it was the sponsorship of a plurality of approaches to religion and the emphasis on meditation that represents the most significant part of the program, a program that Morgan, Griscom (and Mitchell, the probable ultimate source of the donation) shared.

In 1907 Mitchell had published a book on meditation, the first modern book on the subject, according to the historian of religion, Karl Baier.[35] In his book, Mitchell outlined the seven steps that would allow one to pass from the outer world to the inner, the seven dangers to be avoided on that journey, and seven aspects of illumination—the enlightenment of meditation. Mrs. Griscom certainly communicated the centrality of meditation to the Harvard University administration when she made her donation to them. At the Center for World Religions at Harvard, Josep Luis Sert placed the meditation room at the highest point in the building. Morgan probably received the same message and one wonders how much he developed the program for Chapel House in consideration of his donor's wishes or her exposition of Mitchell's beliefs? Laying out a binuclear plan created an exoteric space (the living quarters) and an esoteric space (the chapel).

Mitchell's ideas may also have led Griscom to conclude that Colgate offered a reasonable place for their largesse. While at Columbia University, Mitchell had chaired the Committee on Instruction and they had advocated a course on the fundamentals of religion. The course would be "wholly non-sectarian in character, and should therefore not be given by a clergyman of any denomination."[36] Mitchell perhaps, strayed over the line when he tried to appoint his theosophist colleague Charles Johnston to teach the course—and the president of Columbia refused the appointment, preferring someone in the Department of Religion instead. Mitchell's commitment to a plural religious education, therefore, must have been one key to deciding how the money should be distributed.

There is much to reflect on in this story of theosophy and architecture. There is much to admire in the humility of the Society's indrawl. Humility, as Iris Murdoch reminds us "is a selfless respect for reality and one of the most difficult and central of all virtues."[37] Morgan and Severinghaus matched the humility of the theosophist indrawl, with their own architectural modesty.

Mrs. Griscom's willingness to accept the reality of the world as it was beyond her own circle (and taste) and Morgan's ability to connect with this eccentric benefactress are key parts of the story. SOM's characteristic application of new solutions to traditional problems—better known at Terrace Plaza, at Lever House, at Manufacturers Trust—plays out here too, even though Severinghaus' defining work at the firm was not as a designer. Perhaps Morgan's description of the site recalled to Mrs. Griscom, her own vision published in *Theosophical Quarterly*: "I went up into the mountain to commune with my own heart, and stood there looking at the stars."[38] But about that we know nothing; she died before seeing the building, never saw the site and left no personal record of her thoughts.

4. The Character in Renovation

The inauguration of Chapel House took place in March 1959 and the student newspaper named Kenneth Morgan the "Maroon Man of the Year."[39] It was, for all intents and purposes, the first modern building on campus with a symbolic (as well as a functional) program—an arrival that passed without notice in the campus newspaper.[40] Its first name was the Upstate New York Meditation Chapel but it became "Chapel House" before inauguration. Like Venturi's later "Guild House," it was without a definite article in Morgan's Quaker tradition. Chapel House was soon home to Quaker Meetings and Jewish services (in the Chapel), to lectures and presentations on Eastern religion, and to visitors who appreciated its quiet and peace and welcomed the chance to seek for themselves.[41] (Morgan retired in 1974 and was succeeded by John Ross Carter, Robert Ho professor in Asian Studies; Steven Kepnes, professor of philosophy and Jewish Studies became director in 2013.)

Severinghaus' building had proven remarkably durable—over time refreshed inside with paint but little else. Indeed, to walk into Chapel House half a dozen years ago was to walk back in time: every detail, railings, handles, and bathroom fittings were those of half a century ago: comprehensive, immersive, evocative. Morgan's enthusiasm for the role of art as a stimulus to religious thinking had, perhaps, filled the walls more than was good for the architecture, but the reflective tranquility of the building was persuasive even as the single pane windows, the lighting, the curtain wall, and the fixtures begged for the inevitable modernization.

The work recently completed by Coldham & Hartman, Amherst, Massachusetts, has sought to update the building without destroying its character. Some changes were more or less essential: removal of asbestos; a geothermal heat pump; an energy recovery ventilator; the replacement of the existing curtain wall in the west and its replacement with modern assemblies to minimize heat loss; new accessible bathrooms; roof replacement to improve drainage and increase insulation. Only the thickened roof profile damages the original building's lines. Other changes will have some implication for the experience of users: the glass connector has been breached by doors on the south side to make it possible for individuals or groups to access a little patio. The original corridor glass has been swapped for a more energy efficient but highly banal replacement. A new addition on the west side of the domestic house includes an elevator and the windows have been opened wider. Kitchen facilities have been updated with dining moved from what seemed like a corridor into a room with a window; the space liberated by removing the dining function will become a sitting room as originally envisioned. The removal of the cross from the chapel seems possible; its presence has been praised as the acknowledgement that this is a place of worship, but its signification is probably too narrow by contemporary standards—even though a curtain is available to close it off. In what will be a challenge to the old order of Chapel House culture, informal student-faculty groups will meet within its walls, an attempt to familiarize more students with its functions—the solid masonry walls provide soundproofing. It will be a site for interfaith discussion on special occasions—an activity planned when Mrs. Griscom conveyed the gift to Colgate. The new interior color is Sherwin & Williams "alabaster," and the art that gave the building something of the air of a religious gallery will be winnowed and rotated over time.

The clarity of the original design creates a peaceful effect: the luminescent non-figural glass in the chapel, the white wide-flanged beams, and the warmth of the stone. The building rests in its natural amphitheater. When Reinhold Niebuhr wrote about "ethos" for *Architectural Record* in 1953, he introduced the word to wonder whether the Gothic style, "is the most perfect expression of the ethos of the Christian faith or whether it mirrors the ethos of the Middle Ages too much to express contemporary" belief; and yet found that it, "expresses something more universal [...] than the ethos of a bygone age." Perhaps Chapel House, in its earnest catalog of whatever Breuer found in uneven stone and whatever Mies found in white steel, is much the same, both of its time and for all time. Owings probably never made it to Colgate; the fizz of the pinwheel and July 4th nightmares seem far away when you sit on the gentle slope that leads down to Chapel House with its spiritually therapeutic birch trees and spruces. It is a place for meditation. A line from Philip Larkin's much-anthologized poem "Church Going" comes to mind: "A serious house on serious earth it is ...." And that's as it should be—even if you're the kind of person whose thoughts turn first to architecture before they turn to religion.

Acknowledgements: I am grateful for generous help from the current and the former directors of Chapel House, professors Steven Kepnes and John Ross Carter (Colgate University). David Morgan (Wesleyan University) kindly allowed me to study his father's papers and welcomed discussion of Chapel House in the context of his father's life. Elizabeth Morgan, Alan Morgan, and Scott Morgan generously read the manuscript and I have tried to reflect their comments. John Severinghaus (Norwich, Vermont) shared recollections of his father's pride in the building. Philip Purcell and John Winkler helped me appreciate the quality and character of J. Walter Severinghaus. Sandra Galuten kindly showed me around Fair Hill (today Fieldstone) in Riverdale, a building she has lovingly brought back to life. A lengthy and fruitful conversation with Mrs. Griscom's granddaughter, Joanie Griscom, helped clarify many issues. Paul Ivey (University of Arizona) discussed the issues at Chapel House and provided insights into the history of theosophy. Wayne Kempton (Episcopal Diocese of New York) provided information on the Chapel of the Comforter. Thomas Hartman of C&H Architects, Amherst, MA, showed me through Chapel House while under renovation. Robert Dwyer and Robert McVaugh (Colgate University) filled me in on the architectural history of Colgate University. This essay is offered to David Schenck as a small token for a lifetime of friendship.

1 Nathaniel Alexander Owings, *The Spaces in Between: An Architect's Journey* (Boston: Houghton Mifflin Company, 1973), p. 3

2 An examination of the drafts for *The Spaces in Between* among the Nathaniel A. Owings papers in the Library of Congress, Washington, DC, reveals the opening dream as one of the constants in a changing text. See Adams, "Belonging as a Corporate Ideal: Nathaniel A. Owings of Skidmore, Owings & Merrill writes *The Spaces in Between,"* in *L'architetto: ruolo, volto, mito,* ed. Guido Beltramini and Howard Burns (Venice: Marsilio, 2009), 323–42.

3 J. A., "SOM: The Chicago Office of Skidmore, Owings & Merrill," *Interiors* (January 1959), pp. 90–109.

4 I am grateful to David Morgan, emeritus professor of history at Wesleyan University, for the opportunity to study and quote from Kenneth Morgan's autobiographical manuscript, "Memories." Copies of this work are with the Morgan family and will be deposited at Colgate University, Special Collections and University Archives.

5 Morgan, "Memories," p. 40.

6 Morgan, ed., *The Religion of the Hindus* (New York: Ronald Press, 1953; *The Path of the Buddha* (New York: Ronald Press, 1956); *Islam—The Straight Path* (New York: Ronald Press, 1958).

7 The architect of the Harvard Center was Josep Luis Sert (1960). On the foundation of the Harvard Center, Morgan, "Memories," pp. 239–44. See also, "The Building," in John B. Carman and Kathryn Dodgson, *Community and Colloquy: The Center for the Study of World Religion 1958–2003* (Cambridge: Center for the Study of World Religions, 2006). Mrs. Griscom had no apparent influence on the architecture at Harvard though the placement of the meditation room at the highest point in the building parallels the importance of meditation at Colgate. Charles Hallisey, senior lecturer at the Harvard Divinity School refers to the two buildings as "siblings."

8 Morgan, "Memories," p. 246. The charge from Griscom to Colgate had overtones of her theosophical past and recollects the terms of her gift to Harvard. "We wish to encourage the sympathetic study of the religions of the world in order to show the fundamental unity and reality. Back of all religions—their common root in the spiritual world—from which each person may gain a clearer insight and firmer faith in the truth of his own religion." See *Mid-York Weekly,* December 13, 1956. See Morgan, "Memories," p. 350.

9 Morgan, "Memories," p. 40. Morgan left a three-page statement of the principles for Chapel House dated May 12, 1958. See Colgate University, Special Collections and University Archives, A1000, Box 29. A copy is also in the SOM Marketing Division Archives, New York.

10 Her desire for anonymity has been fully respected by Colgate University and the Morgan family. She told Morgan: "I am an old woman and soon I shall be going over to the other side where I'll see all my friends. If I had done something for the Lord and added my name to it, I'd be ashamed to see them." Quoted in *Chapel House: Introduction to the Works of Art and How and Why Chapel House was Created,* undated mimeographed volume, presumably by Morgan, p. 48. One further reason for her anonymity is that the money she was giving to Morgan was not hers. Morgan knew two of her legatees, Marjorie Kilpatrick and Annette Lewis. The latter also lived at Chapel Farm. Some part of her disposable wealth came from Ernest Temple Hargrove (1870–1938). In a messy court case before the New York State Supreme Court, Hargrove's children unsuccessfully contested his will. See below, n. 17.

11 Morgan was class of 1929; Severinghaus was class of '28.

12 Morgan does not mention her theosophy but she did leave Chapel House theosophical books (as reported by professors Carter and Kepnes.) See also Morgan, "Memories," Appendix C, p. 350 and p. 351.

13 I am indebted to Wayne Kempton, archivist of the Episcopal Diocese of New York for information on Clark and the Chapel of the Comforter.

14 The compound consisted of a mansion, four residences and several small cottages. Her estate was valued at $5.4 million dollars on her death. She left $500,000 to her son and the remainder in trust to "Outer Court Inc. of the Order of the Living Christ, a religious and educational organization." *Herald Statesman* (Yonkers) November 30, 1962. The architect of the compound is unknown. Mrs. Griscom may have known the California theosophist and architect Birger Elwing (1867–1935) who designed the cover for Henry Bedinger Mitchell's book, *Meditation* (see n. 16). Elwing may have been the source of the flowered scroll ceilings found today in Fieldstone. It has been asserted (see, for example, *Wall Street Journal,* May 18, 2012) that the group was waiting for the Second Coming and kept the house empty in preparation. The source of this information seems to have been Mrs. Griscom's lawyer who has been suspected of disloyalty (oral communication from Joanie Griscom, October 3, 2016). There is no evidence from *The Theosophical Quarterly* that the group had any illusions about Christ's return—that is, some believed return was always possible, but it hardly had the importance that something called "a second coming" would seem to imply.

15 *Fragments* (New York: Quarterly Book Department, three volumes 1916; 1920; 1925)

16 See New York State Supreme Court Appellate Division—First Department in the Matter of the Last Will and Testament of Ernest Temple Hargrove, May 1941.

17 *Herald Statesman* (Yonkers), June 2, 1958.

18 See *The Theosophical Quarterly* 34, no. 4 (October 1938), unpaginated but after p. 352.

19 See n. 17.

20 By contrast, the Center for Study of World Religion at Harvard University, though modernist at root, made references to the architecture of East and West through Sert's Mediterranean connection. It was, wrote its first director, "a setting which should make both East and West feel very much at home." Quoted in "The Building," in John B. Carman and Kathryn Dodgson, *Community and Colloquy: The Center for the Study of World Religion 1958–2003* (Cambridge: Center for the Study of World Religions, 2006), p. 92. Mrs. Griscom had no direct input on the design for Harvard. Based on the house at Chapel Farm, Mrs. Griscom's taste seems to have been traditional. The architect of Chapel Farm is unknown though Griscom is explicit about her demanding character as a client. What she knew about Irving Kane Pond's headquarters for the Theosophical movement, the L.W. Rogers Building in Wheaton, Illinois (1927) is unknown. She makes no reference to the best known of the theosophical architects of the 1930s, Claude Bragdon (1866–1946).

21 *Chapel House: An Introduction,* p. 48.

22 Landscape and planting plans are located in the Facilities Department, Colgate University, dated April 24, 1959. The author of the plans is not recorded on the sheets. The only attribution is to Skidmore Owings & Merrill. The probable author is Joanna Diman about whom relatively little is known. She is noted as working at SOM from ca. 1950–1963. Robert McVaugh kindly sent me photographs of the plans and was generous with his insights into the building and its site.

23 Photographs of the model suggest a sculpture might have been envisaged to sit in front of the chapel. The only surviving photograph of the model does not show the sculpture in sufficient detail. See The *Colgate Maroon,* March 12, 1958.

24 The place of the cross in the Chapel is vexing. It can be justified ("because those that made Chapel House were Christians") or because the donor was a Christian and had a large cross on her property at Chapel Farm.

25 The masons solved the coursing problem only on the fourth attempt. Likewise, on the origins of the stone, see Morgan, "Memories," p. 258. Morgan may also have wished to echo Zen Buddhist stone-laying practices.

26 Owings, *The Spaces in Between*, pp. 73–74.

27 Severinghaus was related by marriage to the Luce family, a fact that may explain the generous coverage SOM received in *Fortune*, *Architectural Forum*, and *Time* magazines.

28 Severinghaus was responsible for designs for the Celotex Corporation as part of SOM's work on prefabricated housing. See Hyun-Tae Jung, "Technologically Modern: The Prefabricated House and the War Time Experience of Skidmore, Owings Merrill" in *Sanctioning Modernism: Architecture and the Making of Postwar Identities,* ed. Vladimir Kulic, Timothy Parker, Monica Penick (Austin: University of Texas Press, 2014), pp. 186–218. Some at SOM have questioned Severinghaus' authorship—he was so rarely a designer. I raised this question with SOM's long-term lawyer, Philip Purcell, and former head of the New York office, John Winkler. Both agreed if Severinghaus said he had done something, he had done it.

29 A comparable figure in the Chicago office was William Hartmann (1916–2003) who described Severinghaus as "a tower of strength." *Oral History of William Hartmann,* interviewed by Betty Blum, Chicago: Art Institute of Chicago, rev. ed. 2003, p. 166.

30 See, for example, the Thompson House (1947), the Robinson House (1948), the Breuer House (1948), the Clark House (1949) and many others.

31 Niebuhr, "Religious Building: Tradition and Today's Ethos," *Architectural Record* 144, no. 6 (December 1953), pp. 117–18.

32 Robert Allen Nauman, *On the Wings of Modernism: The United Air Force Academy* (Urbana and Chicago: University of Illinois Press, 2004), chapter 5.

33 Quotations from Richard Kieckhefer, *Theology in Stone: Church Architecture from Byzantium to Berkeley* (Oxford: Oxford University Press, 2004), p. 124.

34 Kieckhefer, *Theology in Stone,* p. 125–26.

35 Henry Bedinger Mitchell, *Meditation* (New York: Quarterly Book Department, undated but either 1906 or 1907). German and Latvian translations appeared thereafter. See Karl Baier, *Meditation und Moderne: Zur Genese Eines Kernbereichs Moderner Spiritualität in der Wechselwirkung Zwischen Westeuropa, Nordamerika und Asien* (Würzburg: Konigshausen & Neumann, 2009), vol. 1, p. 397.

36 See material in the Columbia University Archives, Series I: Central Files 1890, Box 662, Folder 12. The quotation is from a letter to the president of Columbia University, Nicholas Murray Butler dated June 10, 1909. Thanks to Lindsay Cook for undertaking research in the Columbia University archives.

37 Iris Murdoch, *The Sovereignty of Good* (London: Ark Paperbacks, 1985), p. 95.

38 Cavé, *Fragments,* vol. 1, p. 18.

39 *The Colgate Maroon,* May 20, 1959.

40 A dormitory by McKim Mead & White (1954) was the first modernist building on campus. It was followed by the University Library (1959) by O'Connor and Kilham and the Reid Athletic Center (1959) by Oscar F. Wiggins.

41 In a lecture at Bryn Mawr College Morgan noted that books, music, and art were the three essential mediums "to transmit religious insight." (Lecture notes dated November 21, 1961).

National Commercial Bank, Jeddah, 1983

"I Think I Said What They Probably Said": Rhetorical Ethos in the Work and Words of Gordon Bunshaft

Oren Abeles

Blum: Had you been misquoted?

Bunshaft: No, I think I said what they probably said [I said].

Blum: I understand that [the National Commercial Bank building] has been termed "zoned."

Bunshaft: That's words.

From transcript of Oral History Interview with Gordon Bunshaft by Betty J. Blum, April 4–7, 1989

First Paradox: Rhetorical Ethos and the Body

The word *ethos*, when we hear it today, prompts an association *about* associations: we understand it to connote something about all that's commonly and customarily understood and valued by an associated community—especially about how things are, or should be, done. The sound of the word approaches the syllables in *ethics*: virtue, the way to be good, or the essential precept of a design or device—sometimes opposed to *aesthetics*, which are merely a matter of style, of habit, of taste, although some have suggested that virtue can be expressed through style. But the deep history of the word *ethos* as it has come down to us from the Greeks and their interpreters, reveals something quite different. Ethos is not primarily a way of being—especially not a silent and self-evident demonstration of ethics. Ethos is a way of talking.

The Greek thinkers of the fourth century BC, as we understand them through Aristotle's *On Rhetoric*, were interested in the art of persuasion. They understood that logic alone—*logos* they called it—was generally not enough. Any logos had to eventually come to rest upon a fundamental premise that was itself not provable by that train of deductions. A persuasive argument, therefore, had to also offer something in addition to logos, something that transcended but substantiated the logical premises themselves. One additional tactic was pathos, an emotional appeal, by which a speaker stirred the audience's emotions and, thereby, their receptivity to his argument's premises. Of course, it was this reliance upon emotion, and the manipulation of it, which for millennia made rhetoric the enemy of many philosophers. And in the popular imagination, it was rhetoric's use of emotional appeals that made it so fundamentally untrustworthy and ultimately undermined whatever logic it communicated.

Usually this is where discussions about rhetoric end. Yet *On Rhetoric* allowed that something more than logos and pathos was called for. If one could trust that the rhetorician's argument was founded on good lived experience then there was nothing wrong in being swayed by either the speaker's premises or his clever use of emotion. If one could respect the speaker's ethos, his life itself—as understood through his circumstances and spirit, his position and disposition—then this could simultaneously legitimize both his pathos and logos. Today the Latin fragment *ad hominem*—to the man—has the association of a specious argument, resorting itself to addressing the speaker, not the spoken position, yet the Greek ethos is perhaps the converse in effect. To a degree, it was ethos, the quality of the speaker's life, which saved rhetoric from falling into a closed loop between the incompatible yet mutually dependent benefits of logic and emotion. Of interest to architects is that in the history of the word's usage, as Aristotle might have used it and learned it in Homer, its early applications were to a physical or spatial location: an "accustomed place," as we might think of a habitat for a species, or specifically in the *Iliad*, a stabled horse.

But ethos does more than just make logos and pathos more plausibly persuasive. It also points to a fascinating dimension within the philosophy of communication that we might call the dimension of the "body." The thing that is interesting about the body of the persuader is that it is not supposed to matter in persuasion, and yet it so clearly does. We want to imagine that it is only the disembodied argument that sways us to one side or the other, that the speaker himself is immaterial to our assent. Yet the rhetorical ethos shows us that this embodied origin that is often essential to an argument's persuasiveness and certainly its creativity. Therein lies the first paradox of rhetoric and also one of its greatest philosophical contributions. Rhetoric argues that even the premises of logic, which are supposed to be independent of whoever happens to be the speaker of those premises, not only profit from their origin in a body but can logically come from nowhere else. That is particularly the case when the logic voiced by the speaker pushes beyond the bounds of established logic. The genuinely new thought can only emerge from the ethos of a body. Ideas, which are supposed to be fundamentally incorporeal, always find their invention and their credibility in the ethos that composes them. Rhetoric's first argument with philosophy was that bodies are fundamentally creative in this way and that ethos and logos are inseparable.

This paradoxical dependence of a disembodied argument on an embodied speaker—this complication between what we might consider objective and subjective, universal and personal—has a striking parallel in the discourse of modernity in design. On the one hand, rhetoric around modernism in design historically asserted the possibility of a new formal, technical, and material *practice* that transcends the persona of any single practitioner. One the other hand, from the 1920s to the 1960s, modernism had been advanced by and associated with singular larger-than-life figures and would-be heroic master builders.

Second Paradox: Bunshaft's *Ethos* of Creativity

The modern persona of the architect as a public figure is, rhetorically speaking, generally one of either noise or silence. On the side of noise there are the personas of a Frank Lloyd Wight or a Le Corbusier—given to marathon lecturing, publishing, and talking. On the side of silence are differently larger-than-life figures like Mies van der Rohe or Louis Kahn, whose public utterances were famously and deliberately gnomic, and framed by significant silences. Among this latter group, in a complicated way, is the figure of Gordon Bunshaft, the longtime designer for SOM during its mid-twentieth-century heyday.

Bunshaft's public persona was paradoxical from its beginning: a singular and influential individual situated in the American architecture firm that in scale and organization most closely resembled the private corporations that exemplified the cultural ethos of mid-twentieth-century America, and that constituted its most significant clientele. For each term used to describe Gordon Bunshaft's own ethos as a designer, it seems that one could just as easily give its opposite and have an equally reasonable description: unerringly rational but simultaneously inspired and artistic; he was methodical but messy; confrontational but quiet; dictatorial but collaborative. Some of the ambiguity around Bunshaft is simply the result of his having provided an unusually restricted account of his work, in interviews or writings, speech or text. Left having to guess, we often end up relying on the polysemous vagaries of hearsay and anecdote.

Bunshaft, as a recorded and quoted and cited articulation—Bunshaft as rhetoric—exists primarily in only two well-known texts: briefly but famously in the May 1959 *Newsweek* magazine profile, "Designers for a Busy World," and, thirty years later, with much greater length and complexity, in the extended oral history interview he gave to historian Betty J. Blum over the course of four days in April of 1989. The public and private trauma of the first experience, the anecdote goes, explains the public silence that preceded the second. A consideration of both documents, and of how Bunshaft addresses the former in the latter, reveals a very real sense in which he seems to have consciously cultivated the paradoxes that surrounded him.

When *Newsweek* attempted an article that would try, as its headnote promised, to get, "behind the façade of one of these firms to follow the process which leads to a new building," their reporter appears to have had his investigative efforts stymied at every turn by Bunshaft's refusal to pin down his methods. The generally accepted hearsay is that Bunshaft's dissentious claim, quoted in the article, that, "I'm in charge of design," and that every design committee needed such a "dictator," upset the firm's other partners, who had hoped the article would highlight SOM's collaborative methods. Yet the genuinely strange thing is that *Newsweek* piece begins precisely with statements by Bunshaft directly opposed to the ones that got him into hot water. He began by telling Newsweek that, "We deliberately try to have a sloppy organization, because if we got terribly efficient, I'm afraid our architecture might dry up. We have no set chain of command, no set way of operating. Our methods would make a management expert tear his hair, but the important thing is they work." Yet he followed up that account of an unstructured, limitlessly flexible organization with a second description that seems to run directly against it. Asked by Newsweek's reporter to tell him about SOM's already well-documented ethos of, "design by conference," (compared by the article for its, "enormous and assiduous activity and production [to] "something like the General Motors of the architectural world") Bunshaft shot back, "There's no such thing as design by committee. There always has to be one dominant force, someone who comes up with the original design." The reporter, who by this point must have felt that something was getting away from him, appears to have done the honest thing and put the contradictions Bunshaft had handed him front and center. His lead sentence reads, "Obviously, Gordon Bunshaft has a fine flair for paradox."

Here the rhetorical categories of logos and pathos illuminate the exchange. Bunshaft's fine flair—his tone and affect, his tendency and maybe his ethos—situate him in another paradox between logos and pathos. One can almost hear and project, reading his words, their emotional content: the gruffness, the crankiness, the cantankerousness that is the pathos, perhaps primarily of anger, in Bunshaft's attitude, as he sharply corrects the reporter's assumptions; and yet one can also hear, tacitly and explicitly, a logos in which Bunshaft speaks as if he is the last reasonable man in the room: surely, he seems to say, you can understand the basics of how the world works. When he most vividly enacts personality and the emotional, he is most explicitly articulating a defense of logic and the rational. Is this paradox only resolvable in the third rhetorical category of ethos?

Bunshaft enacts further evasions and equivocations when, in her extended oral history interview, Blum asked him to revisit his comments in the *Newsweek* piece. Even thirty years later, Bunshaft inserted ambiguity into any account of the role he played in the designs produced by SOM (even the canonical projects like Lever House and Manufacturers Hanover Trust, in which he is understood to be lead designer). Blum introduces the subject by observing, "With Lever House, Manufacturers Hanover Trust, Connecticut General, and Chase, the critics all knew your work. Whether SOM wanted anonymous coverage or not, the critics knew your work. How did you feel about them identifying you when the policy of the firm was supposed to be no identification?" Bunshaft defends against pathos—an enquiry into his feelings—with a recourse to logos: a questioning of the framing of the question, "Well, you know, when you say 'policy,' it sounds like a law. It was the effort of the firm. I think I'd like to cover this now."

And yet just as Bunshaft says he'd like to cover it (the effort of the firm and the *Newsweek* incident) now, he reverses the framing logic and asserts and emphasizes the press' desire to locate a single master builder author: "The press would not accept it. Take Lever House. Bill Brown played a great, important part of it. But they would not mention him. They only wanted what I used to call "the decorator," the designer. They wouldn't accept anything else. It was a difficult battle. In my case, it was these three other partners. I didn't want to hurt their feelings, and I couldn't avoid what was going on."

But after that reversing deflection, Bunshaft appears to reverse himself again—in feeling if not logic, in pathos if not logos, appearing to concede that the difficult battle was one that, perhaps, he was happy to lose. "I rather liked it. I'm not trying to say I'm a saint. But there was nothing I could do about it. It caused some real trouble.

There was a big article in Newsweek, I think, about the firm. They came to see me, and I said some things ...

But after that feint toward accountability—authorship of both design and his participation in his self-presentation in the media—Bunshaft dissociates himself from the article as its subject, saying he never read it and he was far away: a disposition towards displacement that is its own kind of ethos: "... and right after that I went to Europe. I didn't see the article."

At that moment, in a kind of irony, Blum's cassette runs out of tape and the conversation is paused, and maybe a spell broken. Bunshaft resumes his account—presenting his original statement to the reporter less as something he said, than as a kind of a quote of a quote of a quote that he heard in a of game of telephone: an implication in a telegram of a mood based on an impression based on a quotation:

> I got a telegram from Walt Severinghaus saying that the firm's partners were terribly upset about an article in Newsweek. They were so concerned they wanted to see me as soon as I got home. That was an ominous sort of telegram. I don't know whether I'd seen the article or whether they sent me a copy, but the essence of it was I sort of casually said, "Well, I do the design, and the rest of them do all the work, all the other partners carry it out." You know, like I'm the prima donna and they're slaves. Not quite like that, but it was bad. Owings earlier had once seriously tried to fire me, and Skid wouldn't let him. But this time, the partners of my own group— we were closely knit—asked me to leave when I got home over this remark.

Blum, an apparently sympathetic interviewer, asks if the Newsweek reporter misquoted him; Bunshaft doesn't take the bait: "No, I think I said what they probably said. I wouldn't say misquoted. I was sort of casual, and I sort of said something like, 'Well, I do the design and the rest of them carry it out.' I don't know."

Here, Bunshaft's avowal and disavowal is especially complex: he quotes himself, mediated by a "sort of," and in his concluding passage continues a remarkable trajectory in which he asserts one thing and then its opposite:

> It was stupid. I wasn't misquoted. This was the final blow of this publicity business with the partners. They knew that the magazines wouldn't mention them, but, nevertheless, they didn't like it. Now, it's just the opposite. So, that's been a problem. They got reconciled to it. That's the only stupid one I did. The reputation now is that I've been trying to explain that I'm part of a team, and I really believe that. I think I've told you before I don't believe any man who sits alone can create architecture. It's a team effort. There just happens to be some man that has to make a decision on things, that's all.

Third Paradox: Single Surface, Multiple Space

Blum immediately shifts the conversation to the nature of architectural creativity, saying there has to be, "a man with the creative idea." Bunshaft, in what we can only call another paradox, both entirely agrees and then partially disagrees with Blum's assertion:

> Oh, creative nothing. They have the idea that I tried to explain to you that a creative idea comes out of some brilliant, imaginary mind. It doesn't. It comes out of the sweat that I took you through in Connecticut General. That's how it comes out. You add something to it, which is your architectural training and a certain amount of imagination or a concept. The only building that I think has a major concept that's unique and my own is the National Commercial Bank in Jeddah. And that is rationalized, not just whimsy, those great big holes. That's why I think that's my best building. It is a totally new approach to solving an office building in an extremely hot and dry climate.

Architecture Bunshaft says, is *never* the product of a single imaginative body, but *sometimes* it also is. And Bunshaft was not done being paradoxical: a few hours further into the interview, he suggested that critical elements of the National Commercial Bank's (NCB's) design—its system of three large shifted apertures both shading and revealing the glass-lined interior of a three-sided concrete monolith—emerged from work he did with another senior designer, and even that it was the other designer who may have initially identified that feature.

510 Fifth Avenue, New York (Manufacturer's Trust), 1954

Interviewing Bunshaft, with his simultaneous avowals and disavowals, Blum must have started to feel like the hapless *Newsweek* reporter did three decades before—except that maybe by 1989 Bunshaft was genuinely trying to disclose the source of architectural creativity and genuinely struggling to identify the ethos, the body from which it emerges.

If Bunshaft was opaque and oblique about the NCB's creative origin—and to that extent about its ethos as embodied or enacted by its individual creators—he was transparent and direct about the logos that its design embodied, and a rhetorical analysis can be loosely but speculatively applied to the architectural design itself within Bunshaft's body of work. The building was a logical solution, in his argument, to the problem of creating an office building in a place so luminous, so hot, and so dry that it was otherwise unlivable. If Lever House was about appearing to introduce a lightness and transparency among the closed masonry façades and occluded sight lines of Park Avenue, while still maintaining its own spatial integrity and enclosure, then NCB was the reverse: establishing a notional interior occluded from but spatially continuous with the contextual exterior, an "open-air" inside. In Saudi Arabia, all was light and heat, all was sightlines, and all was skyline. Yet the surface by which Bunshaft solves this problem is the same—just, as it were, folded in upon itself: the NCB's glass curtain, lining an interior courtyard, establishes an exterior that also registers as a quasi-interior, the boundary between a covered plaza and the office floors adjoining. The floors could still regard the world—in fact, the equilateral fold of glass suggested a real openness, like an eye looking out, but in a way that simultaneously sheltered that aperture from the light and heat. The layering of opaque and transparent at NCB can be situated in a history of Bunshaft's work at the Beinecke Library building at Yale (glass-like masonry over a masonry-like glass vault), and the Manufacturers Trust Company building (glass over a masonry-wrapped vault). Thus, perhaps a single surface addresses multiple spaces. I think one can successfully begin to think about the ethos of Bunshaft's architecture through that trope. Both library and bank deploy an ethos of material transparency that expresses a logos of open spatial circulation.

Fourth Paradox: Creative Reason

In his interview with Betty J. Blum, one finds Bunshaft extolling the "rationality" of his architecture in a way that Aristotle would recognize as an appeal to virtue. This kind of commitment to "rationalism" is very much aligned with a broader commitment to an idea of modernism, understood as a movement that, extending well beyond any idea of architectural style, believed firmly in the ability of an enlightened humanity to surmount the social, political and technical challenges it faced. Such a modernism represented an unwavering commitment to the potential of human progress—the ability of rational humans to ever-better govern themselves and the world around them. Surely Bunshaft's designs participate in that tradition. Yet for all Bunshaft's belief in the power of rational progress, we have seen that he struggled to identify the source of such rationality. The more the question was put to him, the more paradoxical his answers became.

Bunshaft's paradoxicality, I think, may be similar to a broader hesitancy that scholars and critics in a variety of disciplines (including my own field of rhetoric) have been increasingly feeling, particularly as it becomes clear that the progressive ethos of modernism seems to complicate its rationalist logos. This is not to say that modernist rationality has not brought about vital social goods—it certainly has. But each of these achievements (be it the internal combustion engine, the nation state, the internet, high finance, etc.) seems to have a rationality all its own, in turn having effects upon us which we simply do not expect, some of which are none too salutary. (This may parallel, or compound, a generational tension in modernism in design between the ecstatically emotional affect of prewar practitioners and popularizers, and the performatively rational affect of their postwar successors, especially those situated in large-scale collaborative or corporate settings such as SOM itself—even as both generations generally subscribed to a shared logos of utility, rationality, and instrumentality.) It may be significant, to those concerned with architecture's intramural and incidental encounters with histories of modernism and its notional successors, that Bunshaft's interview with Blum took place seven months after the close of the mid-1988 *Deconstructivist*

Architecture exhibit at New York's Museum of Modern Art, and seven months before the fall of the Berlin Wall in late 1989.

Our response to such tension, however, need not be an anti-modernist, anti-technological conservative regression, but rather a new respect for and engagement with the way things themselves—buildings included—exert creative logics alongside our own. Such a perspective is not at all post-modern, inasmuch as it stipulates the fact of modernity and the virtue of rationality. It simply does not limit the world's rational behavior to human creations alone. For that reason, it may be better thought of as non-anthropocentricism or, stated more affirmatively, post-humanism. Ancient rhetoricians suggested long ago that every logos emerges with an ethos—that every logic starts with a body. What we are learning now is that humanity is not the only body capable of such ethos.

Things have it, too, and by virtue of that they generate their own arguments, their own persuasions, their own logics and rationalities. In exploring surface, I think Bunshaft caught a glimpse of that non-human ethos, a creative body that likely appeared as a dim spark compared to all the stunningly brilliant human creations of high modernism, but which he still noticed nonetheless and had the curiosity to work with. A surface has ethos. Folded, and a new space emerges. Folded into another surface—another logos arises. Enfolded again and a different logic materializes.

Louis S. Kahn's First Unitarian Church, Rochester, New York, 1962

On Modern Memory: A Case Study in Brick

Marco Roth

"There is a certain shade of red brick—a dark, almost melodious red, sombre and riddled with blue—that is my childhood in St. Louis. Not the real childhood, but the false one that extends from the dawning of consciousness until the day that one leaves home for college. That one shade of red brick and green foliage is St. Louis in the summer (the winter is just a gray sky and a crowded school bus and the wet footprints on the brown linoleum floor at school), and that brick and a pale sky is spring. It's also loneliness and the queer, self-pitying wonder that children whose families are having catastrophes feel."

—Harold Brodkey, "State of Grace," from First Love and Other Sorrows, 1987

"For the love of God, Montresor!"

—Edgar Allen Poe, The Cask of Amontillado, 1846

"When you ask brick what it wants, it says 'I'd like an arch.'"

—Louis Kahn, in lectures, 1971–1973

A long time ago, now, my senior year of high school, I opened Harold Brodkey's short story collection *First Love and Other Sorrows* and was captivated by that first sentence, "There is a certain shade of red brick—a dark, almost melodious red, sombre and riddled with blue—that is my childhood in St. Louis." I had almost no acquaintance with bricks, nor of the gateway city to the American West; a child, instead, of whitish, granite-clad apartment buildings on Manhattan's broad avenues, its brownstone side-streets and concrete playgrounds. But this sentence lodged, evocative in its scope and monitory in its reductiveness. I also would never have dared write anything with so simple and so sweeping a copula: a whole phase of life identified with a color and a building material! It's not meant as a metaphor but an actual state of being. Brodkey gave voice to something I'd intuited but didn't have words for: the feeling that buildings both encode and reflect experience. I an echo of the familiar classical rhetorical device of the memory palace, architects, at work, draw on memory, on tours both foreign and domestic, to translate contingent materials into the form of a real place in the real world. And, once that real place is built, whoever subsequently passes through it will, in turn, use some evocative sensation of it as a sign in their search, conscious or not, for their former or definitive selves, for their spirit, their ethos—just as Brodkey's brick was inlaid with something as quicksilver as the, "wonder that children whose families are having catastrophes feel."

That paragraph from "State of Grace" traveled with me over time, and I found it almost suspiciously easy to recall—the way you might wake up humming a few bars of music—after I'd moved to the place where, often to my astonishment, I've spent the greatest share of my adult life. Philadelphia, almost from its colonial beginnings on the swampy flats sixty miles from the estuary where the Delaware River meets the Atlantic, has been very much a red brick city. What started as a sensible practice—the easy availability of clay, the desire to prevent conflagrations like the Great Fire that swept through wooden London a decade before Philadelphia's foundation—has, over the centuries, collected itself into an ethos and an identity, hardened now by law and custom. It's not only warehouses and factories that were brick-built. The crowded, squat three-story houses for laborers and craftspeople were stacked in red grids. In mews and alleyways, still extant, are the brick slave quarters and carriage houses, service buildings retailed now as expensive "historic" properties. Even the mansions of Philadelphia's old Quaker elite and industrialists rose throughout the nineteenth century in layer after reddish layer, along tree-lined, narrow thoroughfares.

Starting in 1955, a series of historic preservation laws enjoined new construction in most of Philadelphia's older neighborhoods between the Delaware and Schuykill rivers to remain as close as possible to the color and the pattern of original stacked red rectangles, when they can't use bricks themselves. These statutes are responsible for some of Philadelphia's signature share of brick modernism—a local style embodying an extreme tension between the willfully forward-looking building forms of mid-twentieth-century modernism and the everyday nineteenth-century historicity recorded by bricks. My eye was drawn first to Saarinen's University of Pennsylvania dormitory, the Finnish architect's combined salute to the colonial college hall along with a nod to his compatriot Alvar Aalto's Baker House at MIT. Without the benefit of the dappled light and contours offered the latter by the curving stretch of the Charles River, and choked by nearby later constructions, Saarinen's building sinks into its position in the heavily-trafficked street grid. It's a reminder that a preservationist or conservationist ethos cannot be maintained by materials alone. The mood around a building is made up of more than its materials.

Walking the alleyways east of old Washington Square, downtown, I stumbled once into a sudden opening, a square tucked between streets fronted by brick Georgians with plaques advertising their former inhabitants from the heroic early days of the American Republic. The square contains a mid-century development of tiny split-level, cuboid houses, fashioned out of brownish bricks—of course—around a brick-laid courtyard eerily lit by globular street lamps. These were I. M. Pei's 1962 Washington Square East Townhouses, a low-rise complex of some forty residences in the shadow of Pei's adjacent Society Hill Towers, a quasi-contextual gesture at the edge of a typical tabula rasa mid-century urban renewal project. Their effect is almost charmingly retro-futurist, a utopian twentieth-century imagined in the idiom of the nineteenth-century novel—but a sinister touch appears in the form of half-story, high walls of the same material, used to mark off the tiny front gardens of each house from the courtyard while also partially obscuring each house's large picture windows and cutting off light to the first floor. These walls make an enclosure within an enclosure, a paean to privacy or paranoia. These homes belong to the era of Philadelphia's depopulation, of white flight, of fear of crime and of integrated neighborhoods. In their material deference to the past and to the code, they only signal how far removed they are from the dreams of liberty and self-evident equality that were given form in meeting houses, made of the same stuff, only several meters away.

Intended to preserve the character of these old neighborhoods, Philadelphia's aesthetic ordinances also, accidentally, help the city to forget. The ubiquity of brickishness may now even be more a matter of settled habit or the market, than of formal regulation. Almost all new residential construction in the old neighborhoods are brick or brick-colored. The ready-made, Tyvek-wrapped, suburban-style townhouses, complete with garage, await their uniform red coat like recruits to the British army. I suppose this makes the owners feel like they're not living in New Jersey. When the zoning board allowed a 375-foot residential tower to be built on Broad Street, mere blocks from City Hall, the building's steel frame arose clad in pinkish and maroon panels of faux-brick, creating an effect the local newspaper's critic likened to "a giant pepto-bismol bottle." The paneling could not have been done in deference to any logic of historic preservation, but seems a compensation paid to residual modesty and tradition, an ambiguous sign of both shame and brazenness. Passing daily under its shadow, I've often thought that if someone were to write a history of ordinary bad taste—not the kitsch, the glam, the garish, but merely the banal, unimaginative, and thoroughly compromised—this building would be worthy of a chapter.

And I've often thought, in an excess of self-pity—one of those emotions Brodkey associates with his bricked-in childhood—about whether I'd ever have had such an idea for a book if I didn't live in such a city. How a populace tends a legacy becomes part of the character of a place. The cumulative effect of years among all this brick, regardless of the varying quality of the buildings—or perhaps because the varying quality generates a perversely heightened awareness of their common elements—is one of monotony or monochromy, shaded by regret. It's as if I found myself constrained to communicate in a language with a 200 word vocabulary. I've been told that this is a hyper-sensitive reaction. Wouldn't I feel this way about other cities where a different material dominates? Among the whitewashed Mediterranean stone of Ibiza, the ochre clays of Marrakech, for instance, or Tuscan hill towns? While custom can stale any experience, I imagine my anomie would have a different palate and take other turns among those maze-like, multi-tiered ensembles.

Partly, it's a question of how the materials interact with their larger environment. Where the stones of Tuscany and clay of Marrakech seem, to willing eyes, to be imitating the natural features around them, or at least fitting in with them, industrial red bricks constitute, in many ways, a quintessentially anthropocene and anthropocentric material. Individually and in assembly they're more an insistent demonstration of human endeavor than an imitation of an existing natural form, "petrifying all human imagination into rock and sand," as William Blake describes the scientific, industrialist spirit of the late eighteenth century. In effect, they tend toward the erasure of specific natural features into a uniform space, almost anti-historical. And yet bricks persist in having a history and in being remembered, even as they seem to celebrate the erasure of a time before their use. It's notable that when bricks—industrially irresistible for economy and uniformity, despite their pre-modern historicity—were significantly incorporated into large-scale modernist architecture of the mid-twentieth century, as in Gordon Bunshaft's epochal 1951 Manhattan House apartment block on East 66th Street and in the many similar buildings that followed, they were made white. A pale pigmented glaze left them as exsanguinated and bone-white, in architectural history, as the plaster or stucco walls of the fantastical fairgrounds and utopian model neighborhoods and show houses of the 1890s or 1920s.

One history preserved in these bricks is, paradoxically, a history that would prefer us to forget about history. Like its brickish trading and manufacturing homologues in the Old World, Manchester and Liverpool, Philadelphia was molded by Protestant ethics and fired by the early industrial revolution. A desire for equality, a distrust of vanity and ornament, a spirit of labor to be stored up in heaven, laid one block at a time, mingled with the wish to turn a profit without showing-up one's neighbor, these founding virtues, given a slight twist of ordinary human failings, could, in the realm of ordinary action and appearance, express themselves as uniformity, blockishness, cheapness, lack of imagination, and false modesty. The utilitarian brick could, in this way, become a kind of false front, an obstacle to the very enlightened construction it was meant to embody. This is what Brodkey is getting at when he associates the reddish shade of St. Louis with "the false childhood," a period of pretense, routine, and conformity without the self-awareness to understand who he was, or why things were expected of him.

An even darker vision of some psychological blockage inherent in the material can be seen in a couple of tales of seemingly motiveless malignancy by a writer who spent six years renting a plumber's North Philadelphia brick house (it still stands on 7th Street, just north of the avenue misleadingly-named "Spring Garden"). In Edgar Allen Poe's "The Black Cat" and "The Cask of Amontillado," descriptions of *bête-noires* being walled-up behind freshly laid masonry are crucial to the scenery of horror. In both cases, the murders are motivated by the narrator's wounded vanity. The offending elements must be erased. Bricklaying is described in pedantic do-it-yourself detail, with a touch of manic compulsion, "Having procured mortar, sand, and hair, with every possible precaution, I prepared a plaster which could not be distinguished from the old," confesses the man who killed his wife and accidentally buries the titular cat alive, along with her; "I forced the last stone into its position; I plastered it up. Against the new masonry I re-erected the old rampart of bones," says Montresor, after ignoring his rival Fortunato's cry for mercy. Preservation or restoration is here represented as an erasure of a crime, or as part of the crime itself. The new wall, with a body behind it, looks just like the old wall! The wall itself remains as an inscrutable emblem of an orderliness that's become terrifying only because we've been allowed to know what's behind it. For Poe, it's not that the bricks perfectly keep the secret of evil, but that they ultimately fail to do so, since no crime is too perfect to withstand the perpetrator's need to brag and confess, to come to the moment when he cries aloud, "I had walled the monster up within the tomb!"

Poe, even in 1846, grasped that absence of ornament, and thus the appearance of business-as-usual, may constitute crimes or complicity in them. (How much these crimes weigh on a city dweller's conscience depends on how much daily imagination he or she can bear.) Reading Poe architecturally, one wonders whether Montresor's fiendish design was conceived in response to the opportunities presented by construction in masonry, as much as any specific redress to Fortunato's perceived offenses: by supplying a neat retroactive purpose for a niche that was the inadvertent consequence of configuring masonry into vaulted and arched passages: "a still interior recess," in Poe's words, "in depth about four feet, in width three, in height six or seven. It seemed to have been constructed for no especial use within itself, but formed merely the interval between two of the colossal supports of the roof of the catacombs." Montresor's new wall, coplanar with the two supports, corrects this anomalous old form and conceals its opportunistic new function.

These figures of masonry wall, vault, and arch became, it so happens, the central characters in mid-century modernism's most famous allegory of materiality and memory—specifically of personal memory as a signal of sensibility, projected onto the imaginary consciousness of a building material itself, and translated into a formal desire. This allegory is the well-known passage from lectures given by Louis Kahn in various versions, primarily in the years 1971 to 1973, about the putative desire of a brick to be part of an arch—as here, transcribed from a 1971 University of Pennsylvania master class: "If you think of Brick, you say to Brick, 'What do you want, Brick?' And Brick says to you, 'I like an Arch.' And if you say to Brick, 'Look, arches are expensive, and I can use a concrete lintel over you. What do you think of that, Brick?' Brick says, 'I like an Arch.' And it's important, you see, that you honor the material that you use. [...] You can only do it if you honor the brick and glorify the brick instead of shortchanging it."

However charming Kahn sounds, I also read this injunction as an implicit critique of what, after all, were the buildings of Kahn's own North Philadelphia childhood—brick building after brick building, reaching a kind of apotheosis in what's generally attributed as Kahn's own first substantial work, 1938's Ahavath Israel Synagogue in the Oak Lane neighborhood of North Philadelphia, whose front façade was an almost unrelieved pure rectangle of dark red brick. Staged within the putatively uplifting dialogue with this building material, Kahn asserts a protest, voiced by the brick itself, against blockish accretion and for vaulting ambition. But nothing is, in fact, tectonically self-evident about bricks wanting arches: to judge by most of Philadelphia, it seems they really want walls, want to be stacked in rows and made to resemble larger versions of themselves: vast walls constituting their own brackish shapes at larger scales. For bricks to do otherwise requires a leap of intention—or in Kahn's case, of recollection—in which the inventive configuration of the arch and keystone allows blocks of clay or stone (heavy but strong under pressure) to be held in compression across a distance far greater than the dimensions of any one block. For Kahn, the recollection would have been of the Roman and Medieval ruins that he admired on his European Grand Tour in 1928, or of vernacular typologies as far afield as the brickworks of Kathmandu, which he visited in the early 1970s.

Among the mid-century modernist masters, Kahn is credited for the leap into the past: for (like Pei after him) remembering, tolerating, and even celebrating the arch that for many of his contemporaries was the ultimate sign of hidebound classicism; for envisioning massive works in concrete and brick that, in mood but not manner, were the equal of classical ruins. He's attributed with describing those projects as "Ruins in Reverse"; some of the reversal was in the behavior of materials themselves, making them the opposite of what they were, using a Roman arch to make Philadelphia brick as fleet and soaring as Chicago steel. The would-be reversal of ruination with its aesthetic equal—a consequence of a Brodkey-esque wonder at catastrophe—was naturally part of the postwar mid-century architectural project. Looking now at those mid-century buildings, we can see how much they desire to break themselves free and yet also to belong—like exiles in a city struggling to maintain a sense of their foreignness, among the welcoming, encircling walls.

Typical eighteenth-century brick rowhouses in Philadelphia

The north wall of Le Corbusier's chapel at Sainte-Marie La Tourette

At La Tourette

Thomas De Monchaux

> Let there be a separate kitchen for […] visitors, that the brethren may not be disturbed when visitors, who are never lacking in a monastery, arrive at irregular hours.
>
> —The Order of St. Benedict, c. 529 C.E.

> Secretly the casual visitor is a little dismayed.
>
> —Colin Rowe, critique of La Tourette, Architectural Review, 1961

The 9th of November at Pierre Chareau's 1928 Maison de Verre at 31 Rue St-Guillaume in Paris; the 8th of November at Royaumont Abbey, a thirteenth-century former Cistercian compound near Asnières-sur-Oise in Val-d'Oise, some fifteen miles north of Paris; the 12th of November at the Four Seasons restaurant in Mies Van Der Rohe's and Philip Johnson's 1958 Seagram Building in midtown Manhattan; the 16th and 17th of April at Charles Rennie Macintosh's 1909 Glasgow School of Art building in Scotland; the 11th and 12th of October at Aalvar Aalto's 1959 Maison Louis Carre in Bazoches-sur-Guyonnes, some fifteen miles southwest from Paris; the 27th of June—Baltic midsummer—at Aalto's own studio in Helsinki, Finland; the 7th of July at Frank Gehry's 1998 DZ Bank building on Pariser Platz in Berlin; the 10th of June at Skidmore Owings and Merrill's offices in Chicago; the 18th of March at their offices in New York.

And, more recently, two chilly gray days in April at Sainte Marie de La Tourette, the Dominican priory at Éveux, just outside of Lyon, France, whose 1960 building was famously the design work of Le Corbusier. Those are—in reverse chronological order until the most recent meeting at La Tourette—the first ten meeting times and places of the SOM Jury. The pattern in that data is generally French, generally modern, and—factoring in the significant precedent of a weeklong session in September of 1962 at Royaumont Abbey by the Team Ten architecture and urbanism group—generally leans toward the mid-twentieth-century. There's a potentially poignant tendency towards outliers and near-outsiders. Alvar Aalto's earthily regional picturesque disqualified him slightly from the most inflexible or polemical versions of the modernist canon; Chareau and Macintosh's careers—both defined and almost delimited by those two singular buildings, the maison and the school—were unhappy, featuring displacement and unfulfilled promise. Chareau was one of the World War II Paris-to-New York émigrés who didn't quite land on his feet; Macintosh spent what might have been his prime years as an architect as an involuntary watercolorist and gentleman traveler. History has yet to be written on Gehry, but it will no doubt tend to celebrate the early sunny California domestic at the expense of the long twilight of big late works, the Berlin bank among them. Imagine a village in time, made up only of these jury meeting places: one art school; one fancy restaurant; one bank; one atelier; two generic central business-district office conference rooms; two luxurious private houses; two ecclesiastical compounds. What kind of place would that be?

The second of those ecclesiastical compounds—appropriately as the site of an architectural jury—represents a monument in the history of architectural criticism as well as a monument in the history of architectural practice. "In the winter of 1961," wrote critic Anthony Vidler in the winter of 2012 (for the journal *Log*), "in his almost modern lodgings in […] Cambridge, England, I witnessed Colin Rowe writing his article on Le Corbusier's monastery of La Tourette, commissioned by the *Architectural Review*. Laboriously typing and retyping on his characteristic yellow paper, Rowe evinced considerable anguish, if not boredom, at having to, as he put it, 'look for so long at a single building.'" Vidler's essay situates his tutor's critical practice within a long and magisterial patrimony of architectural critique—organized both chronologically and anachronistically around complexities of relative attitudes toward the nominally Greek, Gothic, Renaissance, and Baroque;

around degrees of scholasticism and agnosticism in reference to the defining social and economic theories of their days; and between the Academy and the mere Press. (The names are among those you may remember from Art History 101 and Architectural History 102: Vasari begat Johann Wincklemann begat John Ruskin begat Geoffrey Scott begat Heinrich Wölfflin begat Rudolf Wittkower and Nikolaus Pevsner—those Germans whose respective displacements to the United Kingdom and the United States informed the contemporary and subsequent work of Sigfried Giedeon and Henry Russell Hitchcock, Reyner Banham and Kenneth Frampton.)

By the winter of Rowe's struggle with La Tourette, Vidler suggests, architectural criticism was visibly approaching a crisis from which, in the second decade of the twentieth century, a revisiting of La Tourette as perceived by Rowe may help it emerge. "Architectural criticism, where it has not fallen into the conventional realms of functionalism, formalism, or social realism, has been deeply divided between a mode derived from one or other of many structuralisms and post-structuralisms and a supportive role for an architectural tendency." Or, perhaps, to oversimplify: between being reduced to an arcane exercise in the scholasticism of signs and signifiers to which, as an uncannily unrepresentative art, it is especially subject; and being reduced to simple appreciation of a particular formal mode or reinforcement of a style canon as an exercise in curatorial or social power.

Rowe's essay, in Vidler's essay, emerges like Le Corbusier's building itself as somehow both seminal and terminal: a master class and catalog of motifs and techniques, but also, thanks to its virtuosity and close response to a particular circumstance, not easily repeated other than in its most basic tone and mood—however much one would like it to be otherwise. In Vidler's account, Rowe's long attention to a single building (visited by him over three December days in 1960) precluded his usual habit of lateral comparison and relative evaluation between multiple projects, and sent him equally into the particulars of visual and embodied experience and into an acutely site-specific theoretical mode—a way of looking and thinking to which architectural critique, after its later arguable reductions, might return.

Rowe's thinking was especially taken with the dilemma of the vast blank side wall of the compound's chapel, which is generally the first thing the visitor sees: "In 1916, at La Chaux-de-Fonds, Le Corbusier erected a house with a centrally disposed blank panel. Forty years later, in the monastery of La Tourette and at a heroic scale, he has repeated something very like this device. At La Chaux-de-Fonds the blank panel is the central figure of a façade. At La Tourette a largely blank wall composes the north side of the church. But in both cases, in the villa and in the monastery, as the building is first experienced, the focus of the visual field is provided by an element without high intrinsic interest which, while it absorbs the eye, is unable to retain its attention." A dilemma of one's experience of La Tourette is that this monumental facade resists—by both the geography of one's approach and its insistent blankness—approach. It is a front but not a front. Rowe the architecture critic (and non-practicing architect) burrows into Le Corbusier's own architectural criticism, specifically his 1920–21 appreciations and apprehensions of the Parthenon as collected in *L'Esprit Nouveau*, for a resolution. "The apparent disorder of the plan could only deceive the profane," Rowe quotes Corbusier, suggesting similarly that the La Tourette chapel North wall's inability to retain attention is only an apparent disordering, and is in fact part of, "certain patterns of organization—e.g. a compounding of frontal and three-quarter views [...] a tension between longitudinal and transverse movements, above all the intersection of an architectonic by a topographical experience, which may to the initiated suggest that the spatial mechanics of the monastery's precinct are just possibly some very private commentary apron Acropolitan material." The big blank wall first stuns and disappoints and then deflects the attentions of the visitor to an entry sequence at a minor-seeming corner aperture and platform, from which the whole interior composition tends—like Rowe's vision of Corbusier's vision of the Acropolis—into rewarding perspectival obliques and, if you incline toward Rowe, intelligibly classical architectural references.

La Tourette, somewhere between its actual construction and its cultural reception, between its design and its criticism, provides further dilemmas for those who would seek them. The design dilemma is the clearest, deriving from Rowe's, "intersection of an architectonic by a topographical experience": the complex constructs the object but not the operation of a cloister. A central quadrangle is overlooked by a perimeter arrangement of cellular residences on two levels around three sides, with a refectory and library on the third, west-facing side, tucked under the residential cells into the space ceded by the slopping hillside, and that monumental chapel on the north-facing fourth. But there is no ground to that quadrangle. Because the whole is elevated on piers and piles and pillars above the sloping hillside below, that central cloister only notionally and visually suggests potential occupancy—and is literally occupied by only various enclosed staircases and corridors, most notably the small pyramid-roofed oratory perched on its cruciform pier supports. The whole is inward looking, but without, in this sense, an inside. It is somehow a monastery without that defining feature, the cloister—the essential non-liturgical site of monastic life, the outdoor interior. Small balconies and roof terraces overlooking this groundless courtyard constitute a residue of this kind of space, but there is—and I would assert that one senses it from those very overlooks—something, or somewhere, missing; a sensation perhaps not unrelated by the additional tension between the building's seemingly massive scale and, at only some 16,000 square feet, its surprisingly small total enclosed space. The tension of, despite its peak occupancy of only about 100 friars, its strenuously seeming bigness.

This non-cloister cloister, a twentieth-century take on a ninth-century typology, is an expression of another La Tourette dilemma: the notion of a modern construction of a definitively pre-modern, thousand-year-old religious institution and spiritual practice. A chapel with a flat roof prompts, even in the second decade of the twenty-first century, a double-take—this despite the mid-twentieth-century efforts of a figure like French Dominican friar Marie-Alain Couturier, an artisan and art theorist and editor of the surprisingly forward looking journal *L'Art Sacré*, whose intervention had much to do with Corbusier's commissioning for La Tourette, and whose influence was perhaps seen in Corbusier's pilgrimage chapel at Ronchamp a decade earlier, as well. Couturier's stated project was to provide in the built environment and decorative arts of Catholic ritual a tonic to the insipid, the nostalgic, the saccharine, and close-minded conventional to which it was otherwise all too prone. To be sure, at La Tourette, all that massive cast concrete, complemented by details in patinated metal, seems not so much self-referentially modern as tacitly polemical about the modern's ability to equal the sensational effects of the ancient—the lofty acoustics and satisfying gloom of La Tourette's chapel offers something that to the willing congregant feels at the very least Romanesque, if not, with the absence of interior articulations of those great slab-like surfaces, picturesquely Gothic.

The Catholic monastic life is presumably not consciously concerned with antiquity or modernity, but with timelessness—the choreographed repetitions of each day calibrated to suppress worldly and personal calendars in favor of the liturgical (and the seasonal onto which it's mapped). But another dilemma of La Tourette is to what extent the complex might even be considered a monastery as we popularly and casually use the word and as both Rowe and Vidler attached it to the structure. Architects perhaps especially might favor a reading of La Tourette as a monastery—in the sense of an architectural armature for an ethos, for a monastic order, for a precise one-to-one mapping of event onto space, for a delineation of a mode and manner of life that preserved and enforced in a built environment an otherwise abstract or ephemeral mode of interior life.

That all of an ethos might be rendered into a single built environment, and that people would withdraw from the wider world and choose to dwell only there—architectural subjects at an extreme limit condition, and architectural objects of extraordinary influence—has, at least to architects and monks, its appeal. It is a dream of elegant refusal that is not so different—in the sense of being quarantined from the infectious attractions of daily life, into an environment that hygienically edits away decor and decoration into something severe and pure—behind the tuberculosis sanitariums and other clinical or punitive typologies that, as some have theorized, prompted the interwar encoding of modern design itself. It is for this imagined operation of the building, as much as the celebrity of its architect, that architecture critics and thinkers like Rowe and Vidler may be especially drawn to La Tourette. The essential pre-modern model of this might be the famous Plan of St. Gall, the ninth-century document featuring a layout of a prototypical Benedictine monastic compound, and one of the few architectural plan drawings of the European West still extant from before Brunelleschi. The corresponding Rule of St. Benedict, already in place for centuries before its architectural encoding in the St. Gall plan, did indeed order life as it might be lived only in delineated buildings.

But La Tourette is not such a place. The Dominican order to whose tradition belongs had its thirteenth-century origins in precisely the opposite impulse: it was what came to be called a mendicant order: literally, beggars, who sustained themselves not from the predicable harvest of a particular landscape and through the predictable ritual of a stable cloistered life, but through itinerant and mobile—even worldly and cosmopolitan—participation in those two great flourishing developments of that century, universities and cities. The practice was definitively not pastoral withdrawal but urban travel and immersion into the messy and lively world of Western Europe in the late Middle Ages: street preaching. The *couvent* or priory of such an order was not in this sense any kind of pattern of the Eternal, or even merely a permanent residence, but instead primarily a place of preparation, of some book learning and protocol training prior to life in the wider world. Not a sanitarium, perhaps, as much as a teaching hospital.

This might explain—by conscious intention of its designer or not—why, in a sense, there is within La Tourette *nowhere to go*. Or more precisely nowhere to go that encourages you to stay, to simply to be where you are: no cloister, no courtyard, no Great Hall, nowhere in-the-round, no obvious circumambulation, no communal resting space. Any sense of gathered and self-facing attention is absent even in the collective spaces in which we might expect such an effect: the attenuated refectory, suspended below the west-facing rows of cells over the declining hillside with floor-to-ceiling fenestration on the downhill side, is the glassiest and most outward-looking space, with views across the immediate valley, it feels like a kind of shelf or perch, not a place to stay; the chapel, similarly attenuated, feels with its two shallow ranks of seating, sideways-facing to the axis of the chapel and celebrant, a little like a vast subway car with bench seating along its sides: a place to ride for a certain number of stops and signals, but not the destination. In that space, even such familiar mid-century modern formal tropes as slit windows at the intersections of planes, or the complex retraction of the floor plane from the base of the walls, and its complex articulation into slopes and steps and landings, seem also to urge the visitor to keep it moving. The insistent narrowness of the cells themselves, of the corridors and slit-windows and balconies—all may be not only artifacts of the undersized-seeming ergonomics of a half-century ago, or of some willful application of the arcane Modulor metrics, but also combine to confer restlessness. This difficulty of *staying* and *being* in the spaces of La Tourette is surely the essential complement of the quality that most enervated Rowe: the difficulty of its approach, the blankness of reception, that, "while it absorbs the eye, is unable to retain its attention."

During our visit, this restlessness conferred itself on our jury as well; as visitors to the priory for two nights and three days, we convened in a drafty conference room, one wall all cool-to-the-touch single-paned glass. Aligned orthogonal to the slope of the hillside, slung under the south wing opposite the Chapel, the room felt—just like the refectory—to be a kind of shelf or ledge, tilting the occupant visually and notionally out onto the meadow below. An SOM jury, with its tradition of pilgrimage and—even for the span of only a day—residency, re-enacts in miniature a Dominican cycle of temporary withdrawal from the world directed toward reemergence, with something of a preacher's exhortations at the ready, back into it. Through each jury cycle and at each pilgrimage site we imagine, with whatever self-aware fancy, that we will absorb from the *genus loci* some quality of the setting's original patrons or designers—the cosmopolitan melancholy of Dalsace and Chareau, the tasteful rusticity of Carre and Aalto, the deluxe urbanity of Mies and Johnson and Lambert. At La Tourette the effects were surprising. Willfully Romantic, we timed our deliberations to be suspended at the sacerdotal hour of Vespers, where we joined the dozen or so mostly elderly friars in residence at the Chapel. Typically, the text is from the Book of Psalms: "Let my prayer be set forth before thee as incense; and the lifting up of my hands as the evening sacrifice. Set a watch, O Lord, before my mouth ..." For an austere yet somehow cozy moment inside the chapel the result was perhaps what we expected: modal evensong resonating off those cold high concrete walls, and mellow dusk visibly gathering through the narrow horizontal slots that Rowe described,

La Tourette's interior "groundless" courtyard

seen from the outside, as "gashed." Then, in a ghoulish flash, we were shocked into the twentieth century, or into our own young century of machines and violence perhaps as recollected or foreseen by Le Corbusier, with the flickering on of the chapel's electric lights—gashes narrower still, fluorescent lights in tubes as thin as neon lights, incised, in what was apparently the original design, along the sills of those windows. In that unrelenting light, the chapel as tight and bright as an operating theater.

La Tourette, as a building, pushed us would-be visitors and guests back out into the world. A few times we left the conference room to tread briskly through the meadow to be seen through its glass wall, melted morning frost soaking into our city shoes. Early one morning we crowded into a jerky-clutched rental car and rattled down into the town for market day. Our best conversations happened not in timeless cloistered seclusion but jammed into those cars and into an insistently halogen-lit cafe, tinny Europop on the radio and silent soccer on the flat screen television over the bar and clatter everywhere, as the mercantile and school-day rituals of the town came to life around us. Another day we stayed out late. We returned in a chemically scented minivan, its hired driver murmuring in the usual way into his Bluetooth headset. As we pulled up there was a brief but restless play, on the vast concrete flank of the chapel, of the automobile headlights—as enervated and searching as the eyes of Rowe's dismayed visitor, as comic and ominous as spotlights on a vaudeville prison wall, as if searching there for something not to be seen by mere light of day.

中世纪现代主义

作者：Karrie Jacobs

如果你用 Google 搜索——为何这个词条与众不同？——它会告诉你，术语“中世纪现代主义”或“中世纪现代风格”在 20 世纪最后二十年开始被广泛使用。由于 Google 的历时词频统计工具 Ngram Viewer 不显示 2008 年以后的结果，尚无法确切地说，这一用法是否已达到顶峰，或者我们是否正处于中世纪现代主义的高峰期。

然而，我们可以确定其上升趋势的开始时间。这个词明确始于一本出版于 1984年、名为《中世纪现代风格：20 世纪 50 年代的家具》（Mid-Century Modern: Furniture of the 1950s）的书籍，作者为设计专家 Cara Greenberg，她曾是《都市住宅》（Metropolitan Home）等杂志的知名作家。书中的一排 Eames 椅子、George Nelson 收纳系统，以及少量 Saarinen 和 Jacobsen 风格的装饰造就并推广了这种刚刚崭露头角的风格。奇怪的是，虽然“现代”一词频频出现于整本书中，“中世纪”的出现次数却很少，直到 48 页中标题为“一个时代的结束”章节才能看到这几个简短的字。“中世纪现代风格的黄金时代已经结束，”Greenberg 如是写道，她认为能真正体现制造技术、非传统材料的使用，以及以实用功能性为导向形式的家具时代始于 1947 年、结束于 1957 年。她将中世纪现代风格的没落归咎于一场劣质仿制品灾难和一个易变的公众群体；对于他们来说，现代主义只是另一种类似意大利风或中国风的风格。

从 Greenberg 的书中显而易见，虽然 20 世纪 50 年代素有遵从一致与媚俗的名声，它也是一个高度创新的年代。由于二战中没有什么建筑可供 Eero Saarinen 和 Arne Jacobson 等建筑师设计，他们将注意力转移到了支持新形式和材料的家具。战后，一度被压抑的需求推动了家具销量上升，而且一种新的审美观——简约且注重非传统——被大众欣然接受。连我那原本对设计丝毫不感兴趣的父母，也挑选了一个非常简约的沙发和扶手椅放置在客厅，搭配成丹麦现代风格。我确定这些家具不是来自斯堪的纳维亚附近的任何地方，而是购买于新泽西高速公路旁的折扣店。即使是童年家中一丝丹麦风格的气息也意味着，中世纪是我们轻松摆脱传统的时期，而当时我们未必意识到自己正在这样做。

一般而言，中世纪现代风格是一个让我们如今无需太过纠结的词语。一提起它，就会有案例研究住宅（Case Study Houses）或由彩球环绕的 George Nelson 钟表映入脑海。它是一种用于轻松打造一定风格亮度的方式，也是一种让材料呈现新形式的倾向：弯曲的胶合板、玻璃墙、高强度塑料等。与 Bauhaus、De Stijl 以及其它大型欧洲运动的战前现代主义不同，中世纪现代主义意味着美国的活力。它主要不是为了设计一台居住机器，而是为了建立一种美学，以表现这个国家在战后的冷漠。（请注意，我们所提到的中世纪现代主义通常不是指相同时期的某些作品，例如曾成为现代主义缺点象征的 Pruitt Igoe 住宅 [1954]、代指愚昧强塞官僚势力的现代主义，让我们与 20 世纪 70 年代一系列现代主义联系在一起。）

那么，中世纪现代风格的概念来源于哪里？Greenberg 还著有关于住宅内饰的文章；她认为是她创造了这个词。当我提到最早使用这个词的可能另有其人时，她颇为恼火。但是，当我搜索《纽约时报》档案时，我很快找到了一篇刊登于 1953 年、标题为“现代家居正变得越来越花哨”（Modern Furniture is Getting Fancier）的文章，其中提到了这个词。这篇文章很简短，讲的是 Wanamaker 百货公司商店内的一系列家具：“实际上，当今流行的图案与材料都能在这些新款家具身上找到…… J. Stuart Clingman 将它们称为‘中世纪现代风格’。”文章中提到，Clingman 主要因其传统家具而出名，但他实际上是一位非常有意思的设计师，他的名字已被历史所遗忘，或至少被 Greenberg 时代的读者所遗忘。他是家族中第二代家具制造商，并在家具中心城——密歇根大急流市担任 John Widdicomb 有限公司的设计总监。他的作品多为斜线条和偏重心设计，现在仍可在 eBay 等网络商城上看到。

我发现不可思议的是，Clingman 能在中世纪有足够的自我意识来创造一个词汇，用于定位他当时的作品。不过，也许他并非特别与众不同：根据曾任“牛津英语词典”的词典编辑 Jesse Sheidlower 所说，“20 世纪 50 年代的人绝对意识到他们正处于中世纪。”但 Sheidlower 提醒道：“这并不表示‘中世纪现代风格’的意思与现在的意思相同。”Sheidlower 的话引发了我的疑问，大约在 1953 年的“中世纪”是否实际上是指我将其与之关联的高度乐观主义，或者“中世纪”概念是否还包含即将来临的毁灭威胁，类似“千禧年”的观点预示着半个世纪后将出现世界末日。

无论“中世纪现代主义”这个词语在 1953 年启发了什么，Clingman 的聪明见解都未跟上脚步。这个词还有一些其它早于 Greenberg 的出处，频率为每十年一到两次。例如，《华盛顿邮报》中有一篇预告 Smithsonian's Renwick 艺廊的文章，其第一句提到“可以说，中世纪现代风格已翩然而至。”而且，鉴于展览中有 Knoll 和 Herman Miller 制造的作品，这一表述对于《华盛顿邮报》记者的含义与 9 年后对于 Greenberg 的含义相同。Greenberg 坚称：“我对那场展览一无所知。”

最终，我查到了 Clark Malcolm。过去 33 年内，他一直担任 Herman Miller 公司的内部作家编辑。这家家具制造商生产了 George Nelson 的所有标志性设计作品，而 Greenberg 曾将这些设计评价为“理性的声音和灵魂，优雅的设计”。我有 个疑问是，“中世纪现代主义”如何应用于 Herman Miller 公司？这个词本应对 Herman Miller 公司具有极为重要的意义。他对这个疑问的第一反应简单明了：没有应用。Malcolm 将这个词归功于 Greenberg 并解释说，“Greenberg 的书出版于 20 世纪 80 年，当时 Herman Miller 公司对这个词语所描述的人和产品兴趣不大。正是那一年，George Nelson 曾四次前往安娜堡的建筑学校讲课，而 Herman Miller 公司无人腾出时间与他一起用餐。我们已停止生产许多他和 Eameses 设计的作品，而且将在品位的摆钟开始摆向另一个方向前停止更多产品。”

意识到这一点，那么中世纪现代主义不属于 Herman Miller 企业文化的一部分就不足为奇。我在 20 世纪 80 年代首次开始探索设计文化；当时，评论家和理论家大多将现代主义称为我们最终——最终——超越的东西。所有深度思考皆与后现代主义有关。我津津有味地阅读了由 Hal Foster 编辑的《The Anti-Aesthetic: Essays on Postmodern Culture》 (1983) 和由 John Thackara 编辑的 《Design After Modernism: Beyond the Object》（1988）散文集。这些书中传递的信息是，作为当代生活中一股强大力量的现代主义已经过时，原因在于：a）它已被简化为一种风格 b）它不再是一种激进的反独裁运动，而是权力机构表现自我的默认方式。现代主义无趣，平庸，而且已经走上末路。Thackara 选编的典型情绪可在建筑师兼作家 Nigel Coates 的文章中看到：“60 年代中期，当现代主义的旧思想运动似乎已展现胜利之姿时，本世纪的建筑视角已从伦敦到莫斯科的郊区一同成形。尤其是住宅已成为一种模式，可以复制、标记和堆叠……”

20 世纪 80 年代亦是如此。现代主义不再流行。我们已移步向前。20 世纪 90 年代复苏潮造就的一切，从巴西利亚建筑、东德 Plattenbau 公寓楼到纽约长期受人诟病的泛美大厦，既在意料之中，又在意料之外。这种中世纪设计复苏兴起后，得到了创刊于 1996 年的《墙纸设计》（Wallpaper）杂志的大力推动。该杂志最初支持中世纪风格，因为其创始人 Tyler Brûlé 最近告诉我，这种风格曾伴随着他和他的同龄人（当时他 28 岁）一同成长。“它有一种熟悉感”，Brûlé 说。“这些是曾帮助你蹒跚学步的桌子。”换言之，《墙纸设计》在现代主义建筑风格复兴潮中发挥的作用，是由人们对家具，尤其是丹麦现代家具的怀旧情怀所引发的；这些家具也许就是我父母带回家中的低价丹麦现代家具。从那之后，杂志编辑开始培养一种建筑品位，用于探寻和出版现代主义建筑，通常为堪培拉或横滨等带有异国情调、能吸引伦敦或纽约读者的建筑。

因此，在建筑业界宣布取代解构主义等温室变种的现代主义划下句号十年后，《墙纸设计》杂志开始兴味盎然地展示中世纪建筑，并普及酷炫、冷峻的建筑。Brûlé 称，某种程度上，杂志受到了一种保护主义者的敦促，“与时间赛跑，记录那些让我们意识到可能会失去的地方。”但毫无疑问，《墙纸设计》杂志将建筑变成了时尚。而且当这种时尚出现后，中世纪现代主义已成为一种可变通、容易参考且跟随复兴而复兴的通用语言。

如今，这些战后年月的标志，无论是 George Nelson 的棉花糖沙发还是 Eero Saarinen 的 TWA 航站楼，都是如此的广受欢迎，以致于你往往很难在这个国家思考现代主义，而不联想到其熟悉的修饰语。这是一个历史和哲学问题，可以说，人们对中世纪现代主义的普遍热情宣判了现代主义（Modernism）的死亡——M 为大写——因为它的形容词削弱了它作为名词的意义。

Greenberg 可以告诉你原因：“现代这个词总是意味着相同的东西。我的理解是，它代表着相同的时刻。”如果接受她对“现代”的定义——这也是兰登书屋词典中的定义——并将这个词与历史时刻联系起来，那么它将成为一个悖论。如果现代主义（Modernism）是 60 年前的“相同时刻”，那现在是什么时刻？

虽然我经常写到 20 世纪 90 年代的大多数建筑，但我并未对中世纪现代主义的概念进行太多思考，直到我开始为创刊于 2000 年的《Dwell》杂志工作。这本杂志专门推广现代住宅建筑和设计。当你从事刚起步的工作时，经常发生的一件事是，你得花大量时间来解释你在做什么。我在这本新杂志中总要对同一个烦人的问题做出成百上千次的回答：你们只刊登“中世纪”住宅吗？答案——我认为显然是——否。而且至少最开始，我不明白为什么会有人问这个问题。

当时，美国杂志关注的现代住宅完全集中在 20 世纪 40 年代到 60 年代建造的住宅。其中许多建筑，例如加州先锋开发商 Joseph Eichler 建造的建筑以及 Gregory Ain 和 Garret Eckbo 设计的 Mar Vista Tract 等作为试验性战后住宅小区的建筑，皆非常出色，且在空间的灵活运用、室内与室外的模糊界限以及结构简约性方面都具有创新性。不难理解，为何住宅的主人会珍惜且痴迷于还原他们的中世纪地标。

但这不是《Dwell》的兴趣所在。我意识到，我必须找到一种方法来清楚无误地告诉别人，我们所指的现代主义不同：我们不打算往后看。因此我做了任何可敬的现代主义者（Modernist）都会做的事情；我写了一篇宣言。我们在首本杂志中宣布：“我们不认为现代主义是 20 世纪上半叶历史运动的遗留和回温，而是一种思潮。“M”（现代主义）一词意味着对材料、方法的诚实与好奇，对大规模制造与美并不互相排斥的信念，以及既对未来、也对现在持有的某种乐观态度。

显而易见，现代主义并非发生在过去且已经结束的东西，而是一种看待世界的方式。它是一系列不断变化的技术与机会，一种将不断的激进突破融入平淡历程中的方式。现代主义是一种吸收并收服爆发力的技巧，而这种爆发力在不断重塑人类环境。因此，现代主义是无限的，且具有无尽的相关性。

除非它不是无限或不具有无尽的相关性。

因为还有另一个不容易解决的问题。即使你将它从“中世纪”分离出来，“现代主义”这个词本身也让人联想到过去。如今，“现代”听上去有些古怪，代指未来的符号并未结束。但似乎抛弃这个词是错误的做法，除非我们有替换词。

只可惜我们没有。

据我所知，我们几乎无法定位我们所处的时期。那我们用什么词语来描述这一时期呢？一位作曲家朋友建议用“当代”；这个词常被延伸用于音乐和美术领域，但用于建筑方面却会有些麻烦，因为它通常是轻现代主义的委婉说法。人们提出的所有定义词都含义太窄或没有支撑依据。记得信息时代吗？在建筑学中，没有哪个词比现代主义更有影响力或气势：后现代主义、解构主义、水滴主义、参数主义、被动式设计以及可持续性设计。这些词的含义都不够广泛，不够有远见，或不够简约。

Sheidlower 指出，如“天主教”遇到“教堂”的问题，“现代风格”这个词遇到“主义”时也会出现类似问题。“这种情况普遍出现于，当词语在理论上有广泛的含义，但却指向具体含义时——广泛含义将被具体含义打败”他解释道。

所以我们最后讨论后-后现代主义或元现代主义。（元现代主义甚至有自己的宣言：它与摇摆（oscillation）相关。）Brûlé 通过“重新”这个前缀来描述现在，例如“我认为我们正处于重新复兴和重新启动的阶段。”

也许，建筑当前最广泛的趋势在于由惊人的功能水平所创建的形式，以及可大幅推动社会目标的建筑：净能耗、碳中和或改善健康。但如果不是现代主义，这种全新的建筑类型是什么？确切地说，当今的写字楼和公寓楼只是居住机器。这会让 Le Corbusier 大吃一惊。现代主义从未如此重要；它是一种能将我们轻松带入新世纪中叶的思维方式。除非现代主义确实已十分陈旧，即已如其定义所言而结束。

“你们年轻人是如此确定”：礼拜堂 (Chapel House)（建筑师 J. Walter Severinghaus）之建筑精神：

Nicholas Adams

建筑学，与所有艺术学科一样，需要伟大传统的形成力量以及足够活力，以确保该传统适应当前利益，即适应技术时代的喜好和功能需求。

– Reinhold Niebuhr，“传统与今日道德”，《建筑论坛》，1953年12月

“嗯，它看起来很像一个温室，但你们年轻人是如此确定这是正确的方式，那我们就这么做吧。”

– 礼拜堂的客户 Genevieve Ludlow Griscom 与其主设计师J. Walter Severinghaus, Kenneth W. Morgan 和 Everett Case 在1957年的谈话

1. 两者之间的空间

“一个陀螺仪旋转带来绚丽的结构……轮转焰火焦灼，发出可怕的巨大声响。”在他的自传《两者之间的空间：一个建筑师的旅程》（1973）中，Nathaniel A Owings（1903-1984）这样描述七月四日的噩梦。他看到的不是从轮转焰火中飞向夜空的火箭，而是 Skidmore, Owings & Merrill 的主要建筑物；他被可怕的自我怀疑惊醒了。“这四十年的设计留下的证据是否只是碎屑？它们与哪一部分相关联？他们身在何处？对我来说，这些设计旨在展现“具体形式”，其目的远不止用于居住——但是这些设计最终是这样的吗？[1]

Owings的噩梦展现的是一位创始人在职业生涯即将结束之际，看到一个令人不安的SOM景象[2]。这个梦表明一种恐惧，强加给他生命的意义现在什么都不是，SOM本身只是一个离心的强制任务、一个旋转的发电机。醒来后，Owings想知道：有没有一种逻辑将这一成就整合起来？抵抗这种分裂能量的向心力在何处？答案当然是在手中。《两者之间的空间》表面上看是一个自传，其实是Owings为他在四十多年前创立的公司制定的一个新愿景，反映了Owings对该公司致力于现代设计这个可持续愿景的绵绵信心，同时也讲述了他对自然和环境的集体力量、对社区和社会生活、对家庭以及对建筑师们所取得的小（通常不为人注意）胜利的敬畏之情。

可以肯定，《两者之间的空间》这本书与一位老人有关，讲述一个退伍军人回顾旧日的运动，而对世界重新行成更广泛的理解。这本书努力地想给后人留下些什么，就像预言一样，它所关注的事情在当今时代产生了共鸣。对 Owings 噩梦最坏的解释是，作品的主体在声音和愤怒中燃烧，没有指向任何主体之外或之内的事物。最好的解释是，那个轮转焰火是一种推进装置：一种可以在当今时代得以收获和维持的能量，用于寻找和扩展公分母、识别和培养设计收敛力及原理。 Owings 噩梦的产生，在于认识到超越任何个人控制力——制度、常规、社会、文化等控制力——的力量塑造了公司的各种做法，持平甚至超过公司设计师们的个人或集体用意。Owings 退休后，由内部人员转变成为局外人，他所能做的就是写一本书，指出他认为公司应该前进的方向；可能不足为奇的是，他的前同事们基本上都无视他的信息——或者至少，建筑和写作记录显示他们没有因Owings的这一疑虑而有所影响。在这一点上他不受同伴待见，他的写作技巧有限。以前和现在一样，喂养野兽、让钱流经管道这等事情经常发生。无论如何，建立实践参数、定义企业精神，可能不是局外人可以做的，甚至Owings这位特权局外人也不行。

可以说，Owings 关注的是精神：这是两者之间的空间组成部分。这个部分通常未被阐明，但却被深度沟通。当然，SOM从一开始就注重于集体或企业建筑的设计，这点与准英雄气概的现代大师们截然相反。但是，尽管精神依赖于“房屋风格”，却与之大不相同：精神是一种信仰，通常不作声明。它可以提供信心，给人自信——无论是它什么，但能使你足够确信，作出设计决策。应用于建筑公司时、应用于公司内部可变的协作过程时，精神具有包罗万象的性质。那么，历史学家怎样去理解五十年前的实践呢？定义实践有很多东西，在此不必多说——而且，根据定义而未作说明的规则，不是历史学的一部分，也很难从历史中梳理出来。同样，反事实也很难证明：比如，关于未设计通道的视觉证据，很少能找到。因此，我们倾向于专注于我们所看到的，甚至为之奋斗。当今，观察者可能想通过项目名称建立起历史精神：“它是利华大厦（Lever House）、或约翰·汉考

克中心（John Hancock Center）、或美铝大厦（Alcoa Building）”。但是，在以精神定义某一特定建筑物或一组建筑物时，有一些不可抗拒的静态事物——带有持续沟通和调整的动态。我们还必须考虑到Owings发挥的关键作用，他早期参与利华大厦的建设（1952年）；将Graham对待Hancock的脾气体现在塔与塔相叠之上（1965年）；或Goldsmith对Bassett的美铝大厦设计产生的影响（1964年）。这些事件不成系统，但也不是真的反常——在这个意义上，他们是精神的一部分。或者，我们可以将Gordon Bunshaft或Bruce Graham或Myron Goldsmith的作品视为精神的典范。毕竟，他们的作品随着时间的推移而逐渐变化，就像精神发生变化一样。即便如此，在识别一个甚至三个彼此各不相同的人或实践的精神时，也会过于个性化。精神的辨别充满悖论：因为它是在动态的沟通、决策和变革过程中得以表达，而这些过程又是可变的——我们对它进行了定义，它便可以重新进行自我定义。

从外部看，当我们不能确定作者时，也许我们离一个时期和实践的精神更近一步了。一位同事回忆她去一家纽约医院时，发现自己正在看着街上一栋不明身份的建筑物。慢慢地通过分析、拨开迷雾，她意识到，通过她的窗口看到的窗户和竖框，只可能是SOM人员设计的。它们让她想起SOM的其他建筑物——也许，像George Kubler的“链接系列”，形成的是一系列立面解决方案。更具关联性效果的是：《室内设计》杂志1959年1月刊一篇早期文章描述的室内设计，由SOM芝加哥办公室进行设计，宣传一种独特的“芝加哥”风格的室内设计。但是，芝加哥的设计整体看起来与纽约的设计没有什么区别。SOM有没有一种建筑精神依赖并超越建筑风格及业已确定的权威特性？[3]我将芝加哥的内陆钢铁大厦（1958年）列为当时精神的有效代表，正是因为不能确定作者是Graham, Walter Netsch还是我认为有关键影响的候选人Gordon Bunshaft。它是纯粹的精神，每个贡献者似乎都朝着一个被所有参与者理解、但却没有明确说明的目标而努力。寻找具有这种品质的建筑，其过程充满启发性。一系列的品质组合，构成特定时间和特定地点的精神。我们可以找到某个单一建筑，也许就是一栋无名建筑，并从中找到这种精神？

如果我们怀疑SOM的当代精神完全或部分地来源于对其二十世纪中叶各个作品的理解，也许我们应该在这些作品中找到一个无名建筑物；一个风格要素明显、却不严格执行的建筑物；一个无归属设计师或归属设计师不出名的建筑物；一个设计明确彰显有形与无形关系的建筑物。一个像纽约汉密尔顿科尔盖特大学礼拜堂（1958-1959）这样的建筑。

2. 礼拜堂的精神

在SOM的建筑物列表上找到它后，我便启程首次前往礼拜堂。这个名字令我困惑。六年前，在访问了纽约州上州Oneida社区附近乌托邦式的建筑遗迹之后，我绕道去了礼拜堂。正值盛夏，校园里荒无人烟；远离学术建筑的礼拜堂向游客开放，热情、安宁而又空荡。我漫步过去，想知道这个建筑是哪个SOM人员或部门设计的。《*Skidmore, Owings&Merrill 1950-1962*》（1963）中没有这个建筑，当天的建筑新闻也没有登记。SOM似乎没有人有这个设计师的记录。在夏天的下午，也不能从科尔盖特大学得到解释。然而，很明显它是SOM的50年代建筑。今年春天，我又去了一次礼拜堂，重新审视它，看它是否能激起我的记忆，是否能让我从中读到很多信息。此时，礼拜堂正在进行翻修：这个暂时的改造状态将它剥离、打开，呈现在我面前，等待着它的碎片重新组装成为新的模样。我适时地探索了它的历史，遇见了第一任主任（该建筑的客户）的几个儿子，并与设计师的儿子以及出资人的孙女进行了交谈。

礼拜堂在那个时代不同寻常：它是一个根源于浸礼会、致力于非教派宗教的校园建筑。既不致力于在大学做礼拜（因为当时有Memorial Chapel作为周末强制性出席礼拜之地），也不致力于传授新教传统（时至今日，这仍然反映在核心课程上，其中宗教和哲学部门发挥了重要作用）。礼拜堂用于在抽象和单一层面上促进宗教。这个地方，校园内外的任何人都可以独自带着自己的想法进来、可以阅读和思考、可以听音乐、看宗教艺术、打坐、冥思或祈祷。没有定期服务，是所有宗教、尤其是在美国鲜有人知的东方宗教进行个人探索的地方。

礼拜堂的倡议来自大学牧师和宗教教授 Kenneth W. Morgan（1908-2011）[4]。他高校毕业后就读于哈佛大学哲学系，而后进入神学院，获得神学学士学位（1935）。他是一个探求者，对不同宗教找到上帝的方式十分着迷。他最早的宗教经历是在卫理公会。但是，在剑桥时，时间允许的情况下，他定要访问犹太和天主教仪式，以及其他新教教派甚至一些“当地出版物中宣传的”奇怪教派的服务。[5]“1934年，他会见了Ramakrishna-Vivekananda Center纽约分部的负责人

Swami Nikhilananda（1895-1973），并且在他的帮助下前往印度的Ramakrishna ashrams，研究印度教的实践（1935-1936）。作为一个良心反对者，在与公谊会进行合作以及战时服务之后——他后来加入了公谊会——Morgan前往科尔盖特大学担任牧师（1946年）。东方宗教的经验重现，成为他第一本书的灵感，编辑的研究作品集《印度作家笔下的印度教》（1953年）。这本书为之后的佛教（1956年）和伊斯兰教（1958年）书籍建立了模式。[6]这些书籍专为机构或私人场所的学生设计，常被称赞具有公平性和异乎寻常之处，填补了英语读者长久以来的缺口。Morgan以公平对待各种宗教而享有声誉，这给礼拜堂的建设带来直接影响。

1956年初，一位富有的纽约老人 Genevieve Ludlow Griscom（1868-1958）由著名的英国比较宗教支持者J. N. Spalding引荐，联系到了 Morgan。她没有向 Morgan透露自己的个人情况，但明确表示她希望找到一种办法来推进东方宗教及其与美国基督教之间的关系。她怎样才能做到呢？在Morgan的帮助下，Griscom被介绍给哈佛大学的适当人员。随后，Griscom捐赠了50万美元，在神学院设立了世界宗教研究中心[7]。然后，她自发地向科尔盖特大学发送了一张35万美元的支票，给Morgan用于推进在那里进行的伟大的世界宗教研究。[8]受到这个慷慨之举的激励（以及她的鼓励），Morgan提出了一个建议并送给她，“一个小建筑，在那里探求者可以研究所有传统的宗教信仰和习俗在书中、在宗教音乐录音中以及宗教艺术复制品和原件中的呈现方式。”它将是“一个为那些想要更多地了解世界各宗教中关于礼拜、奉献、冥想、无私和关心的人而专门设计的地方。”他设想了一座小教堂、一个图书馆、一间音乐室、一些供过夜游客使用的卧室、以及一个小厨房和餐厅。“这个地方将欢迎来自任何宗教传统的探求者或无宗教信仰的探求者，他们想了解更多关于其他寻求者所遵循的宗教路径；关于他们的个人祷告仪式、诵经、祷告词、冥想以及他们读到的内容。”[9] Griscom夫人为他的冥想中心提供了60万美元（超过他所要求的金额），并有两个要求：她的名字“不能被提到，以及建筑平面图必须得到她的批准。”[10] Morgan说服大学接受这份礼物，然后辞去牧师一职，成为中心的第一任主任。这位高级设计师不是SOM公司一位杰出的设计师，而是J. Walter Severinghaus（1905-1987），他是Morgan在俄亥俄州卫斯理大学（俄亥俄州特拉华）的朋友[11]。

Morgan留下了他与“那位女士”会面的一些记录。他提到“那位女士”——或者“B. 夫人”，他也是这么称呼她的。1956年第一次见面时，她已经八十七岁。他们在她位于纽约Riverdale的Chapel Farm庄园的Fair Hill宅邸（现称为“Fieldstone”）会面。Morgan似乎对她的生活所知甚少，或至少没有记录任何信息，但他们一定大量谈论宗教。他知道，她有着存在已久的灵性兴趣，特别对于东方的灵性传统，而且她有钱（她强调，不是用她的个人财产）可以用于教育。他也知道，她是一个神学家，甚至参与讨论她和她“朋友们”制定的哈佛礼物赠与条款。[12]

虽然Morgan在Chapel Farm见到了她，但他没有记录（甚至可能不知道）有关Fair Hill或Chapel Farm的全部目的。事实上，Chapel Farm是一个名为“活基督秩序外部法院”（或简称，“活基督秩序”）团体的家园。在那时，Griscom夫人是最年长的（如果不是核心的）人物。“活基督秩序”（The Order of the Living Christ）是总部位于纽约市的“神智学协会”或“美国神智学协会”所留下来的神智学者团体。随着神智学运动爆发以及他们的创始人Helena Blavatsky夫人（1831–1891）逝世，追随者之间发生了争端（他们曾经是神智学主要的东海岸中心）。由此，“活基督秩序”于1894年成立。她告诉Morgan，事实上他们组织了一个小组，研究基督教神秘主义和东方宗教的主要文本的精神文本。他们还举行公开演讲、研讨会、静修、年会以推进神智学，给Chapel of the Comforter的Horatio Street使命提供赞助。他们在那里安排了一个通晓神智学的牧师Clarence C. Clark。[13]主教制度主义是他们的外表，神智学才是他们深奥的内心。1903年，他们在Fair Hill开始创立杂志《神智学季刊》，并定期出版，直到1938年。这所房子面积巨大，14000平方英尺的本地花岗岩建成一个改良的法国乡村风格的豪宅。[14] Fair Hill一直是《神智学季刊》及其许多活动的所在地，Chapel Farm的小屋一直是许多神智学者的家。 Griscom自己以笔名“Cavé”（借指埋没的古代知识）在《神智学季刊》的一个常规专栏进行创作。常规专栏名为“碎片”，而她的文章被收集成三册书籍，取名《碎片》。[15]
虽然她和她的丈夫Clement A. Griscom（1868-1918）（热交换器工程公司Griscom-Russell的主席）是神智学协会的主要支持，他们却不孤独。该组织的领导人是恼人的Ernest Temple Hargrove （1870–1939）。Hargrove的个人生活有相当阴暗的一面，他死后的一个法庭案件就显示了这一点。[16]关键的智慧光是爱尔兰作家和编辑查尔斯·约翰斯顿（1867-1931）。作为一名俄罗斯和梵文专家，他将薄伽梵歌以及其他精神文本翻译成英语。他还将诗人W. B. Yeats（威廉·巴特勒·叶芝）引荐给Blavatsky夫人，并与Blavatsky的侄女Vera结婚。最重要的成员之一是Henry Bedinger Mitchell（1874-1956），他在哥伦比亚大学教数学，1903 – 1938年担任《神智学季刊》的编辑，人们都称他为“教授”。他的弟弟John（1877-1956），是一名华尔街律师，也是一个成员，也许是最先与Morgan接触的人。Henry Mitchell于1956年7月去世时，他的遗产价值110万美元，留给了“活基督生命秩序”的领导人Griscom。[17]正是Mitchell的钱（以及其他人留下的资金）成为了建设礼拜堂的基础－－她说她给科尔盖特大学的钱不是她的，这也是其中的原因之一。

然而，到1956年，神智学协会便不复存在。1938年《神智学季刊》停止出版。给订阅用户的信函（1938年10月发行，但日期为1938年12月31日）写道，循环定律“教导我们，外部活动在一个时期有益，在另一个时期则危害多过益处；精神进步只能通过Indrawl（内省）来实现”。“Indrawl（内省）”是一种新术语。它并不像在“withdrawl（撤退）”中一样意味着“放弃”。相反，它指的是一个等待期，团体停下来期待一个更吉祥的时刻。“《神智学季刊》”，编辑们写道，“已经证明了它知道什么时候说话以及如何说话；现在它要证明它知道什么时候该保持沉默。”[18]具体是什么原因促使《神智学季刊》停刊，并不清楚－－但显然没有足够的第二代人员继续为此工作。Johnston在1931年去世；Hargrove在此后第二年去世；而1938年，Griscom夫人年满七十岁；Henry Bedinger Mitchell是六十四岁，他的弟弟John六十岁。

在《神智学季刊》（以及神智学协会）关闭后，那些继续留下的人，他们的行动无人知晓。据推测，他们致力于自己的精神需求；他们参观了Chapel of the Comforter（尽管该教堂也于1950年并入了韦弗利广场的圣约翰教堂）。“活基督秩序”状态良好，Griscom和Mitchell为其利益进行辩护——在1941年，于纽约最高法院就Hargrove的遗嘱进行激烈的斗争。[19]也许，他们找到了更多公共方式来推进他们的事业。Griscom夫人的孙女Joanie Griscom把Fair Hill描述为一个令人毛骨悚然的地方－－Griscom夫人的一个儿子（Ludlow）对他母亲的宗教活动深感羞耻；而另一个儿子（Clement）则是一个怪胎。关于这些，Morgan应该所知甚少。他描述的是司机驾驶的汽车以及人量形式的东西；Joanie Griscom回忆，她祖母身后跟着“教授”，称她为“我的女士”。

在看到Griscom夫人传统的房子后，Morgan决定打电话给他的朋友Walter Severinghaus和SOM。这是一次冒险行为。Morgan清楚地知道，需要淡化建筑象征主义：他认为建筑“必须为自己说话”，拥有包容性的野心意味着它不能采用共同的教会象征主义：现代建筑是可取的。[20]在制定平面图的过程中，Morgan让Griscom夫人知道，SOM是建筑师，现代艺术博物馆（商业和政府建筑）的展览会展出他们的一些作品（展览时间1957年2月26日至5月5日）。据Morgan说：“她立即打电话说她不明白建筑师如何允许他们的作品在现代艺术博物馆展出，这点她不会批准，因为该博物馆展出的作品没有一样是她会穿过街头去看的”。几个星期后，Severinghaus，Morgan和科尔盖特大学校长Everett Case带来了一个模型和平面图。他们这么做了，但却有些担心。“她听了该平面图的详细解释，没有任何评论，然后沉默了很长时间，看着模型，最后说，“嗯，它看起来很像一个温室，但你们年轻人是如此确定这是正确的方式，那我们就这么做吧。”[21]

礼拜堂位于科尔盖特大学校区的西边，由两个矩形连接，在开放的草地上组成“L”形状，像一只张开的手，俯瞰着梦莲湖和远处的山谷。建筑物上的景色十分美丽，成排的树木形成一个密集的窗帘，一直延伸至西边。人们沿着两旁都是树木的陡峭小路前进，就能找到开放的呈“L”形的礼拜堂及其玻璃走廊：这个建筑被Andrew Jackson Downing现代化版本乡村环境中的树所包围。这个地方形成了天然的露天剧场，是校园里一个独特的风景园林。没有它，校园的呼吸空间很少：西部和南部都是高松树；南边的挡土墙上是丁香花、卫矛和荚莲；北边的云杉树（原本是山茱萸）沿着石头路一直通往大门；草坪上也栽满了桦树。[22]南边就是教堂，像一个躺在水泥通道上的长方形箱子，里面有三十五个座位，正面安装了橙色的德国大教堂玻璃，角落的四条白色宽缘梁十分醒目，支撑起往外延伸的平屋顶。[23]双层玻璃使得教堂内部空间沐浴在金色的光芒中，嵌花式屏风与这金色相映成趣。晚上，灯光从里面照亮，教堂变成了一个中国灯笼，在黑暗中发出橙色光芒。悬挂的山墙天花板，尽管采用二十世纪中期的规范，完全呈现现代化，但也让人想起传统的中殿形式或帐篷内部的折叠。椅子带有扶手、靠垫和直背，以帮助人们平坐。教堂的后面是私密的木制座位室，Morgan称之为“祈祷室”，但让人想起天主教的告解室——只是没有祭司的地方。这里布置有窗帘，可以拉起来保护隐私。在祈祷室的前面是一个木制的座位区，一排六把椅子，分隔开来。这样，人们面向前边时，不会看到左边或右边的人。如有需要，还可以增加座椅。尽管可以拉起窗帘盖住，但祭坛墙上的十字架似乎有点突兀，彰显着这座建筑的目标，即服务所有的宗教。[24]教堂外部的两端有色彩丰富的花岗岩墙（带有从杨克斯带来的石头），放置成不规则的锯切图案。Morgan说服Severinghaus不要以平整的方式堆叠石头；那样的话，关于Chapel Farm的回忆就会丢失。[25]

第二个侧厅采用花岗岩墙作为主要的幕墙装置。里面是日常生活环境；实际上，该房子包含：图书馆、音乐室、主任和行政办公室、餐厅和厨房。空间很简单，原来有白色墙壁和白色石膏天花板。用餐区的插图面板含有宗教雕塑，墙上其他地方挂着Morgan收集的折衷派宗教艺术品。 Ezra Stoller的当代照片强调室内空间的简约性，艺术的限制性展示让人想起SOM在办公楼和酒店内放置艺术的成功案例。公共客厅的椅子是加高的，椅子的两侧自成角度，以加强私密性。这些都是用于自我关注的无声空间。欢迎学生、教师和游客（来自本社区及以外）的到来。楼下是七个小客房，供过夜游客使用。客房大多采用修道院的形式，有的甚至采用Morgan在印度之旅中所了解到的静修所的形式。游客来待上一段时间——至少两天——在图书馆阅读宗教文学、听音乐（在耳机上）、打坐或在树林里散步。可能会有来自校园或其他地方的居民，答疑解惑或提出建议。但是，没有安排精神议程、指定方向、或制定议程。这是一个寻找安静和灵魂的地方。交谈仅限于进餐时间。曾经，这里可以观赏到Chenango山谷的美景——当前的翻新再次强化了这些美景。最初，面向山谷的窗户很小，下面允许种植树木，以降低山谷中的车辆声音。没有任何迹象表明自然景观曾经是主要的看点。如果有的话，也是截然相反的情况。其中一个最令人叹为观止的空间位于教堂的南边。在那里，挡土墙相接，放置的一条板凳（后来添加的）可以让游客坐在教堂的裙楼和白梁之上，就像人们右手上的现代化图腾柱一样。树木遮挡，给人一种如绿洲般隔离的惊喜之感，是公园中适合人们休息的安静之地。（其中一些已经被翻修，在玻璃连接器的南边加强了与外部的连接。）

3. 那时的年轻人

J. Walter Severinghaus 是Louis Skidmore最早请来纽约办公室的员工之一。Severinghaus 毕业之后便加入Adams & Prentice，也许当时还参与了Adams & Prentice《耶鲁每日新闻》大楼（1932）项目。1938年，他开始在SOM工作；此前一年，Gordon Bunshaft Owings称Severinghaus“身怀业界良心，是一个思虑者、诚信最终保障者……”。Severinghaus的言辞和行动相当成熟；Owings认为他是最符合“温和的逻辑和理性”概念的人。[26]照片里面，Severinghaus有时看上去更像是一名律师或者家庭医生，而不是一名建筑师。他曾担任合伙人委员会纽约办公室的代表和项目经理，并且以高效闻名，曾大力帮助Gordon Bunshaft 处理Chase Manhattan（1961）项目问题，协助Michael McCarthy处理Texaco Headquarters （1973）项目问题以及其他很多项目，并因此深受赏识。[27]然而，Severinghaus并不以设计著名。礼拜堂设计来自他大学同学的委托，可能是他唯一成熟的作品。[28]可是从历史的角度来看，如果要说哪位代表了SOM作风传承，那肯定是像Severinghaus这样的人，他们将部分变成整体，随时准备好面见客户，裁决纠纷，管理合伙人委员会，同时又大部分时候居于幕后。[29]他们有可能是当代精神的定义者吗？

设计礼拜堂时，Severinghaus认真研究了当代设计。简单的平屋顶和抽象形式主义是SOM此前秉承的，体现在Connecticut General （1955） 、加州卡梅尔市美国研究生技术学院（1955）（United States Post Graduate Technical School （1955））以及一些小学，其中比如纽约斯克内克塔迪市 Grout Creek小学(1954)的设计当中。然而，礼拜堂在某种程度上却给人一种失败者的感觉。建筑两部分弯曲的平面图让人想起Marcel Breuer独具特色的双核心式平面图，有如Geller House （1947）、McComb House （1951)或者Ferry House （1952）的感觉，甚至让人回想起Frank Lloyd Wright的Unity Temple （联合教堂）(1908)。入口庭院处堆砌的花岗岩墙采用一种类似于细致的摊铺地砖的图案，也是最受欢迎的Breuer 图案。[30]然而这些墙，与白色的宽翼结构搭配在一起令人惊奇。柱子位于外侧，与支撑的横梁形成层流，让人想起Mies van der Rohe为伊利诺伊州普莱诺市设计的Farnsworth House（1951）；后来在旧金山SOM崭露头角的Myron Goldsmith （1918–1986)也设计过。这里的横梁让人联想起日本的寺庙，佛寺，甚至最简单的原始小屋或者是《走向新建筑》（*Vers Une Architecture*）(1923)中带有Le Corbusier“原始寺庙”建筑特点的帐篷。平面图中还可以看出对Eero Saarinen MIT 教堂（MIT Chapel）(1955)的回忆，如教堂内部的金色色调，风格简洁的玻璃走廊（作为最初构造），装饰有垂直移位矩形的竖框，连接着两侧的附楼。通过使用与众不同的方式，Severinghaus设计的马赛克墙甚至与Harry Bertoia在MIT 教堂（MIT Chapel）内圣坛屏风雕刻中那逐渐消失的浴室在感觉上有几分相似。

礼拜堂是在类型学陷入危机之时对当代宗教建筑的重要贡献。神学家Reinhold Niebuhr曾在《建筑实录》（1953）（*Architectural Record* (1953)）一书中一篇名为《宗教建筑：传统与当代之精神》（“Religious Building: Tradition and Today's Ethos”）、十分具有影响力的文章中指出，人们将哥特式建筑融入当代所做的努力饱受“拟古主义”影响，因而证明“宗教或建筑传统中没有足够的活力让传统能够适应并运用到当代利益中去”。[31]一年之后，Walter Netsch设计的美国空军学院机械化哥特式教堂(1954)（Chapel for the Air Force Academy (1954)）正面挑战了这一观点。[32]当然在宗教圈中，Rudolf Schwarz (1897–1961)设计的建筑要比其他教堂建筑更受欢迎，比如Mies van der Rohe设计的伊利诺伊州理工大学的教堂（1952）（Robert F. Carr Chapel (1952)），尽管一开始这一教堂是由美国新教圣公会资助的，但后来成为了非宗派的“上帝的盒子。”礼拜堂异乎寻常的宗教特点，遵循的是另一条路，更接近比利时天主教作家Frédéric Debuyst (b. 1922)阐述的原则。对于他和他的美国新教信徒Edward Sövik (1918–2014)来说，教堂应当作为一个“庆祝审美提升、庆祝仁慈用的客厅。”教堂应当为接待客人而设计，并创造像家一样的环境，让人舒适。丰富的艺术空间创造了一个“平静、充满回忆且让人易懂的庆典。”[33]随后，Sövik到访日本，他发现日本的茶屋——在一个融合环境和精神的建筑中，其茶道不失为一个有效典范。[34]Severinghaus可以说是身临其境。Colgate的修行之所（“ashram”）带有住宿、餐饮功能以及用于冥想和祈祷的室内空间，同时还附带有教堂，提供适当升华机会，具有与原来的宗教活动类似的效果。

Morgan和Severinghaus是否在礼拜堂的设计中反应了Griscom的神智学理念还很难说。“礼拜堂”这个名字的选择则明显是对应了“教堂农场（Chapel Farm）”。这一石头堆砌的概念（不去说石头的来源）可能也是对Griscom的Fair Hill宫殿的一种认可。在 Fair Hill宫殿上方，房子后头的岩石景观中伫立着一个十字架。在教堂的屏风上竖立一个十字架也可能让人联想起Morgan为主顾设计的房屋。然而，最后，是对宗教的多方面赞助以及对冥想的强调代表了这一项目最重要的部分。这一项目由Morgan、Griscom（以及Mitchell——很可能是捐赠的最终来源）共同承担。

1907年，Mitchell出版了一本关于冥想的书；根据宗教历史学家Karl Baier的说法，这是现代第一本有关这一主题的书。[35]在他的书中，Mitchell列出了让人一路从外部世界到得以窥探内心世界的七个步骤以及这一路中要避免的七种危险、启明的七个方面——冥想的启蒙。很明显，Griscom夫人在捐助时，曾就冥想的核心与哈佛大学的管理人员做了交流。在哈佛大学的世界宗教中心（Center for World Religions），Josep Luis Sert将冥想的房间设计在了建筑物的最高点。Morgan也可能收到了同样的信息，有人想知道他在礼拜堂项目开发中有多大程度考虑到捐赠者的愿望或她对Mitchell信念的阐述？双核平面图的布局，创造了一个通俗的空间（生活区）和一个深奥的空间（教堂）。

Mitchell的理念也可能使Griscom认为Colgate为自己的捐助提供了一个合适的场所。在哥伦比亚大学期间，Mitchell曾任教育委员会主席，他们一道倡导宗教基础的课程。这门课程应当“特点是完全非宗教的，并且不应当由任何一个宗派的神职人员任教。”[36]也许Mitchel在试图任命他神智学同事Charles Johnston教授这门课程时就已经超越了这一底线。当时的哥伦比亚大学校长否决了这一任命，取而代之的是宗教部的某位人员。因此，Mitchell对多元宗教教育的奉献必定是决定有多少款项分配的关键因素。

这个关于神智学和建筑的故事，可以反映很多东西。在神智学协会的“内省”式谦逊中，有许多令人钦佩的东西。正如Iris Murdoch提醒的那样，谦逊“是对现实的无私尊重，是所有美德中最难做到但却最重要的一个”。[37] Morgan和Severinghaus完全符合神智学者“内省”式谦逊，他们有着自己在建筑学方面的谦逊。

Griscom夫人愿意接受她圈子（和品位）以外的现实世界，以及Morgan能够与这个不同寻常的利益相关者取得联系，这两点是这个故事的关键部分。 SOM别具一格地将新式解决方案运用于传统问题上——在Terrace Plaza、 Lever House、Manufacturers Trust上的应用更为人所知——这种做法也在这里发挥作用，即使Severinghaus在公司的主要工作不是设计师。也许Morgan对该场地的描述勾起了Griscom夫人的回忆，她在《神智学季刊》中发表观点：“我上山去与我自己的心进行交流，站在那里看着星星。”[38]但是，关于这一点，我们一无所知；她去世之前，从没见过这栋建筑物，从没看过这个建筑场地，也没有对她的想法做过任何个人记录。

4.翻修的特征

礼拜堂的揭牌仪式于1959年3月举行，学生报纸将Kenneth Morgan列为“Maroon年度人物”。[39]就其意图和目的而言，这是校园内第一座具有符号性（以及功能性）的现代建筑——其到来没有在校园报纸上刊登。[40]它最初取名“纽约上州冥想教堂（Upstate New York Meditation Chapel）”，但在揭牌仪式之前，更名为“礼拜堂”。像文丘里后来的“公会议事厅（Guild House）”一样，它在Morgan的贵格会传统中没有一篇文章加以定义。礼拜堂很快成为了贵格会会议和犹太教服务（在教堂）的举办地、介绍东方宗教的讲座和演示场所，以及喜欢其安静和平环境、寻求自我机会的游客聚集地。[41]（1974年，Morgan退休，由专注于亚洲研究的John Ross Carter和 Robert Ho教授继承；2013年，哲学和犹太研究教授Steven Kepnes成为主任。）

事实证明Severinghaus的建筑十分耐用——时光流逝，建筑内部上了油漆，仅此而已。事实上，十几年前走进礼拜堂，即是走进了时光倒流：每个细节、栏杆、把手和浴室配件都是半个世纪前的样式：样式齐全，令人身临其境，回味无穷。或许，Morgan使用艺术刺激宗教思维的热情，充斥着各个墙壁，对该建筑十分有利。但该建筑更有力地反射出宁静的特性，即使单一的窗格、照明、幕墙和装置都不可避免地极力彰显现代化气息。

Coldham&Hartman位于马萨诸塞州阿默斯特市，在其最近完成的工作中，试图在更新建筑物的同时保全其性质。或多或少的改变是有必要的：清除石棉；安装地热热泵；能量回收通风机；把西侧现有的幕墙更换成现代化的组件，以尽量减少热损失；新的无障碍浴室；更换屋顶以改善排水，增加绝缘，只有加厚的屋顶轮廓会损坏原有建筑的线条。其他改变对于用户体验具有一定的意义：南侧的门将玻璃连接器分开，为个人或团体提供通道进入小庭院。原来的走廊玻璃更换成更节能、但极度普通的样式。房子室内的西侧新添加了电梯，窗户也更宽敞了。厨房设施也已更新，从用餐区经过一个类似走廊的通道，进入一个带窗户的房间；如原来所设想的那样，用餐功能区会被移除，其空间将用于建造客厅。

将教堂里的十字架去掉，似乎是可能的；十字架的存在被人们称赞，认为其承认这是一个礼拜场所，但是按照当代标准，它的意义可能太狭隘——尽管有一个窗帘可用来把它遮住。对礼拜堂文化旧秩序构成挑战的是非正式学生——教师团体将聚集教堂内，试图让更多的学生熟悉其功能——实心砖石墙具有隔音功能。礼拜堂将成为进行宗教间讨论的特殊场所——这也是Griscom夫人将礼拜堂这份礼物送给科尔盖特大学时所设计的一项活动。室内更换了新的颜色，采用Sherwin&Williams“雪花石膏”。为建筑物增添宗教画廊气氛的艺术，也将随着时间的推移而越发显得精致和经典。

清晰的原始设计创造出安宁的效果：教堂中的素色玻璃散发着光芒，宽缘梁呈现白色，石头透着温暖。这个建筑展现着它与生俱来的圆形剧场特性。Reinhold Niebuhr在1953年《建筑实录》中写到“精神”，他引入了这个词，想知道哥特式风格是否“是基督教信仰精神的最完美表达，或是否反映出太多的中世纪精神，而不能表达当代精神”的信念；然而他发现它“表达的东西比一个过去时代的精神更加普遍[......]。”也许对于礼拜堂而言，不论是Breuer在粗糙的石头中的发现，还是Mies在白钢中发现，都是一样的，都是来自于它所处的时代，也同样服务于任何其他时代。Owings可能从没去过科尔盖特大学；礼拜堂白桦树和云杉具有精神治疗功效，坐在通往教堂的柔软的斜坡上，轮转焰火的嘶嘶声和7月4日的噩梦看起来很遥远。它是一个冥想的地方。菲利普·拉金（Philip Larkin）的诗歌“去教堂”浮现在脑海：“在严肃的土地上，一栋严肃的房子.....”教堂本应该这样——即便你先想到建筑，然后才想到宗教。

致谢：非常感谢礼拜堂现任和前任主任Steven Kepnes和John Ross Carter教授（科尔盖特大学）的慷慨帮助。David Morgan（卫斯理大学）允许我研究他父亲的文章，并从他父亲的生平中对礼拜堂进行讨论。Elizabeth Morgan、 Alan Morgan 和Scott Morgan阅读了手稿，我也试图将他们的意见反映出来。John Severinghaus（佛蒙特州诺维奇）分享了他父亲在回忆建筑物时展现的自豪感。 Philip Purcell和John Winkler帮助我分析了J. Walter Severinghaus的品质和性格。 Sandra Galuten非常热情地带我参观了Riverdale附近的Fair Hill（今天的Fieldstone）。这座建筑是她满怀深爱，努力使其恢复生机的。我与Griscom夫人的孙女Joanie Griscom进行了漫长而卓有成效的谈话，这帮助我弄明白许多问题。 Paul

Ivey（亚利桑那大学）讨论了有关礼拜堂的问题，并对神智学的历史提出了深刻见解。Wayne Kempton（纽约圣公会主教辖区）提供了关于Chapel of the Comforter的信息。马萨诸塞州阿默斯特C&H Architects的Thomas Hartman在翻修期间向我介绍了礼拜堂。Robert Dwyer和Robert McVaugh（科尔盖特大学）为我填补了有关科尔盖特大学建筑史知识的空缺。谨以本文献给David Schenck，致我们终生不变的友谊。

1 Nathaniel Alexander Owings，《两者之间的空间：一位建筑师的旅程》（波士顿：霍顿·米夫林出版公司，1973），第3页。

2 华盛顿特区美国国会图书馆对Nathaniel A. Owings论文《两者之间的空间》初稿的审查，揭示开篇所描写的噩梦是这篇变化无常的文本中的一个常量。参见Adams，“归属感作为企业理想：Nathaniel A. Owings of Skidmore, Owings & Merrill writes The Spaces in Between,”《L'architetto: ruolo, volto, mito》，编辑Guido Beltramini 和Howard Burns（威尼斯：Marsilio出版社，2009），第323－42页。

3 J. A., “SOM: The Chicago Office of Skidmore, Owings & Merrill,” 《室内设计》（1959年1月），第 90–109页。

4 I感谢卫斯理大学历史名誉教授David Morgan，给我提供机会研究和引用Kenneth Morgan的自传手稿“回忆”。这项工作的副本与Morgan家族有关，将存放在科尔盖特大学的特色文献和大学档案。

5 Morgan, “回忆”，第40页。

6 Morgan，编辑，《印度教的宗教信仰》（纽约：罗纳德出版社，1953）；《佛陀之路》（纽约：罗纳德出版社，1956）；《伊斯兰教——笔直之路》（纽约：罗纳德出版社，1958）。

7 哈佛中心的建筑师是Josep Luis Sert（1960）。在哈佛中心的基础上，Morgan，“记忆”，第239-44页。另见，John B. Carman和Kathryn Dodgson的“建筑物”，《社区与科学：世界宗教研究中心1958-2003》（剑桥：世界宗教研究中心，2006）。Griscom夫人对哈佛建筑没有明显的影响，尽管在该建筑最高处的冥想室与科尔盖特大学的冥想室有同等重要性。哈佛神学院高级讲师Charles Hallisey把这两座建筑称为“姐妹”建筑。

8 Morgan，“回忆”，第246页。 Griscom给科尔盖特大学的费用暗示了她过去的神智学经历，也让人想起她给哈佛的赠礼条款。“我们希望鼓励对世界宗教的同情心研究，以彰显所有宗教的基本统一和现实背景——它们在精神世界中的共同根源——每个人都可以从他所信奉宗教的真相中获得更清晰的洞察力和更坚定的信念。”见《Mid-York Weekly》，1956年12月13日。见Morgan，“回忆”，第350页。

9 Morgan，“回忆”，第 40页。Morgan留下了一本三页的礼拜堂原则声明，日期为1958年5月12日。见科尔盖特大学特色文献和大学档案，第29栏，A1000。副本也存于纽约的SOM营销司档案中。

10 她不想透露姓名，这点得到科尔盖特大学和Morgan一家的充分尊重。她告诉Morgan：“我是一个老妇人，很快我会去另一边与我的朋友们见面。如果我为耶和华做了一些事，并添加了我的名字，看到他们时我会感到羞愧。”引自《礼拜堂：在教堂：艺术作品介绍以及礼拜堂的建设方式和原因》，无日期油印卷，推测为Morgan所著，第48页。她隐藏姓名的另一个原因是她给Morgan的钱不是她的钱。Morgan认识她的两个律师，Marjorie Kilpatrick和Annette Lewis。后者也住在Chapel Farm。她一部分可用财富来自Ernest Temple Hargrove（1870-1938）。在纽约州最高法院的一个凌乱的法庭案件中，Hargrove的孩子们在遗嘱争夺中失败了。见下文，注解17。

11 Morgan是1929级；Severinghaus是1928级。

12 Morgan没有提及她的神智学，但她的确给礼拜堂留下了神智学的书籍（据Carter 和Kepnes教授所述）。另见Morgan，“回忆”，附录C，第 350页和第 351页。

13 感谢纽约圣公会主教辖区的档案管理员Wayne Kempton提供有关Clark和Chapel of the Comforter的信息。

14 该建筑综合体由一个豪宅、四个住宅和几个小别墅组成。她去世时，她的地产价值540万美元。她留下了50万美元给儿子，其余的委托给“宗教和教育组织——

活基督秩序外部法院公司”。《先驱政治家》（杨克斯），1962年11月30日。该建筑综合体的建筑师不为人知。Griscom夫人可能认识加利福尼亚州的民族主义者和建筑师Birger Elwing（1867-1935），他设计为Henry Bedinger Mitchell的书《冥想》（见注解16）。今天在Fieldstone找到的花朵卷轴天花板，可能来源于Elwing。人们断言（例如，参见，《华尔街日报》，2012年5月18日），该团体在等待第二次回归，把房子空置，以做准备。这些信息似乎来自Griscom夫人的律师，他被怀疑不忠（2016年10月3日，来自Joanie Griscom的口头交谈）。《神智学季刊》中没有任何证据表明该团体对基督的回归有任何幻想——也就是说，一些人认为回归总是可能的，但是这点几乎没有重要到以“第二次回归”作为暗示。

15 《碎片》（纽约：季度图书部，1916、1920和1925三册）

16 见1941年5月纽约州最高法院上诉庭——Ernest Temple Hargrove最后遗嘱第一司审判。

17 《先驱政治家》（杨克斯），1958年6月2日。

18 见《神智学季刊》第34期，编号 4（1938年10月），第 352页之后，但页码不详。

19 见注解17。

20 相比之下，哈佛大学世界宗教研究中心虽然源于现代主义者，但通过Sert的地中海联系，从而参考了东西方的建筑。第一任主任写到，它是“一个应该使东、西方都感到宾至如归的环境”。引自《建筑物》，John B. Carman 和Kathryn Dodgson，《社区和学术：世界宗教研究中心1958-2003》（剑桥：世界宗教研究中心，2006），第92页。 Griscom夫人对哈佛的设计没有直接的了解。从Chapel Farm的房子可以看出，Griscom夫人品味似乎很传统。虽然Griscom客户对自己严苛的个性毫不遮掩，但无法从她那儿得知Chapel Farm的建筑师。关于Irving Kane Pond的神智学运动总部——位于伊利诺斯州惠顿L.W. Rogers Building大厦（1927），她所知道的有多少，我们也无从得知。她也没有提到20世纪30年代最著名的神智学建筑师Claude Bragdon（1866-1946）。

21 《礼拜堂：简介》，第48页。

22 景观和种植平面图由科尔盖特大学设施部于1959年4月24日制定。平面图的作者没有记录在工作表上。唯一归属人是Skidmore Owings&Merrill。作者可能是Joanna Diman，但很少有人知道她的信息。有标注显示，1950-1963间她从加州来到SOM工作。Robert McVaugh很友好地给我寄来了平面图的照片，并慷慨地提供了他对这栋建筑及其场址的见解。

23 模型的照片表明，教堂前面可能有一个雕塑。唯一幸存的一张模型照片没有足够显示雕塑的细节。参见《Colgate Maroon》，1958年3月12日。

24 教堂里的十字架十分恼人。它可以被正当解释为（“因为修建礼拜堂的是基督徒”），或是因为捐助者是一个基督徒，而且在她Chapel Farm地产上也有一个大十字架。

25 经过四次尝试，才解决了建筑物的这个问题。同样，关于石头的起源，见Morgan，“回忆”，第 258页。Morgan也可能希望参考禅宗佛教的砌石做法。

26 Owings,《两者之间的空间》，第73-74页

27 Severinghaus通过婚姻与Luce家庭产生了关联，这可能足以对SOM在《财富》，《建筑论坛》和《时代》杂志上收到的慷慨报道作出解释。

28 Severinghaus负责Celotex公司的设计，作为SOM预制房屋工作的一部分。参见Hyun-Tae Jung，“Technologically Modern: The Prefabricated House and the War Time Experience of Skidmore Owings and Merrill”，《 Sanctioning Modernism: Architecture and the Making of Postwar Identities》，编辑 Vladimir Kulic, Timothy Parker, Monica Penick（奥斯汀：德克萨斯大学出版社，2014），第186-218页。有些SOM人员对Severinghaus的作者身份表示质疑——他一点都不像设计师。我向SOM的长期律师Philip Purcell和纽约办事处前主管John Winkler提出了这个问题。两人都同意，如果Severinghaus说他做过某些事情，那么他就的确做了。

29 芝加哥办公室的一个类似的人物是William

Hartmann（1916-2003），他把Severinghaus描述为“一座力量之塔”。《William Hartmann的口述历史》，由芝加哥Betty Blum进行采访：芝加哥艺术学院，2003修订版，第166页。

30 参见，例如，Thompson House（1947），Robinson House（1948），Breuer House（1948），Clark House（1949）等等。

31 Niebuhr，“宗教建筑：传统和今日宗教”，《建筑实录》第144期，编号6（1953年12月），第117-118页。

32 Robert Allen Nauman，《现代主义的翅膀：联合空军学院》（乌尔巴纳和芝加哥：伊利诺伊大学出版社，2004），第5章。

33 引自 Richard Kieckhefer，《石头神学：从拜占庭到伯克利的教堂建筑》（牛津：牛津大学出版社，2004), 第 124页。

34 Kieckhefer，《石头神学》，第125-26页。

35 Henry Bedinger Mitchell，《冥想》（纽约：季度图书部，无日期，1906年或1907年）。此后，德语和拉脱维亚语翻译出现。参见Karl Baier，《Meditation und Moderne: Zur Genese Eines Kernbereichs ModernerSpiritualitätin der Wechselwirkung Zwischen Westeuropa, Nordamerika und Asien》（Würzburg: Konigshausen, Neumann, 2009），第一部，第397页。

36 参见哥伦比亚大学档案馆的材料，系列一：中央档案1890，第662号文本，第12号文件。引自写给哥伦比亚大学校长Nicholas Murray Butler的一封信，日期为1909年6月10日。感谢Lindsay Cook在哥伦比亚大学档案进行的研究。

37 Iris Murdoch, 《The Sovereignty of Good》(London: Ark Paperbacks, 1985)，第95页。

38 Cavé, 《碎片》，第1册，第18页。

39 《The Colgate Maroon》，1959年5月20日。

40 McKim Mead&White（1954）设计的宿舍是校园内的第一座现代主义建筑。其后是O’Connor和Kilham设计的大学图书馆（1959）和Oscar F. Wiggins设计的瑞德运动中心（1959）。

41 在布林茅尔学院的一次讲座中，Morgan指出，书籍、音乐和艺术是“传播宗教见解”的三个基本媒介。（1961年11月21日的讲义）。

关于现代记忆：砖块案例研究 作者：Marco Roth

“红砖有其特定的色调——一种深暗、几乎和谐的红色，暗淡，且缀满蓝色——这是我在圣路易斯度过的童年。不是真正的童年，应该是从启蒙到离家上大学的那段假童年时光。那种红砖色调和绿色树叶象征着圣路易斯的夏季（冬季只有灰色的天空、拥挤的校车和学校油毡地板上的湿脚印），而那种红砖和浅淡的天空象征着春季。还有孤独、古怪和自怜，想探究那个家中有大难来临之感的孩子。”
—*Harold Brodkey,*“恩宠的状态”（State of Grace），出自（*First Love and Other Sorrows,1987*）

“为了上帝之爱, *Montresor*！”
——*Edgar Allen Poe,The Cask of Amontillado,1846*

“当你问砖头想要什么，它说‘我想要拱门’。”
—*Louis Kahn,*讲座内容，*1971–1973*

很久以前，当我还是高中毕业生时，我像现在一样翻开 Harold Brodkey 的短篇小说集《*First Love and Other Sorrows*》，并被第一句话深深吸引，“红砖有其特定的色调——一种深暗、几乎和谐的红色，暗淡，且缀满蓝色——这是我在圣路易斯度过的童年。”我对砖块的了解不多，对美国西部的门户城市也所知甚少；我的孩童时光只有曼哈顿宽阔大道上泛白的、有花岗岩覆盖的公寓楼，褐砂石小路和混凝土游乐场。但小说中这句话的含义有引发性，它的简约风格有训诫性。我决不敢用如此简洁、如此总括的联系词写作：只用一种颜色和一种建筑材料来表达整段人生！这不是隐喻，而是一种实际的存在状态。Brodkey 为我能感受到但无法形容的东西赋予了声音：一种让建筑编码并反映经验的感觉。作为一名建筑师，我是记忆宫殿中熟悉的古典修辞手法的回声；工作时，我调动国内外旅途中的记忆，将临时材料转化为真实世界的真实地点。而且，当真实地点建成之后，无论后续有谁经过，无论是有意识还是无意识，他们将依次使用一些能唤起记忆的感觉作为搜索标志，可搜索他们的过去或明确的自我，他们的精神，以及他们的思想——正如 Brodkey 的砖块中嵌入了如以下这句话中多变而又玄妙的含义“想探究那个家中有大难来临之感的孩子”。

“恩宠的状态”这段话一直伴随我旅行；我发现令人不敢置信的是，我竟然能轻松回忆起——我醒来后哼几段歌曲的样子——令我惊讶的是，这是在我搬到一个地方并在这里度过大部分成年生活之后。几乎从殖民地时期开始，位于距特拉华河与大西洋交汇口六十英里远的平坦湿地上的费城，一直是一个红砖城市。城内最开始的明智做法——随处可得的粘土、预防类似伦敦大火（曾在费城建立十年前席卷伦敦的木质建筑）等火灾的渴望——在历经数个世纪后，变成了一种精神和身份，并在如今得到了法律和习俗的加强。砖块不仅修建了仓库与工厂。为工人、手工艺人修建的拥挤、低矮的三层楼房也由红砖格栅堆砌而成。在尚存的马厩街和巷道中，还有一些用砖头砌成的奴隶宿舍、马车房和服务房，这些如今已成为昂贵的“历史”财产。在整个 19 世纪，即使是费城老牌贵格会精英人士和工业家的豪宅也由一层层红砖砌成，并配有二条狭窄的过道。

自 1955 年开始，一系列历史保护法责令位于特拉华河（Delaware Rivier）与斯古吉尔河（Schuykill River）之间大部分老区的新建筑，应尽量与原始红砖的颜色和样式保持一致，而它们自己不能随意选择砖块。这些法规负责保护费城砖块现代主义的一些标志性建筑——这种现代主义是一种当地风格，体现二十世纪中期现代主义的意向前瞻性建筑形式，与砖块记录的 19 世纪日常历史性之间的极度紧张的气氛。我的目光首先被 Saarinen 设计的宾夕法尼亚大学宿舍所吸引；这位芬兰籍建筑师在向殖民地学院大厅以及由他同胞 Alvar Aalto 设计的麻省理工大学贝克宿舍楼（Baker House）致敬。由于宾夕法尼亚大学宿舍不具备贝克宿舍楼的优势：有蜿蜒曲折的查尔斯河提供充足的采光和轮廓线，而且被附近后来修建的建筑所遮挡，这栋由 Saarinen 设计的建筑在街道网格中黯淡失色。这提醒人们，保护主义或环保主义的精神不能只用材料来保持。建筑情绪的构成因素并非只有材料。

沿着市中心老华盛顿广场漫步而行，我曾遇到一个突然开阔的地方；那是个夹在街道之间的广场，前面铺有砖块，乔治·华盛顿雕像的饰牌宣示着美利坚共和国人民在早期英雄年代的丰功伟绩。广场内有一些建造于中世纪、被细致分割开的立方体建筑，由棕色砖块打造——当然——周围环绕着砖砌庭院，还立有神秘的球形路灯。这些是贝聿铭于 1962 年修建的华盛顿广场东部联排住宅；建筑群由 40 套低层住宅组成，静静伫立在附近社会山塔的阴影里。在空白的中世纪城市更新项目中，社会山塔发挥了近似承上启下的作用。这些联排住宅几乎具有复古未来主义（19 世纪小说中的词语，用于描述想象中的乌托邦）的效果——但它们的半层形式和同材质高墙带有一种暗黑气息；这些高墙用于分割每套住宅门前的小花园和院子，同时对每套住宅的大落地窗进行部分遮挡，并切断到达一楼的光线。这些高墙是围墙内的围墙，是对隐私或被害妄想症的赞歌。这些住宅属于费城人口减少、白人群飞、人们害怕犯罪率或社区种族融合的时代。它们的建造材料遵从历史和法规，仅显示出它们与自由的梦想以及不言而喻的平等相距多远，而这些自由与平等是在仅数步之遥的同材质会议建筑中成形的。

为了保持这些老社区的特性，费城的美学条例也意外地让这座城市学会了遗忘。如今，普遍存在的砖制风格在更大程度上是一种固定的习惯或市场，而不仅仅是正式的法规。几乎老社区的所有新建筑皆为砖制或砖制颜色。这些陈旧、包有特卫强(Tyvek) 汽膜的郊区风格联排住宅配有车库，统一等待着它们的“红色外衣，犹如英国军队的新兵一样”。我想，这让业主有一种未住在新泽西的感觉。当区划委员会允许百老街（Broad Street）上修建一栋高 375 英尺的住宅大楼——市政厅，委员会仅允许这栋楼的砌块和钢框架覆盖粉色及栗色的仿砖镶板，形成一种本地评论家所比喻的效果：“一个巨大的pepto-bismol瓶”。镶板没法遵从任何历史保护逻辑，却似乎是对残余的谦虚与传统的补偿，是羞愧和无耻的一种模糊标志。每天从它投下的阴影中经过时，我经常想，若有人要写一段关于普通差品位的历史——不是指媚俗、华丽或花哨，仅仅指平庸、缺乏想象力和毫无个性——这座建筑就值得写一章。

在过于自怜的情绪中——Brodkey 将这种情绪与他的砖块童年联系在一起——我还经常想，如果我没有在这个城市居住，我是否会有这样的想法。民众将遗产变成了一个地方的一部分特征。无论建筑质量有何不同——也许是由于不同质量造成了对其共同元素意识的强行提高——经过日积月累后，所有这些砖块的效果皆在遗憾中千篇一律，或呈现单一的色调。这就像，我受到限制，只能用 200 字的词汇与人交流。别人告诉我这是一种过敏反应。若是由另一种材料主导建筑风格的其它城市，我也会有这种感觉吗？例如，遍布白色地中海石头的伊比萨岛，满地赭色粘土的马拉喀什，或是托斯卡纳山城？虽然习惯可以让经验变得陈旧，但我想我的失范会带来不同的品位，并在迷宫般的多层住宅楼之间引导其它方向。

一定程度上，这是一个关于材料如何与其大环境互动的问题。对乐于接受的人来说，托斯卡纳的石头和马拉喀什的粘土似乎是在模仿它们周围的自然风貌，或至少是在融入其中；而工业红砖在许多方面皆是一种典型的人类纪或人类中心主义材料。无论是单独呈现还是整体呈现，它们更像是对人类努力的不断演示，而不是对现有自然形式的模仿。如 William Blake 对 18 世纪末科学和工业精神的描述，它们“将人类所有想象力石化成石块和沙子”。实际上，它们倾向于抹灭特定的自然特征，并将其变成统一且几乎反历史的空间。然后，砖块保持了其固有的历史，并被人们所牢记，即使这些砖块在使用前曾庆祝过另一段历史的抹灭。值得主意的是，当砖块——因经济性和统一性而有着无法抗拒的工业用途，虽然它们有其前现代历史性——被大量融入 20 世纪中叶的大规模现代主义建筑中，例如 Gordon Bunshaft 于 1951 年设计的划时代作品：位于 East 66th Street 的 Manhattan House 公寓大楼，以及之后的许多类似建筑，它们变成了白色。一种淡色釉让它们产生了一种失血后的骨白色；建筑史上，它们被用作幻想游乐场或乌托邦模式社区的石膏或灰泥墙，并用于展示 19 世纪 90 年代或 20 世纪 20 年代的住宅。

矛盾的是，这些砖块所保留的历史希望我们忘却另一段历史。如旧世界（Old World）、曼彻斯特和利物浦的砖块交易及制造有同源性一样，费城由新教伦理塑造，并由早期工业革命激发。对平等的渴望、对虚荣和花哨的不信任以及备受推崇的劳动精神，一次垒起一座建筑，交织着对利润的追求却不显山露水的希望；鉴于普通人类弱点的轻微扭曲，这些基础美德在普通行动和外表方面，可以表现为统一性、封锁性、廉价性、缺乏想象力和假谦虚。如此一来，功利的砖块成为了一种虚伪的面子，并且阻碍了它原本想要展现的开明建筑。这正是 Brodkey 将圣路易斯红色色调与“假童年”联系在一起时所表达的含义——一段假装、例行且墨守成规的时期，没有要了解自己是谁、为何他要这样做的意识。

一位作家在他的几个故事中谈到了似乎毫无动机的恶意，并对材料中一些固有的心理封闭状态进行了更黑暗的解读。这名作家在北费城一位水管工的砖房中租住了

6 年（这栋住房依然伫立在第 7 街，位于被错误命名为“春天花园”的大道北侧）。在 Edgar Allen Poe 的《黑猫》和《一桶白葡萄酒》中，关于 *bête-noires*（令人讨厌的人或物）被封在新砌体后的描述对恐怖场景的描写至关重要。这两本小说中，谋杀都起源于叙事者受伤的虚荣心。他们一定要消灭那些曾冒犯过他们的因素。小说用卖弄式的操作步骤以及一丝狂躁的冲动感来描述砌砖过程，“我弄来了石灰、黄沙和一些毛发，做好一切准备，我就调配了一种与旧灰泥无法区分的新灰泥，”杀死妻子后意外将小猫与尸体一起砌起来的男人如此承认道：“我把最后一块石头塞好，抹上灰泥。再紧靠着这堵新墙，重新堆好尸骨，”Montresor 忽视敌人 Fortunato 的求饶声说道。此处的保留或恢复表示犯罪的抹灭，或是犯罪本身的一部分。砌在尸体外的新墙看上去就像旧墙一样！墙壁本身是一种神秘的秩序象征；只有我们得知它暗藏的东西时，它才变得可怕起来。在 Poe 看来，并不是砖块将邪恶的秘密完美地掩盖起来，而是邪恶的秘密本身是无法掩盖的，因为没有犯罪能彻底天衣无缝，以致于无法承受犯罪者的吹嘘和坦白，直至他大声喊道，“我把那个怪物砌在坟墓里了！”

即使在 1846 年，Poe 依然认为不加修饰与一切如常的外表下也可能蕴含着犯罪或合谋。（这些犯罪对城市居民的良知有多大影响取决于他或她每日能承受的想象力）若在建筑学中解读 Poe，人们想知道 Montresor 的残忍设计是否是根据砖体建筑所展示的机会而构想出来的，正对应他感受到 Fortunato 的冒犯后所作出的纠正：为壁龛提供一个有序的追溯目的，而这个壁龛正是将砖体砌成拱形通道的无意结果：“里面还有一个壁龛”，用 Poe 的话形容道，“深约四英尺，宽达三英尺，高六七英尺。似乎当初建造后并没打算派什么特别的用处，不过是墓窖顶下两根大柱间的空隙罢了。”Montresor 的新墙与两根大柱子在同一平面上，纠正了这种异常的旧形式并隐藏了投机取巧的新功能。

这些砖墙、拱顶和拱门的图形恰巧成为了，中世纪现代主义最著名的实质性寓言以及记忆的中央符号——尤其是作为情感信号的个人记忆，投射到建筑材料本身的虚构意识上，并转变为正式的欲望。这个寓言出自 1971 年至 1973 年间，路易・康（Louis Kahn）各个讲座版本中一段著名的话，谈论一块砖想变成拱门材料的假定愿望——此处转录自 1071 年路易・康在宾夕法尼亚大学的研究生授课中：“你问砖，‘你想要什么?’砖告诉你，‘我喜欢拱门。’如果你对它说，‘造一座拱门太昂贵了，我可以在你上面做一个混凝土过梁。你说好吗？’砖答道，‘我喜欢拱门。’”尊重你所使用的材料是非常重要的。[……]只有尊重它，成就它，而不是欺骗它，你才能用好这块砖。”

然而，无论路易・康的话多么动听，我还是将这段警言视为一种含蓄的批判：路易・康在北费城童年时期的建筑——一栋又一栋的砖体建筑，在发展到他自己的首个实质性作品时达到了一种顶峰；该作品是设计于 1938 年、位于北费城橡树街（Oak Lane）的 Ahavath 以色列犹太教堂（Ahavath Israel Synagogue），其前立面是由深红色砖块砌成的单调的纯矩形。这种建筑材料上演了一段令人振奋的推定对话，路易・康表示了一种抗议，由砖块本身发声，反对顽固的堆积和成为拱门的野心。但实际上，没有什么东西的结构能清楚地表示砖想成为拱门；由费城大多数人来判断，似乎砖块真的想成为墙，想被堆积成排然后做成类似更大号砖块的版本：巨大的墙组成更大片的砖块形状。若要让砖块做别的事情，须进行思维跳跃——或者在路易・康的情况中是回忆的跳跃——其中，拱门和拱心石的创新性布局可以由粘土块或石块（很重，但善于承压）受压支撑，而且它们跨越的距离远大于任何粘土块或石块的尺寸。对于路易・康，他的回忆将是他在 1928 年欧洲大巡航时曾表示钦佩的罗马及中世纪废墟，或是远至加德满都砖体建筑的民间建筑（他曾于 20 世纪 70 年代初访问加德满都）。

在中世纪现代主义大师中，路易・康因其对过去的探寻而饱受赞誉：对过去（像他之后的贝聿铭）的铭记、容忍，甚至对拱门的赞扬，而他的一些同辈人将拱门视为呆板古典主义的最终象征；以及按照心境、而不是方式，设想了大量与经典废墟遗迹类似的混凝土和砖块作品。他将那些作品归结为“颠倒的毁灭”；一些“颠倒”为材料自身的行为，将材料变成与本来相反的样子，例如利用罗马拱门将费城砖变得像芝加哥钢铁一样敏捷、高耸。这种破坏般的准颠覆及其审美平等性——Brodkey 式灾难探究的结果——自然是战后中世纪建筑作品的一部分。回望那些中世纪建筑，我们会发现它们是如此渴望自由的突破，却又希冀着归属感——犹如一些城市流亡者努力在热情、环绕的围墙之间保持一种外来感。

Contributor Biographies

Oren Abeles

Oren M. Abeles is a teaching fellow and doctoral candidate at the University of North Carolina at Chapel Hill, where he studies and teaches rhetoric and composition. His current research focuses on the intersection of rhetoric, science, and modern culture, particularly the ways rhetorical style and figures of speech help scientists epitomize and articulate new theories and concepts. His most recently published work appears in the *Quarterly Journal of Speech* and the journal *Poroi*. He is currently working on a book that traces Charles Darwin's engagement with theories of agricultural breeding, the enclosure of the commons, and early-modern rhetorics of agricultural improvement.

Nicholas Adams

Nicholas Adams is the Mary Conover Mellon professor in the history of architecture at Vassar College and is the author of *Skidmore, Owings & Merrill: SOM Since 1936* (2007); *Firearms and Fortifications: Military Architecture and Siege Warfare in Sixteenth Century Siena* (1986); *Gunnar Asplund's Gothenburg and the Transformation of Public Architecture in Interwar Europe* (2014). He is currently working on a critical biography of Gordon Bunshaft. He is a member of the editorial board of the Italian architectural magazine *Casabella*, and his essays, articles, and reviews have appeared in international architectural periodicals.

Thomas De Monchaux

Thomas De Monchaux is an architect and writer. He teaches design at Columbia University's Graduate School of Architecture, Planning and Preservation, and did his graduate work in architecture at Princeton University. His architectural criticism and journalism has appeared in the *New York Times* and *The New Yorker*'s Culture Desk column, in the journals *n+1*, *Perspecta*, and elsewhere. He received the inaugural Winterhouse Award for Design Writing and Criticism, and delivered the 2011 Myriam Bellazoug Memorial Lecture at the Yale School of Architecture entitled "Seven Architectural Embarrassments." A contributing editor at *Architect* magazine, De Monchaux is currently at work on *Dream House*, a book about cultural and personal histories of American houses and homes.

Karrie Jacobs

Karrie Jacobs is a professional observer of the man-made world with a deep interest in the ways in which humans are re-engineering nature. She's a contributing editor at *Architect* magazine, a regular contributor to Curbed, and a faculty member at School of Visual Arts' graduate program in Design Research, Writing and Criticism. The author of *The Perfect $100,000 House* (2006), Jacobs was the founding editor-in-chief of *Dwell* magazine and the founding executive editor of Benetton's *Colors* magazine.

Marco Roth

Marco Roth is a cultural critic and founding co-editor of *n+1* magazine, a journal acclaimed since 2004 for its deft mixture of literature, culture, and politics, and the author, most recently, of *The Scientists: A Family Romance* (FSG, 2012), a memoir of growing up in a family riven by the AIDS crisis in 1980s New York. He lives in Philadelphia.

Juror Biographies

Brandon Haw

Educated at the Bartlett School of Architecture and Planning in London and subsequently at Princeton University, where he received his Masters in architecture, Brandon began his professional development working in the New York offices of SOM, where he immersed himself in the commercial development side of the profession until 1987. On his return to London, he spent the next twenty-six years working in the office of Lord Norman Foster, where he became a Senior Partner and Board Director responsible for numerous high profile international projects ranging from large master planning initiatives to major corporate headquarters buildings such as the Commerzbank Headquarters in Frankfurt; HSBC World Headquarters in London; the World Trade Center competition in New York and subsequent Tower Two project; the Hearst Tower in New York; and the Faena House residential project in Miami, among others. In 2010 he returned to the US to run the New York offices of Foster and Partners. In July 2014 he set up his own architecture and design studio, Brandon Haw Architecture in the Seagram Building.

Sylvia Lavin

Sylvia Lavin is an internationally known critic, historian, and curator whose work explores the limits of architecture across a wide spectrum of historical periods. Her most recent book is *Kissing Architecture* (2011); *The Flash in the Pan and Other Forms of Architectural Contemporaneity* is forthcoming. She was the curator of *Everything Loose Will Land*, a large-scale exhibition focusing on the intersections between art and architecture in Los Angeles during the 1970s. Her next exhibition, *Creative Spaces*, explored the relationship between architecture and the radical redefinitions of creativity that have taken place since the advent of computing. She is currently the Director of the Critical Studies and MA/PhD programs in the Department of Architecture and Urban Design at UCLA, where she was Chairperson from 1996 to 2006, and The Curatorial Project, a collaborative design and research group that supports the critical engagement with experimental architecture in the public realm. Ms. Lavin has taught at Princeton, Harvard, Columbia, and numerous other institutions, and has been recognized by many grants and awards, most recently from the American Academy of Arts and Letters, the Getty Research Institute, and the Graham Foundation.

Zoe Ryan

Zoe Ryan is the John H. Bryan Chair and Curator of Architecture and Design at the Art Institute of Chicago. Since joining the museum in 2006, she has taken an interdisciplinary approach to curating exhibitions on graphic design, furniture, fashion, and architecture. Her most recent exhibition is *Making Place: The Architecture of David Adjaye* (2015). She is a Lecturer in the Art History Department at the School of the Art Institute and an Adjunct Assistant Professor in the School of Art and Design at the University of Illinois at Chicago. In 2014, she was the curator of the second Istanbul Design Biennial.

Project Credits

Al Ahmadi Cultural Center
Al Ahmadi, Kuwait
Designed 2013-16

Client: ISSNAD Urban Development, Kuwait National Council for Culture, Arts and Letters
Design Partner: Roger Duffy
Managing Partner: Anthony Vacchione
Managing Director: Thomas Behr
Project Manager: Emily Mottolese
Senior Design Architect: Jon Cicconi
Senior Technical Coordinator: Thierry Landis
Technical Coordinator: Maja Paklar
Team Members: Sarah Jester, Miguel Brochado, Sara Dionis, Ina Ko, Nathan King, Dorothy Xu
Structural Design: Skidmore, Owings & Merrill
Structural Director: Charles Besjak
Structural Engineer: Preetam Biswas
MEP: Al-Farooqi
Lighting: BPI
Theater Consulting: Harvey Marshall

Chhatrapati Shivaji International Airport Terminal 2
Mumbai, India
Designed: 2007-14

Client: GVK, Mumbai International Airport Pvt. Ltd.
Design Partner: Roger Duffy
Managing Partner: Anthony Vacchione
Project Manager: Laura Ettelman
Senior Aviation Planner: Derek Moore
Design Architect: Peter Lefkovits, Scott Duncan
Technical Architect: Narin Gobindranauth
Structural Design: Skidmore, Owings & Merrill
Structural Director: Charles Besjak
Structural Engineer: Preetam Biswas
Structural Engineering team: Bonghwan Kim, Alexandra Thewis
Architect and Engineer of Record: Larsen & Toubro Limited
MEP Designer: Skidmore, Owings & Merrill
Lighting Design: Brandston Partnership Inc.
Acoustics: Cerami & Associates
Cultural Design Collaboration: Abu Jani – Sandeep Khosla
Signage: Pentagram, Entro

CITIC
Shenzhen, China
Designed: 2014 – ongoing

Client: CITIC Securities Co., Ltd & Goldstone Zexin Investment Management Co., Ltd.
Design Partner: Craig Hartman
Technical Partner: Keith Boswell
Structural Partner: Mark Sarkisian
Managing Partner: Gene Schnair
Project Manager: Lucy Ling
Senior Design Architect: Fernando Herrera
Senior Technical Architect: John Kuchen
Senior Interior Designer: Federica Carrara
Design Team Members: Qianqian Cai, Chris Dehenzel, Huan Fang, Qinghua Fan, Ross Findly, Benjamin Golze, Yanli Hao, Lisa Hedstrom, Sunnie Hwang, Jann Johnson, Tracie Kelly, Kibum Kim, Seong Koo Lee, Yi-Hsin Lin, Leo Lung, Glen Marquardt, Jon Sargent, Jeremy Steiner, Sargam Tandon, Abdel Tarabieh, William Wallace, Xiling Weng, Julia Wu
Senior Structural Engineer: Neville Mathias
Structural Engineer: Alessandro Beghini
Structural Engineering team: Lachezar Handzhiyski, Yue Hua, Zhao-fan Li, Bin Pan
High Performance Design: Olivier Brouard, Brian Griffith
Landscape: Tom Leader Studio, Inc.
Traffic: CHS Consulting Group
MEP & Lighting: WSP/PARSONS BRINCKERHOFF
Vertical Transportation: Edgett Williams Consulting Group, Inc. (EWCG)
Retail: BENOY

Closed Cavity Façade
Geneva, Switzerland
Designed: 2011-14

Client: Japan Tobacco International
Managing Partners: Jeffrey McCarthy, Anthony Vacchione
Structural Partner: William F. Baker
Structural Director: David Horos
Design Director: Kent Jackson
Senior Design Architect: Yasemin Kologlu
Project Manager: Julia Skeete
Co-Designer: Josef Gartner AG

Denver Union Station
Denver, Colorado
Designed: 2007-14

Client: Denver Union Station Project Authority, Regional Transportation District (RTD), Continuum LLC, East West Partners
Design Partner: Roger Duffy
Managing Partner: Anthony Vacchione
Planning Partner: Marilyn Jordan Taylor
Structural Director: Charles Besjak
Project Manager: Kristopher Takacs
Senior Design Architect: Jon Cicconi, Themis Haralabides
Team Members: Peter Glasson
Senior Planner: Derek Moore
Structural Engineering team: Dmitri Jajich, Aurelie Seblani
Urban Design: Stefano Ceccotto
General Contractor: Kiewit
MEP Engineering: AECOM
Transportation Design: AECOM
Urban Design Consultant: Ron Straka
Landscape Architect: Hargreaves

Shenzhen Rural Commercial Bank Headquarters
Shenzhen, China
Designed: 2012-14

Client: Shenzhen Rural Commercial Bank
Design Partner: Mustafa Abadan
Managing Partner: TJ Gottesdiener
Design Director: Scott Duncan
MEP Director: Luke Leung
Structural Director: Charles Besjak
Project Manager: Brant Coletta, Walter Wang
Senior Design Architect: Ryan Culligan
Senior Technical Coordinator: Eric Van Epps, Saul Hayutin
Senior Structural Engineer: Ronald Johnson, Alexandra Thewis
MEP Engineering: Joseph Dilenno

SOM TOOLS: SOM HPD Methodology + SOM Wind Tunnel 260
Design: 2011 – ongoing

Managing Partner: Jeffrey McCarthy
Structural Partner: William Baker
Structural Team: Joel Putnam, Bradley Young, Christian Hartz
High Performance Design Team: Arathi Gowda, Olivier Brouard
Wind Tunnel Construction collaborator: Aaron Bladon
Western University collaborator: Nicholas Isyumov

The University Center at The New School
New York, New York
Designed: 2005-13

Client: The New School
Owner's Representation: The Durst Organization
Design Partner: Roger Duffy
Managing Director: Mark Regulinski
Project Manager: Chris McCready
Senior Design Architects: Colin Koop, Jon Cicconi
Senior Technical Coordinators: Angelo Arzano, Kevin Peters, Kimberly Garcia
Technical: Adam Letcher
Team Members: Adam Casey, John Locke, Samantha Stein, Mauricio Ulloa, John Locke, Daekyung Jo, David Hood, Aung Barteaux, Mikako Oshima
Interiors: Ece Calguner Erzan, Cynthia Mirbach
General Contractor: Tishman Construction Corp.
MEP Engineer: Cosentini Associates
Structural Engineer: DeSimone Consulting Engineers
Civil Engineer: Langan Environmental & Engineering Services
Lighting: Brandston Partnership
Sustainability Consultant: Buro Happold
NYSERDA Consultant: ADS Engineers
IT/AV/Security: Shen Milsom Wilke
Vertical Transportation: Van Deusen Associates
Commissioning: Fulcrum
Acoustics: Cerami Associates
Theater: Fisher Dachs Associates
Signage: Integral Ruedi Baur Paris

Image Credits

Acknowledgements

The Partners of SOM extend their thanks to Thomas De Monchaux, the Jurors, and to all those who have contributed to the represented work. We would also like to thank Katie George, Lydia Ciaputa, Candy Guo, Li Shao, Wayne Chen, and Steve Wang in assembling, writing, and coordinating the materials for this SOM Journal 10.

Editor:
Thomas De Monchaux

Managing editor:
Amy Gill

Copyediting:
Eugenia Bell

Graphic design:
SOM

Typesetting:
perfect image, Ostfildern

Typeface:
Arial MT

Production:
Ines Sutter, Hatje Cantz

Project Management:
Carolin Schulz, Hatje Cantz

Reproduction and printing:
DZA Druckerei zu Altenburg GmbH, Altenburg

Paper:
LuxoSatin, 150 g/m²

Binding:
DZA Druckerei zu Altenburg GmbH, Altenburg

Published by
Hatje Cantz Verlag GmbH
Mommsenstraße 27
10629 Berlin
Tel. +49 30 3464678-00
Fax +49 30 3464678-29
www.hatjecantz.de
A Ganske Publishing Group Company

Hatje Cantz books are available internationally at selected bookstores. For more information about our distribution partners, please visit our website at www.hatjecantz.com.

ISBN 978-3-7757-4303-7

Printed in Germany